MUSCLE CARS
FIELD GUIDE

John Gunnell

AMERICAN SUPERCARS 1960-2000

©2004 by Krause Publications, Inc.

Published by

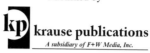

kp krause publications

A subsidiary of F+W Media, Inc.

700 East State Street • Iola, WI 54990-0001
715-445-2214 • 888-457-2873
www.krausebooks.com

Our toll-free number to place an order or obtain a free catalog is (800) 258-0929.

All rights reserved. No portion of this publication may be reproduced or transmitted in any form or by any means, electronic or mechanical, including photocopy, recording, or any information storage and retrieval system, without permission in writing from the publisher, except by a reviewer who may quote brief passages in a critical article or review to be printed in a magazine or newspaper, or electronically transmitted on radio, television, or the Internet.

Library of Congress Control Number: 2004093866

ISBN 13-digit: 978-0-87349-869-2
ISBN 10-digit: 0-87349-869-0

Designed by: Wendy Wendt
Edited by: Brian Earnest

Printed in U.S.A.

CONTENTS

CONTENTS

CONTENTS

CONTENTS

MERCURY

OLDSMOBILE

PLYMOUTH

CONTENTS

INTRODUCTION

Long ago, in the Prehistoric Era (before World War II), American cars were real "dinosaurs"—huge, heavy and definitely slow. If you wanted to travel fast in American Iron, you had to buy an old Ford and build yourself a hot rod. If you wanted it to look fast, you had to add some "Kalifornia Kustom" accessories.

Dearly departed Oldsmobile changed all this in '49 by dropping its powerful Rocket V-8 into a dressy new small-bodied car called the 88. In addition to inspiring the first rock-and-roll record, the Rocket 88 proved that Detroit could build hot rods, too. It was the beginning of the "muscle car" concept, though a long way from what would come later on.

The term "muscle car" has no strict definition, especially if you consider the more modern variety. Some muscle cars are small, and some are large. Some have a four-cylinder engine or a V-6, and some have a V-10 (though the V-8 is predominant). Some do the quarter-mile in under 12 seconds, and some need over 17 seconds to cover the same distance. Some are as plain as they can be and some carry all kinds of decorations.

It is probably best to think of muscle cars as "factory hot rods." They are cars that the factory modified to go faster and look different than the cars they are based on. A true muscle car will go *much* faster than its progenitor. As far as the appearance changes go, they can be very subtle (such as a Chevy Z11), or outrageous (such as a Plymouth Superbird), as long as they make the muscle car stand out in the enthusiast's eye.

The years between '64 and '72 are regarded by most to be the Muscle Car Era. The '49 Olds 88 was the first step towards that period. Chrysler took the next step with its 300 Letter Car—the first production automobile to put 300 hp in the hands of John Q. Public.

Suddenly, Detroit was talking "high performance" and getting seriously involved in NASCAR stock car racing. By 1957, Chevy and Chrysler were offering engine options that delivered one horsepower per cubic inch. Some Chevys and Pontiacs could have mechanical fuel injection, while Ford was toying with superchargers. Chrysler experimented with EFI. Dual-quad and tri-power carburetor setups were popping up in all kinds of cars.

Jerry Heasley

1965 CHEVROLET CORVETTE STING RAY 427

Automakers soon discovered that winning stock car races on Sunday brought more customers into the showroom on Monday morning. To qualify their high-performance parts as "stock" equipment, the car builders had to sell a certain number of the parts to customers. Since this was taking place shortly after Cornell University's famous study on auto safety, a combination of factors was raising eyebrows. These factors included an increase in highway fatalities, some headline-making auto-racing accidents and heavy promotion of speed and performance.

Things were almost getting out of hand—or at least the government thought so. There was talk in Washington of stuffing safety regulations and advertising bans down Detroit's throat. To prevent such official action, the Automobile Manufacturer's Association got the automakers to sign on to a self-imposed ban on the advertising of high performance and racing involvement. All factory support of NASCAR teams and drag racers was supposed to stop.

From that point on, factory backing of motorsports was strictly an "under-the-table" effort for the next several years. Since racing wins still sold cars, some automakers continued to funnel speed equipment to enthusiasts, but the really hot hardware was available only through the parts department—not in the cars that sat in the showroom.

Things continued this way for about four years. Big V-8s and multi-carb setups were available, but only in larger, heavier cars. These cars were powerful and, with some tweaking, did well in drag racing at that time. However, in strictly stock form, they were best suited for blasting down the new superhighways, rather than covering the quarter-mile.

Some interesting developments took place at the same time. For instance, soon to be "trademark" muscle car features like bucket seats, four-speed gearboxes and floor shifters (which actually reflected the '50s interest in foreign sports cars) became available in sporty domestic models. The four-seat Thunderbird even had bucket seats and a center console as *standard* equipment. This was a clear sign that the muscle car image was starting to shape itself between '58 and '61. By 1959, Pontiac had designed its famous "8-lugs," one of the first styled rims.

Jerry Heasley

1967 DODGE CORONET R/T

The mid-'61 release of the Super Sport package for the Chevy Impala was another muscle car milestone. The term Super Sport came from racing and the dealer-installed kit included heavy-duty underpinnings, SS emblems, special tires, "spinner" wheel covers, sintered metallic brakes and a tach. Though available on any Impala, the trick setup at the time was to put it on a car with Chevy's 409 big-block V-8. In stock form, with a single four-barrel carb, this motor delivered up 360 hp. With bolt-on items, that could be raised to about 1 horse per cube.

By this time, Detroit was off to the races again and the AMA ban was history. The big Cadillacs and Lincolns that formerly led the cubic-inch race were no longer players. Chevy, Ford, Pontiac, Plymouth, and Dodge were the forces to be reckoned with and it wouldn't be long before Buick, Mercury, and Oldsmobile got sucked into the high-performance whirlpool. Chrysler continued to offer the Letter Car for a few years and the Thunderbird managed to blend performance with luxury in a related-but-different market niche.

The high-performance cars of '62-'63 were mainly large machines with even larger engines: 409 Chevys, 421 Super-Duty Pontiacs, 426 Max Wedge Dodges and Plymouths, and Ford Galaxie 427s. The Z11 Chevys and monster Mopars tended to be Plain-Janes with bench seats and bottle cap hubcaps, big-block V-8s, and very business-like stick shifters. The Pontiacs and Fords looked more like street cars, but with hood scoops and wheels that hinted at their special nature. These cars certainly had lots of muscle, but Detroit hadn't quite gotten around to packaging it up in factory hot rod style.

As the pace of the racing picked up, it didn't take a genius to realize that small cars with big engines would go faster that big cars with the same engine. By '63-'64, Pontiac was stuffing Super-Duty "mills" into Tempests and Tempest Safaris (converted to rear-drive of course), and Ford countered with its legendary 427-powered Fairlane-bodied T-Bolts. Chrysler had the Dodge Dart to stuff full of wedge and Hemi motors. Burning rubber was becoming the national pastime and it was '57 all over again—but better!

Then came the "Goat" ... the Gran Turismo Olomogato ... the GeeTo ... the Tiger. This one snuck out of the factory to make waves on Woodward Avenue. Some Pontiac engineers who were into racing and a dragging PR guy named Jim Wangers envisioned a factory hot rod that they could take out at night to whip the Plymouths and Fords in local stoplight grand prixs. It was the Rocket 88 theme all over again, but with a catch. General Motors had a corporate restriction about selling a midsize car with a 300-cube "big-car" engine. But Pontiac boss John Z. DeLorean winked and his tire-frying engineers created a package for the Tempest LeMans that included a souped-up version of the Bonneville's 389 V-8.

The GTO wasn't exactly an engine option. It was like the original Super Sport package, except with the engine added in. The GM brass didn't notice this mid-season sleight of hand and the GTO took off, carving out a new market category called muscle car. Like we said, it was not just an engine, it was an American sports car with buckets, badges, bolt-ons, and a V-8 that packed much more power than a midsized car needed for grocery getting. With sales around 32,000 cars for a half of a year, the GTO lit the fuse for a dynamite new era in American motoring.

Timing was part of the GTO's success, since about the time the car came out, GM ordered all of its divisions to get out of racing again. While GM was bowing out of NASCAR, Ford was pushing its "Total Performance" program and very happy to take up the slack. Mopar had its "Race Hemi" engine all set to dominate the field, which it did until it was finally outlawed. As in the past, all the hardware had to be "legalized" for competition by selling a certain number of cars with the same parts to John Q. Both Ford and Chrysler began to follow the GTO path, creating muscle cars to put the special equipment in.

What followed was a glorious '65-'66 period in which one manufacturer after another tried to outdo each other while playing GTO copycat. Chevy created cars like the SS 396 Chevelle and the Nova SS, not to mention awesome big-block versions of the Corvette. Dodge kicked things off with the hot Coronet and the beautiful Charger fastback and soon made such cars available with a "Street Hemi." Ford's Fairlane became its GTO fighter with up to 7 liters of V-8 underhood. Hot Mustangs started a new niche for muscle pony cars. (Carroll Shelby stepped in to heat up the Mustang even more than the factory

1971 FORD MUSTANG MACH 1

Jerry Heasley

dared.) Mercury shoehorned big engines into its Comet and had a very serious factory-backed drag racing team. Plymouth turned to its Belvedere intermediate to create models like the GTX and Satellite that offered big blocks up to the Hemi.

The car wars weren't just corporate battles, either. Buick and Oldsmobile, which were once regarded as hotter rides than a Pontiac, found themselves losing sales to their cousin, which had managed to nail down third place on the sales chart. Both came up with neat answers to the problem. The Skylark-based Buick GS was a more glittery muscle car with a few more cubic inches, while the Oldsmobile 4-4-2 (the model name meant different things at different times) was simply one of the best muscle cars to be had anywhere.

From mid-'64 until '66, Ford had one muscle-related market niche pretty much all to itself, but by '67 other automakers had their pony cars ready to go. Chevy launched the Camaro, Pontiac followed with the Firebird, and Mercury cloned the Cougar. Plymouth's Barracuda had appeared at the same time the Mustang did, but never quite made it big in its "big window" format. It raced successfully, but just never sold well until later.

As the new "ponies" hit the showrooms, they were merchandised over a wide market spectrum and each brand had a heated-up version to compete with the sizzling Mustang GT. During '67-'68, these smaller new high-performance models stole the spotlight, since they offered the same engines used in midsized muscle cars in a smaller, lighter-weight package. The Camaro SS 396, Mustang SCJ 428, and Formula 400 Firebird were wild and wooly street racers.

In the '68-'69 period, two new trends evolved in the muscle market, as engines and options continued to grown hairier thanks to intense competition. Some mid-sized supercars like the Endura-nosed GTO and the fastback Ford Torino began to look more like their pony car counterparts. Plymouth introduced the bargain-basement Road Runner, which soon inspired cars like the Dodge Super Bee, GTO Judge, and Ford Falcon-Torino. Engines continued to grow larger, with many now over 400 cubes and, while fuel injection and multi carburetion began to disappear from GM models, new ram-air-induction systems were devised to keep up the power level.

During these years, the auto industry experienced the first direct government intervention, with seat belts required by some states in the '61-'63 period and federal safety mandates kicking in by '66. The handwriting was on the wall and, by the dawn of the '70s, insiders understood that it was basically all over for muscle cars. Almost as if in reaction to the clouds darkening over the segment, Detroit used the period from '70-'72 to build some of the all-time ultimate muscle cars.

Mopar's "Winged Warriors"—the Plymouth Superbird and Dodge Daytona—got the ball rolling, with a bit of help from the GTO Judge. A restyled Camaro proved more popular than ever and the Mustang line shook the streets with its "Boss" models and Mach 1s. Dodge and Plymouth entered the pony-car parade with a new Dodge Challenger and a reconstituted Plymouth sportster now dubbed the 'Cuda. Chevy's Chevelle got a neat-but-not-drastic restyling and some massively strong engine options. Midsize and sports-compact Mopars cars were offered with Hemi V-8s, and these cars turned out to be rarities and great investments.

If the muscle car niche was going to die, it was going to go out swinging some of the best hardware to ever roll down the pike. The 455-powered Hurst/Olds, the Buick GSX Stage 1, the Trans Am 400 H.O., the LS6 version of the Chevelle SS 454, the Plymouth GTX 440 Six-Pack, the Mustang Boss 429, the Cougar CJ-R, the Hemi 'Cuda, the Hemi Superbird, the Hemi Charger S/E, and the Ram Air IV Pontiac GTO were all among '70 models that could do the quarter-mile in the 13s at well over 100 mph!

A new player, American Motors Corporation, also got into the muscle car arena starting around '68 and continuing through the end. As a small, struggling outfit, AMC had to depend on fantastic creativity to carve out order in a neck-and-neck sales race. Cars like the AMX 401, the Rebel "Machine," and the Hurst SC/Rambler were great budget-priced performers that earned the admiration of a youth-oriented generation.

With the move to unleaded fuels in '71, the heyday of high-performance started to fizzle. The following year, American car engines no longer required high-octane gasoline. Compression ratios were lowered and the octane content of regular gas was lowered to the point where owners of older high-compression cars began to worry about using them. The insurance companies gave the muscle cars the second part of the one-two punch by raising rates for high-performance models so high that most young drivers could no longer afford coverage.

If muscle cars were truly factory hot rods, there were still some around in this era, but the rules had just changed. Plymouth's Duster 340 (and its cousin the Dodge Demon) were truly factory-modified versions of production models, as were the last of the Nova SSs or the Ventura GTO. It's probably true that they were not as out-of-the-box fast as earlier muscle models, but they had the technical and visual upgrades needed to qualify, plus some could be insured at reasonable prices. The Hemi survived for a while, and Pontiac struggled to keep things going as late as 1974 with a truly awesome Super-Duty engine for Formula and Trans Am Firebirds.

After 1974, it was clearly "all over." Detroit wasn't dumb and kept making "lick-'em stick-'em" cars that looked like muscle cars with bucket seats, floor shifts, stripes, decals, hood scoops and catchy model names. These qualified as factory *customized* cars, but they were not genuine factory hot rods. Some had big-cube V-8s, but with power-robbing pollution hardware and stuffy exhaust systems they could hardly get out of their own way. In addition, the very same engines were used in regular family sedans.

For quite a long time, it appeared that there would be no more muscle cars as Detroit had to spend all of its money developing systems to meet ever-tightening safety and air-quality regs. And since much of this work was done in a rush, the results were often less than satisfactory. There were horribly complicated devices that may have worked in a laboratory, but failed on the street. A GM employee who purchased a new '76 Nova could not get it to run right and took it to the Tech Center where he worked. His engineer buddies went over the new car and made a list of over 250 problems!

Eventually, the tides turned. Perhaps the growth of the computer age helped, but by the mid-'80s, performance cars began to rear their heads again. The redesign of the Camaro and Firebird in 1982 and the renaissance of the 5.0-liter Mustang in the same year marked a turning point and the beginning of the Gen II Muscle Car Era. This was strictly a Ford and GM movement at first as Chrysler was planning to drop V-8 engines in 1986. But Gen II development eventually reached the point where non-V-8 muscle cars became a reality. High-tech advances in turbocharging made it possible to build four-cylinder cars and V-6s that ran as fast as the V-8s of earlier times. Later, Chrysler would turn to a V-10 to power its Viper, which is a true modern muscle car by any measure.

Jerry Heasley

1970 PONTIAC GTO JUDGE

Musclecar Field Guide is a quick-reference guide to more than 175 of the top muscle cars of all eras. Each entry provides a capsule rundown about a specific car that includes historical facts and product information. This is followed by a table that tells the reader what the cars cost when new and gives certain specifications such as wheelbase, length, weight, engine size, horsepower, 0-to-60 mph performance, and quarter-mile performance. There is also a MCFG "ballpark" estimate of the value of each car in top condition. Estimating prices is a very inexact science, and cars are ultimately worth what a buyer is willing to spend on them, but these figures are meant to provide an estimate based on past sales of these great cars.

Also included is a unique "He Said/They Said – We Said" commentary on each car. The "He Said/They Said" quotes are taken from contemporary or expert sources and sum up their informed opinion of each car. The "We Said" statement is a sentence or two stating our own impression, which may agree with or differ with the first opinion.

Because of the "building-block" nature of many muscle cars, the information presented in different charts may vary slightly. Some give the as delivered price (ADP) of the car. In some cases, this may be the original price of the base model, and in other cases it may be the manufacturer's suggested retail price (MSRP) of the muscle car version. In other cases, where we located an old article about the car, we are giving the as tested price (ATP), which we think better reflects what most people paid for such models. Of course, the ATP includes the cost of options on the old magazine's test car.

Many listings have explanatory notes in brackets, so you will know which version of the car we are providing information on. These indicate such things as the specific engine that was in the car used to determine performance numbers. Most estimates of current prices are based on a magazine that we publish called *Old Cars Price Guide*. However, we have done some additional research on rare models and desirable engine options.

As you can imagine, the amount of information we can pack into a book of this size is limited. However, we want to let you know that Krause Publications produces additional books and magazines on the topic of muscle cars. Should reading this guide lead you to seek additional information, please visit **www.krause.com** to preview our full product line.

1968 AMX 390

1968 AMX 390

AMX meant "American Motors Experimental." The first steel-bodied American two-seater since the '57 T-Bird started as a prototype in '66. The non-running glass show car proved AMC could design a car with pizazz. AMC's youth-image muscle car hit showrooms two years later.

Dateline Feb. 24, '68: The AMX bowed to the press in Daytona and at the Chicago Auto Show. Neat machine! Even the 225-hp 290-cid base V-8 made the two-seater fly. The one-step-up 280-hp 343 V-8 was nastier, but the AMX "390" was the real muscle mill.

A 97-inch wheelbase helped trim the AMX 390 to 3,205 lbs. That gave the 315-hp mini coupe a 10.8 lbs.-per-hp ratio. Top speed was an estimated 122 mph. In February 1968, Craig Breedlove piloted an AMX to 106 world speed records. About 50 special red-white-blue "Craig Breedlove" edition AMXs were sold.

Reclining bucket seats, full carpeting, woodgrain interior trim, and E70-14 Goodyear Polyglas tires were standard. Also included was a four-speed gearbox and H.D. suspension. AMXs built in '68 had a metal dashboard plate bearing a special serial number from 000001 to 006175. The first 550 cars, built in '67, lacked this feature. The '68 production total was 6,725 cars.

Factory ADP	Wheelbase	Length	Shipping Weight	Base V-8	Engine Options	0-to-60 MPH	¼-Mile
$3,245	97 in.	178 in.	3,097 lbs.	290 cid/225hp	343 cid/280 hp 390 cid/315 hp	6.6 seconds	14.80 seconds @ 95 mph

MCFG Says: $20.5K, but extra for a "Breedlove."

They Says: In March 1968, *Car and Driver* said, "This is no Rambler, you guys. It is—to quote a sensitive and eloquent artist friend from the West Coast—"one son-of-a-bitch motorcar!"

We Says: "Rump-rumps like American muscle, but wants to be driven, too. Most enjoyable on twisty Wisconsin roads. Goes, stops and turns like a real sports car."

The 1968 Javelin SST

1968 JAVELIN SST 390

1968-'69 JAVELIN SST 390

The SST was Dick Teague's handsome answer to the Mustang and Camaro. With the right engines, it became a real musclecar. AMC expert Larry G. Mitchell says the AMX 390 was made available in Javelins. "This engine doesn't show up in factory literature because it came out so late, but it makes sense. It was just a question of taking the engine from this pile or that pile."

Car and Driver featured the very first Javelin 390 in March '68. "Its long suit was handling," said the writer. "It felt very much like a British sports car." Of six cars tested—Javelin, Camaro SS, Mustang 2 + 2, Cougar, Barracuda and Firebird 400 HO—the SST handled best.

The '69 Javelin was mostly unchanged. Styling treatments were improved and a few mechanical features were upgraded to create a better product.

Factory ADP	Wheelbase	Length	Shipping Weight	Base V-8	Engine Options	0-to-60 MPH	¼-Mile
'68 $2,692	109 in.	190 in.	3,099 lbs.	290 cid/200hp	290 cid/225 hp 343 cid/280 hp	N/A	N/A
'69 $2,734*	109 in.	190 in.	3,103 lbs.	290 cid/200hp	290 cid/225 hp 343 cid/280 hp	N/A	N/A

MCFG Says: $17K (add 20% for Go-Package; add 30% for Big Bad package)

They Says: *Motor Trend* called the '68 Javelin tops in the sports-personal class, saying "The most significant achievement for an all-new car and the most notable new entry in class."

We Says: "Don't smirk, Doug Thorley—one of the biggest names in drag racing—campaigned a Javelin funny car, and another ran in NASCAR. The 'Jay 390' is a sleeper!"

* The 1969 Javelin SST 390 was also avalible in a 390 Go-Package for $3,943.

Jerry Heasley

1969 AMX 390

1969 AMX 390

The '69 AMX had few changes at first. Power train availability was the same as '68. The desirable "Go-Package" cost $233 on the 343-powered cars and $311 on those with the 390. The option included E70 redline tires on 6-inch rims, a handling package, power disc brakes, Twin-Grip differential and over-the-top stripes.

The mid-year "Big Bad" option packages came in wild colors. Although the Big Bad package was only $34, sales were limited to 284 orange, 283 green, and 195 blue copies. A Hurst Competition Plus shifter for the Borg-Warner four-speed manual transmission was added to the options list at the same time as the Big Bad package. It cost $205.

The most interesting and sought-after AMX of all was the AMX SS. Only 52—or by some reports 53—AMXs were sent to Hurst for drag racing "legalization." The AMX SS 390 was topped by a pair of 650-cfm Holley four-barrels on an Edelbrock aluminum cross-ram intake. Doug's Headers and other modifications resulted in a conservative advertised output of 340 hp. The suggested retail price of $5,994 seems a steal today, but was nearly *twice* the regular sticker price in '69.

Factory ADP	Wheelbase	Length	Shipping Weight	Base V-8	Engine Options	0-to-60 MPH	¼-Mile
$3,297*	97 in.	178 in.	3,094 lbs.	290 cid/225hp	343 cid/280 hp 390 cid/315 hp	7.2 seconds	14.59 seconds @ 96 mph

MCFG Says: $20.5K (add 25% for Big Bad; add 200% for SS)

They Says: In '69, *Drag Racing Magazine* said, "Contrast is represented by the 140 mph speedo in the new AMX. Economy Ramblers were only capable of 90 mph."

We Says: "140 mph probably isn't enough. These cars are really fast with the 390 stuffed under the hood. Prices are climbing fast, too."

1969 SC/RAMBLER

Jerry Heasley

1969 SC/RAMBLER

In '69, AMC hooked up Hurst Performance Products to create the SC/Rambler ("Scrambler," get it?). Simple formula: Small rogue hardtop + big V-8 = Fast. Hurst thought up the idea and AMC bought into it.

The 390/315 V-8 was linked to a B-W four-speed with Hurst shifter. A 3.54:1 axle with Twin-Grip differential took up the rear. The hot little car had a power-to-weight ratio of 10.03 lbs. per hp, putting it in NHRA F-stock class. The factory estimated low 14-second quarter-miles at 98 mph. *Road Test* magazine did even better.

In addition to power, the screaming SC/Rambler included a big ram-air scoop, fat dual exhausts, a column-mounted Sun tach, Bendix front discs, blue-finished five-spoke 14 x 6-in. mags, trim rings, and red-striped Goodyear tires. The plain-looking gray vinyl interior had red-white-blue headrests. These colors were carried in several variations.

The first 500 cars built had red center body-side panels and thick blue horizontal racing stripes on the hood, roof, and deck. A blue arrow pointed towards the scoop, which had large letters spelling the word "AIR" and calling out the engine size. This was the "A"-type graphic treatment. A second batch had new "B"-type trim with a mostly white exterior with narrow red and blue stripes. A third batch of cars reverted to the type-A trim with fewer elements. The A-finished cars seem to be the more common of the 1,512 built.

Factory ADP	Wheelbase	Length	Shipping Weight	Base V-8	Engine Options	0-to-60 MPH	¼-Mile
$2,998	106 in.	181 in.	3,160 lbs.	390 cid/315hp	None	6.3 seconds	14.20 seconds @ 100 mph

MCFG **Says** $18.5K

They Says: MuscleCarPlanet.com says, "This was not your Grandma's Rambler, as quarter-mile times were reported in the low 14s at over 100 mph."

We Says: "Looks like a neat toy and many toy versions were made. You don't see the real ones very often and even a ratty original will pull down 6 grand."

1970 AMX

1970 AMX

"We made the AMX look tougher this year because it's tougher this year," heralded ads for the '70 model. A new 360-cid/290-hp V-8 was included at $3,395 base price.

On the outside, the AMX got new rear lamps and a restyled front end shared with hi-po Javelins. The grille was flush with the hood. A redesigned bumper housed "mutant square" parking lamps. A horizontally divided, crosshatched grille had four very prominent, bright, horizontal moldings. AMX lettering filled a gap at the center of the second and third moldings. The grille also incorporated circular rally lights. The bumper included an air scoop to cool the front brakes. The restyled hood had a large ram-induction scoop. A longer nose made the '70 AMX look more like its pony car rivals. This should have helped sales, but didn't. AMC built only 4,116. The metal dashboard plates affixed to '70 models were numbered 014469 to 18584.

New contoured high-back bucket seats had integral head restraints. There was a completely new instrument panel. An exclusive Corning safety windshield was also available. A four-on-the-floor transmission with a Hurst shifter was standard. Performance options included the 390 V-8 with 325 hp and a close-ratio four-speed. A "Go-Package" was available on 360-powered AMXs for $299 and on 390-powered AMXs for $384. It included power front disc brakes, F70-14 RWL tires, a handling package, H.D. cooling and a Ram-Air hood scoop.

Factory ADP	Wheelbase	Length	Shipping Weight	Base V-8	Engine Options	0-to-60 MPH	¼-Mile
$3,395	97 in.	180 in.	3,126 lbs.	360 cid/290hp	390 cid/325 hp	6.56 seconds	14.68 seconds @ 92 mph

MCFG Says: $20.5K

He Says: *Motor Trend* magazine's Eric Dahlquist said that the '70 AMX was, "One of the better constructed cars around."

We Says: "The rarest of the two-seat AMXs should have something special going for it with muscle car collectors, especially as time goes by."

Jerry Heasley

1970 JAVELIN SST 390

1970 JAVELIN SST 390

Racer Mark Donahue and racecar builder Roger Penske won the '68 and '69 Trans-Am titles and signed a contract with AMC to drive Javelins in Trans Am. One modification they made was a spoiler. To make it race legal, the spoiler had to go on 2,500 factory cars.

These Javelin SSTs also included dual exhausts, power front disc brakes, E70 x 14 white-letter tires, 14 x 6-in. wheels, a handling package, and a AMX ram-air hood. The signature of Mark Donahue was seen on the right-hand side of the spoiler. The "Mark Donahue Signature Edition" was offered with a 360- or 390-cid V-8 and console-shift automatic or four-speed with a Hurst shifter. Actually, 2,501 cars were built this way.

Trans-Am editions were replicas of Ronnie Kaplan's racing cars with a red-white-and-blue paint scheme by industrial designer Brooks Stevens. The Trans-Am edition had a $3,995 price. Only 100 copies were built, just enough to qualify for Trans-Am racing.

Total Javelin production for '70 dropped down to 28,210 cars (a 31 percent decline) of which 19,714 were SSTs, including the Mark Donahue and Trans Am special editions.

Factory ADP	Wheelbase	Length	Shipping Weight	Base V-8	Engine Options	0-to-60 MPH	¼-Mile
SST $2,942	109 in.	192 in.	3,130 lbs.	304 cid/210hp	360 cid/245 hp 360 cid/290 hp	7.6 sec. (w/390)	15.1 seconds (w/390)
TRANS-AM $3,995	109 in.	192 in.	3,340 lbs.	304 cid/210hp	360 cid/245 hp 360 cid/290 hp	7.6 sec. (w/390)	15.1 seconds (w/390)

MCFG Says: $14.5K (add 20% Go-Package; add 30% Big Bad package), $16K for Mark Donohue Edition

They Says: *Motor Trend* called the '68 Javelin tops in the sports-personal class.

We Says: ""This perfect rocket made some fast changes in AMC's old "Kenosha Cadillac" image."

Janet Kaufmann

1970 REBEL "MACHINE"

1970 REBEL "MACHINE"

"Standing before you is the car you've always wanted," said a December 1969 *Hot Rod* magazine ad showing the Rebel "Machine," which bowed at the NHRA World Championship drag races two months earlier. Ad copy warned, "Incidentally, if you have delusions of entering the Daytona 500 with the Machine, or challenging people at random, the Machine is not that fast. You should know that. For instance, it is not as fast on the getaway as a 427 Vette, or a Hemi, but it is faster on the getaway than a Volkswagen, a slow freight train, and your old man's Cadillac."

The Machine's "standard stuff" included a four-speed gearbox, Hurst shifter, a hood tach, Ram-Air, H.D. suspension, low-back-pressure dual exhausts, styled wheels, high-back buckets, and disc brakes.

The first 100 cars were white with blue lower beltline stripes and hood. The upper body sides were red striped. Red-white-blue stripes ran across the rear fender tips and deck. "Machine" emblems decorated the front fenders and rear trim panel. For buyers who didn't like the color scheme, AMC said, "You can order the car painted in the color of your choice." Such cars had silver striping and a blacked-out hood. "The Machine" was an AMC-Hurst joint venture. AMC built 2,326 Rebel Machines.

Factory ADP	Wheelbase	Length	Shipping Weight	Base V-8	Engine Options	0-to-60 MPH	¼-Mile
$3,475	114 in.	197 in.	3,640 lbs.	390 cid/340hp	None	6.4 seconds	14.40 seconds @ 98 mph

MCFG Says: $19K

He Says: AMC sales VP Bill Pickett said the Machine was another youth-oriented car introduced in recognition of the important marketing axiom: "Youth must be served."

We Says: "The stripes are eye catching, but don't blow your budget on a Machine unless you're a dyed-in-the-wool AMC fanatic. Buyers are as limited now as they were when this car was new."

Jerry Heasley

1971 HORNET SC/360

1971 HORNET SC/360

AMC's Hornet SC/360 was a sensible alternative to money-squeezing, insurance-gouging muscle cars. When the Hornet arrived in '70 it was a compact, but its wheel wells were big enough to accommodate racing slicks. Kenosha saw a niche and whipped up the SC/360 version.

AMC stuffed a 245-hp 360 V-8 under the hood and hooked it to a floor-mounted three-speed via a H.D. clutch. 14 x 6-in. mags and fat D70 x 14 Polyglas tires said "muscle." Rally stripes and reclining seats were among few amenities. For $199 extra you got the Go-Package with a four-barrel carb, dual exhaust, Ram-Air hood scoop, handling hardware, RWL tires, a tach, and 40 extra ponies.

Options included four-on-the-floor or a B-W Shift-Command automatic. You could add a Dana Twin-Grip axle. Only 784 cars were made.

Factory ADP	Wheelbase	Length	Shipping Weight	Base V-8	Engine Options	0-to-60 MPH	¼-Mile
$2,663	108 in.	179.26 in.	3,057 lbs.	360 cid/240hp	360 cid/280 hp	7 seconds	14.80 seconds @ 94.63 mph

MCFG Says: $13K

He Says: Can-Am driver Steve Diulo summed up the S/C360 as "a great little car with slow steering that was really a lotta car for the money!"

We Says: "Lots of appeal for the AMC lover, but you're not going to see one pulling down six figures at Barrett-Jackson. You *can* get 17 mpg, though!"

Jerry Heasley

1971 JAVELIN-AMX 401

1971 JAVELIN-AMX 401

After '71, Javelins and AMXs shared bodies, though the four-seat AMX had a cowl-induction hood, spoilers, badges, and special trim. A 245-hp two-barrel 360 V-8 was standard. A four-barrel gave you 40 extra ponies. The real muscle-car mill was a new 330-hp 401 based on the AMC 390. The 401 made the Javelin-AMX a muscle car. Driver George Follmer took the '71 and '72 Trans-Am titles with Javelins.

Only 2,054 Javelin-AMXs were produced in '71, and only a fraction of those had the 401. Besides being the most powerful Javelin engine ever, the '71 version of the 401 was the last to require premium gas. The 401 was also used in some '71 Javelin SSTs, such as a fleet of 100 Alabama State police Interceptors.

After '71, the 401 was de-tuned for unleaded. It dropped to 255 *net* hp, but the '72 (0 to 60 mph in 8.3 seconds/16.1-second quarter mile) and '73 (0 to 60 mph in 7.7 seconds/15.5-second quarter-mile) Javelins with the 401 were still pretty hot cars. Javelin-AMX output increased to 3,220 in '72 and 5,707 in '73, before tapering to 4,980 in '74, the final year. A "Trans-Am Victory" package was offered only in '73. It included commemorative fender decals.

Factory ADP	Wheelbase	Length	Shipping Weight	Base V-8	Engine Options	0-to-60 MPH	¼-Mile
$3,432	110 in.	192 in.	3,244 lbs.	360 cid/245hp	360 cid/285 hp; 401 cid/330 hp	7.1 seconds	14.70 seconds @ 95.5 mph

MCFG Says: $14K tops + 15% for Go-Package: ('72)$14K; '73) $11K; ('74) $10K; ('75) $8.5K

They Says: *Hot Rod* noted, "It must be doing something good for the performance image of AMC because you don't hear people calling them 'Nashes' anymore."

We Says: "No matter what you call them, the '71-and-up Javelin AMXs are cool—and hot, too."

1965 SKYLARK GS

1965 SKYLARK GS

The Skylark GS was Buick's GTO. With a big four-barrel V-8 and 10.25:1 compression, the GS tested by *Motor Trend* in May '65 had a top speed of 116 mph.

Buick engineers said the Skylark GS was completely different than the regular Specials because all three body styles—coupe, hardtop and ragtop—used a beefed-up ragtop-type frame that resisted torque flexing. The GS package was $253 with a three-speed, $420 with a four-speed, and $457 with Super Turbine 300 automatic. H.D. shocks and springs and a stiffer front anti-roll bar were included. "Like a howitzer with windshield wipers," said Buick's marketing folks.

Other features of the first Skylark Gran Sport included H.D. upper control arm bushings, dual exhausts, 7.75 x 14 tires, and a choice of 2.78:1, 3.08:1, 3.23:1, 3.36:1, 3.55:1, and 3.73:1 rear axle ratios. To show what a Skylark Gran Sport could do set up with 4.30 gears and cheater slicks, *Motor Trend* mentioned that Lenny Kennedy's race-prepped example clocked a 13.42-second 104.46-mph quarter-mile run.

"It seems to us that Buick has another winner in the Skylark Gran Sport," said *Motor Trend's* assistant technical editor, Bob McVay. "The point is that better cars are being built—and Buick is building them!"

Factory ADP	Wheelbase	Length	Shipping Weight	Base V-8	Engine Options	0-to-60 MPH	¼-Mile
*(CPE) $2,805	115 in.	209 in.	*(CPE) 3,479 lbs.	400 cid/ 325 hp	None	7.8 seconds	16.6 seconds @ 86 mph

With three-speed: Factory ADP: (HT) $2,945; (RT). $3,095. Shipping Weight: (HT) 3,428 lbs.; (RT) 3,532 lbs.

MCFG Says: (CPE) $17.4K; (HT) $19K; (RT) $28.8K;

They Says: "There is mounting evidence that our engineers have turned into a bunch of performance enthusiasts," said Buick. "First they stuff the Wildcat full of engine. Then the Riviera Gran Sport. And now this, the Skylark GS, which is almost like having your own, personal-type nuclear deterrent."

We Says: "A-bombs away!"

This is what mountain country looks like to the tuned car.

What makes one car so styling, performance, ride and handling. Only when they're all tuned together is the car a Buick. Like this '66 Skylark Gran Sport.

As a matter of fact, it's what enjoyable traffic looks like to the tuned car. And valley, midcity road. And a "most rated country." "cars," too.

For the tuned car makes a habit of making cumbersome sights disappear.

Which makes the tuned car a most welcome sight indeed.

The Skylark Gran Sport—one of the tuned cars. The Skylark GS in the picture is, like every tuned car, a beautiful blend of styling, performance, ride and handling. Which means it rides as smoothly as it performs. (A suspension designed specifically for the GS sees to the side. A 325-hp Wildcat V-8 sees to the performing.) And it handles as briskly and responsively as you'd expect a car that looks like this to handle. (Also, some cars don't live up to the way they look. The tuned car always does.)

Here the tuned car works its wonders. If you're intent on making mountains so remote, you've got to get out of the tail, so say. So we do a lot of our product development out in the real world, on real roads, where real people drive.

For instance, in the mountains of West Virginia. (The residents of Pott's Mountain are getting used to seeing Buicks coming up and down, up and down.) For another instance, at Pikes Peak. (A lot of cars are tested in dizzying drives up Pikes Peak. Ours are tested in breath-driven dozen Pikes Peak. That's one of the best ways we know to learn about ride and handling and bucking.)

All this means you aren't likely to run into a dizzying situation that we haven't already seen. And that means the tuned car is tuned to your kind of driving.

Tuned safety equipment, even. Built-in blended into every Buick are padded sun visors and a padded dash. Two-speed electric wipers and windshield washers. A shatter or sixteen mirror inside and a rear-view mirror outside. Back-up lights. And seat belts all around, which we submit you may, plead with you—to buckle up. (Is there nothing we can't do to make sure you're in fit shape to come back in more Buicks? Nothing.)

How to turn your country into tuned car country. The only thing standing between you and the tuned car is your Buick dealer. And an easier obstacle to surmount you've never met.

Unless you rated membership.
Wouldn't you really rather have a Buick?

**1966 Buick.
The tuned car.**

BUICK

1966 GS 400

The GS became a separate hi-po Skylark series in 1966. Gran Sports had most of the plush Skylark features, plus bright simulated hood scoops, side stripes, a blacked-out grille, GS badging, a black rear panel, H.D. suspension, all-vinyl notchback bench seats, full wheel covers, and 7.75 x 14 whitewall or red line tires—and no hood ornament.

A 325-hp Wildcat 401 V-8 with 10.25:1 compression and four-barrel was standard. It developed 445 lbs.-ft. of torque at 2800 rpm. To placate GM brass, it was advertised as a "400." That made it "legal" for use in a GM midsize car. A 340-hp midyear option was added.

Motor Trend tested two GS hardtops with the Super Turbine automatic. One was loaded, the other had no power options and mild upgrades like a 4.30:1 rear axle, racing slicks, headers, shimmed front springs, and a transmission kick-down switch. The second car did 0 to 60 in 5.7 seconds and the quarter-mile in 14 seconds at 101 mph!

Buick built 1,835 GS coupes, 9,934 hardtops and 2,047 ragtops.

Factory ADP	Wheelbase	Length	Shipping Weight	Base V-8	Engine Options	0-to-60 MPH	¼-Mile
(CPE) $2,956; (HT) $3,019; (RT) $3,167	115 in.	204 in.	(CPE) 3,479 lbs.; (HT) 3,428 lbs.; (RT) 3,532 lbs.	400 cid/ 325hp	400 cid/340 hp	7.6 seconds	15.47 seconds @ 90.54 mph

MCFG Says: (CPE) $17K; (HT) $23K; (RT) $24K

He Says: Sports car racer Masten Gregory said, "I didn't like the car at first, because I thought it was too soft, but as I got used to it, I started liking it quite a bit."

We Says: "The '66 Skylark is about as soft and cuddly as Kevlar. Get the big engine and go have some big fun with this baby!"

IN

'67 BUICK

Get in with the In Crowd in a GS-400

The In Crowd knows what's happening, and what's happening is Buick '67. Proof: GS-400. Buick's personal sport car. It has a 400-cu. in., 340-hp V-8, a new brake system with dual master cylinders, energy absorbing steering column, bucket seats, heavy-duty suspension and a list of standard equipment features—including all the new GM safety items—so long it takes a Buick dealer to do it justice. (He'll also tell you how four out of five new-car buyers pay Buick-sized prices to begin with.) The In Crowd's at your

1967 GS 400

1967 GS 400

In '67, Buick got serious about its mid-size muscle. The old "nailhead" V-8 disappeared and a new 400-cid V-8 replaced it. "GS 400" was now the higher-performance model's official name. Bulging front-facing scoops decorated the hood and front-slanting air slots appeared behind the front wheels. Other standard equipment included a rallye stripe, GS badges, foam-padded vinyl seats, and twin exhausts.

The hydraulic-lifter engine was modernized and smoother and tolerated higher rpms. It had 10.25:1 compression and a big four-barrel carb. Hooked behind it you could get a three-speed or a four-speed stick shift or a new three-speed automatic that could be shifted manually. Options included a tach and a 3.90:1 posi rear.

This year the GS 400s were in their own series. Hardtop, post-coupe. and ragtop versions were offered. As in 1966, all body styles used the beefier ragtop-type frame. A big, sturdy chassis rode on F70x14 Wide-Oval tires. The GS 400 offered superior handling. *Motor Trend* said it had "the best road behavior of any car we've driven in quite a while." Power front disc brakes were a new $147 handling option.

Buick prices were higher than those of rival muscle cars. This tended to hold sales down. The company built just 1,014 post-coupes, 10,659 hardtops and 2,140 ragtops.

Factory ADP	Wheelbase	Length	Shipping Weight	Base V-8	Engine Options	0-to-60 MPH	¼-Mile
(CPE) $2,956*	115 in.	205 in.	(CPE) 3,439 lbs.*	400 cid/340hp	None	6 seconds	14.7 seconds @ 97 mph

* Factory ADP: (HT) $3,019; (RT) $3,167. Shipping weight: (HT) 3,500 lbs.; (RT) 3,505 lbs.

MCFG **Says:** (CPE) $16K; (HT) $18.5K; (RT) $23K

He Says: "Before the wheels had made their first revolution, we immediately noticed that the '67 GS 400 was going to be an even far stronger performer than its 1966 counterpart—which itself was no slouch," said *Motor Trend's* Steve Kelly.

We Says: "Ads summed it up best: 'The car that enthusiasts are enthusiastic about.'"

1968 GS 400

1968 GS 400

Swoopier styling with an S-curving body side, a huge scoop in the trailing edge of the hood and chrome finned ornaments behind the front wheel openings characterized the '68 GS 400. A new 112-inch Skylark wheelbase did not affect overall length.

The 340-hp 400 V-8 was carried over. Standard equipment included a three-speed manual gearbox and a 3.42:1 rear axle. A H.D. three-speed was $84.26 extra, a four-speed was $184.31, and THM cost $205.24. Cars with stick shift had 3.64:1 and 3.91:1 rear axle options. A 2.93:1 rear was standard with automatic. Several other ratios were optional.

Buick built 10,743 GS 400 hardtops and 2,454 ragtops. *Motor Trend* tested a ragtop and got figures like those in the table below. *Hot Rod* magazine's Eric Dahlquist did better in a hardtop with a homemade cold-air package: 14.78 seconds at 94 mph in the quarter. He noted that January 1, 1968, would bring factory cold-air packages. Stage 1 and Stage 2 packages were offered, along with forged-aluminum pistons, a special intake manifold gasket that blocked the heat riser; oversize rods, fully grooved main bearings, 6 percent richer carb metering rods, and special spark plugs and headers.

Motor Trend said the 1968 GS 400 had "surprisingly good" performance and was "very tight." The magazine liked the construction, comfor,t and general quality of the car.

Factory ADP	Wheelbase	Length	Shipping Weight	Base V-8	Engine Options	0-to-60 MPH	¼-Mile
(HT) $3,127; (RT) $3,271	112 in.	201 in.	(HT) 3,514 lbs.; (RT) 3,547 lbs.	400 cid/340hp	None	7.5 seconds	16.3 seconds @ 88 mph

MCFG **Says:** (HT) $19K; (RT) $22K

They Says: "Buick makes all kinds of cars because there are all kinds of people in the world," said Buick. "So we thought we'd cater to the person who truly gets a thrill out of driving. The GS 400 is our contribution to his hobby."

We Says: "We're thinking about taking up a new hobby. Where're the keys?"

1969 Buick GS Series

GS 400

1969 GS 400

1969 GS 400

The '69 Skylark GS 400 had minor styling revisions, but big underhood changes, including a functional air scoop. Cold air passed through chrome grilles decorating the car's much more prominent air scoop. The grille had a thick horizontal center bar, too.

Buick's Stage 1/Stage 2 options came into their own this year, offering drag strip-style performance enhancements for serious muscle car lovers. The calmer Stage 1 was promoted in Buick ads. It incorporated a high-lift cam, tubular push rods, H.D. valve springs and dampers, a high-output oil pump, dual exhausts, big 2 1/4-inch tailpipes, and a modified Quadrajet carb. When it was ordered, the transmission was equipped with a 5200-rpm governor to protect against over-revving the engine.

The hairier Stage 2 had to be ordered from your Buick parts department and home installed. It was *not* recommended for street use on cars with mufflers. It included an even wilder cam, plus all the other above goodies.

Car Life found the GS 400 to be the fastest muscle car it tested. *Motor Trend* tested a 3,706-lb. ragtop with the standard 340-hp engine and got different results. The GS 400 ragtop was the slowest of six muscle cars it tested together.

Factory ADP	Wheelbase	Length	Shipping Weight	Base V-8	Engine Options	0-to-60 MPH	¼-Mile
(HT) $3,181; (RT) $3,325	112 in.	201 in.	(HT) 3,549 lbs.; (RT) 3,594 lbs.	400 cid/340hp	400 cid/350 hp	(ragtop) 6.1 seconds	(ragtop) 15.9 seconds @ 89 mph

MCFG Says: (HT) $20K; (RT) $24K

They Says: "Two 'muffs,' as they're called, reach up from twin air snorkels on the four-barrel air cleaner, compressing against the hood underside, directing only outside air to the fuel mixer," said *Hot Rod*.

We Says: "Air is free—and the GS 400 makes good use of this fact!"

1970 GS 455 STAGE 1

Jerry Heasley

1970 GS 455 STAGE 1

The '70 Buick GS 455 had a new engine derived from the earlier 430-cid V-8. It featured 10.0:1 compression, a Rochester four-barrel carb, and 510 lbs.-ft. of torque at 2800 rpm. This mill could push a 3,800-lb. base Skylark from 0 to 60 mph in 6.5 seconds.

Motor Trend advised that the $199.95 Stage 1 package was a bargain. It included extra-large nickel-chrome stellite steel valves, big-port cylinder heads with special machining and valve relieving, stronger valve springs, a high-lift cam, a carb with richer jetting, blueprinted pistons (notched for valve clearance), and an advanced-performance distributor. You could get a Stage 1 V-8 with a special shift-governed automatic or a H.D. four-speed with a beefed-up clutch.

On top of its outstanding performance, the GS 455 was a real handler and hugged the road even better when equipped with the $15.80 Rallye Ride package. This option gave *Motor Trend's* press car extra stability at high speed.

The GS 455 option could be ordered in two body styles. Buick built 8,732 of the two-door hardtops and only 1,416 of the ragtops.

Factory ADP	Wheelbase	Length	Shipping Weight	Base V-8	Engine Options	0-to-60 MPH	¼-Mile
(HT) $3,283; (RT) $3,469	112 in.	203 in.	(HT) 3,562 lbs.; (RT) 3,619 lbs.	455 cid/350hp	None	5.5 seconds	13.39 seconds @ 105.55 mph

MCFG Says: (HT) $20K; (RT) $25K

They Says: "Buick's Stage 1 was interesting in '69; now with the 455 mill it's an engineering tour de force," *Motor Trend* remarked.

We Says: "On paper, the '70 GS 400 with the Stage 1 kit looks like one of the wildest Buicks ever made."

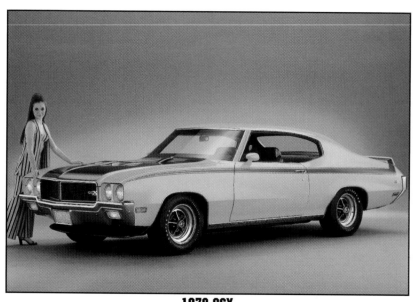

1970 GSX

1970 GSX

In mid-'70, Buick issued the GSX option. For those willing to cough up $1,196 over the cost of a GS 455 hardtop, lovers of mid-size Buick muscle got a four-speed transmission, a Hurst shifter, G60-15 billboard RWL tires on mag-style wheels, a 3.42:1 Posi rear axle, Rallye Ride and Control suspension, power front-disc brakes, H.D. cooling, bucket seats with consolette, a special Rallye steering wheel, front and rear spoilers, and a light-up hood tach.

The GSX came in any color you liked—as long as you liked Saturn Yellow or Apollo White. Black striping underlined its muscle image, but didn't help sell many cars. The Buick factory in Flint, Michigan, cranked out 581 yellows and 187 whites. Records show that 400 GSX buyers added the Stage 1 performance package for an extra $113.75. Buick thought the GSX looked hot and had its advertising agency license The Doors' song "Light My Fire" to help promote it.

Other special GSX features included a trunk tension bar designed to support the rear deck lid spoiler and a baffle incorporated into the rear spoiler. The Buick GSX Registry at *www.buickgsx.net* is a good source of information about these cars.

Factory ADP	Wheelbase	Length	Shipping Weight	Base V-8	Engine Options	0-to-60 MPH	¼-Mile (automatic)
$4,479	112 in.	203 in.	3,562 lbs.	455 cid/350hp	455 cid/360 hp	6.2 seconds	14.2 seconds @ 103 mph

MCFG Says: $30K

They Says: "Buick's GSX—A limited edition and another light-your-fire car from Buick," said the Flint, Michigan, automaker.

We Says: "As things turned out, not too many people had their fires lit, but you have to admit that with a total production of 678 copies, the GSX is truly a limited-edition muscle car."

Jerry Heasley

1971-1972 GSX STAGE 1

1971-'72 GSX STAGE 1

The GSX package was a special option for any '71-'72 Buick Skylark GS from the GS 350 to the GS 455 Stage 1. To order a GSX, your Buick dealer had to check off the Special Car Order (SCO) section of the form.

Like other '71-'72 Buicks, the GSX editions used de-tuned engines with 8.5:1 compression. But the GSX with the Stage 1 option was still one of the hottest muscle cars in town. Buick fans say it could zip down the quarter-mile faster than an LS6 Chevelle.

Both '71 and '72 GSXs used a special frame, a computer-designed Rallye-tuned-suspension and large-diameter sway bars. The use of side stripes and a rear spoiler was continued. These cars varied widely in color and came with an unlimited range of options and accessories. The GSX Registry says very little is known about them, except that the option was added to 124 cars in '71 and 44 cars in '72.

While no where near as muscular as '70 editions, '71 and '72 Skylarks with the GSX package and the Stage 1 engine option are still tremendous performance cars and, since they were rare when new, they are extremely hard to find today.

Factory ADP	Wheelbase	Length	Shipping Weight	Base V-8	Engine Options	0-to-60 MPH	¼-Mile
'71 N/A	112 in.	204 in.	N/A	350 cid/260hp	(455 V-8) 455 cid/315 hp 455 cid/225 hp	5.8 seconds	14.5 seconds @ 101.1 mph
'72 N/A	112 in.	203 in.	N/A	350 cid/260hp	(455 Stage 1 V-8) 455 cid/345 hp 455 cid/275 hp	5.8 seconds	14.10 seconds @ 97 mph

MCFG **Says:** $30K (add 40% for Stage 1)

They Says: "The GSX Registry at *http://www.buickgsx.net/* says "It is very difficult to identify these cars without paperwork."

We Says: "If you want a rare muscle car that hasn't been slandered in the press, this is the one for you; no one knows enough about them to tell the full story. You can be the first!"

1971 GS 455 STAGE 1

1971 GS 455 STAGE 1

The '71 Skylark Gran Sport series included a hardtop and a ragtop with a special 260-hp 350 four-barrel V-8 as standard engine. Gran Sport equipment included Comfort-Flo ventilation, door-operated interior lights, a smoking set, front and rear ashtrays, front and rear armrests, carpeting, dual exhausts, functional air scoops, H.D. springs, H.D. shock absorbers, an H.D. stabilizer bar, a 6,000-mile front lubricated suspension, a full-flow oil filter, a semi-closed cooling system, a Delcotron alternator, 14-in. wheels, composite finned cast-iron brake drums, and G78 x 14 bias-belted black sidewall tires.

The $164 Code A9 option package for Gran Sport models included all GS features plus a specific H.D. battery, a specific H.D. cooling system, and a 455-cid V-8 with a four-barrel carb. Cars so-equipped wore a "455" call-out under the GS letters on the front fenders. The $325 Code A1 Stage 1 option was a modified version of the 455-cid V-8 was an additional package that could be added to GS models that already had the lower-priced 455-cid V-8 GS 455 option added. Cars with this engine option had a "Stage 1" call-out in place of the "455" call-out below the "GS" lettering on each front fender.

Buick built 8,268 GS and GS 455 two-door hardtops and 801 were Stage 1 cars. Convertibles accounted for 902 total GS and GS-455 assemblies.

Factory ADP	Wheelbase	Length	Shipping Weight	Base V-8	Engine Options	0-to-60 MPH	¼-Mile (automatic)
(HT) $3,774; (RT) $3,964 (w/Stage 1)	112 in.	204 in.	(HT) 3,461 lbs.; (RT) 3,497 lbs. (w/o Stage 1)	(GS) 350 cid/260hp	(GS 455) 455 cid/315 hp (Stage 1 V-8) 455 cid/345 hp	6.5 seconds	14.5 seconds @ 101.1 mph

MCFG Says: (HT) $30.2K; (RT) $37K

He Says: Muscle car expert Scott Lewis said, "The Stage 1 had the highest torque rating of any engine GM put in a car during the muscle car era. The Buick had what it took."

We Says: "Put a GS 455 Stage 1 ragtop in your college fund today."

Jerry Heasley

1972 GS 455 STAGE 1

1972 GS 455 STAGE 1

The Red '72 GS that *Motor Trend's* A. B. Shuman tested had a white vinyl top and automatic transmission. It seemed like a grocery getter, except for the timing slips it picked up at the NHRA "Winternationals" in Pomona. The GS won Stock Eliminator and whomped all stock class winners to take the overall category win. With open exhausts, fatter tires and some legal "tweaks," weekend drag racer Dave Benisek set a 13.38-second class record with the same car.

The '70 GS 455 Stage 1 had also ran a 13.38-second quarter-mile, but did it with 10.0:1 compression, 360 hp and taller gears. The no-lead '72 version had 8.5:1 compression, 275 hp and a 4.30:1 rear axle, which made its performance more impressive.

Despite such a positive appraisal, Buick made only 7,723 GS hardtops and 852 GS ragtops in model year '72, and that total included GS 350, GS 455 and Stage 1 production. In addition to a choice of three V-8s—350/190 hp, 455/225 hp or 455/275-hp Stage 1—all '72 Gran Sports had four-barrel carbs, dual exhausts, functional hood scoops, and an H.D. suspension. GS monograms appeared on the front fenders and rear deck.

Factory ADP	Wheelbase	Length	Shipping Weight	Base V-8	Engine Options	0-to-60 MPH	¼-Mile
(HT) $3,225; (RT) $3,406	112 in.	203 in.	(HT) 3,471 lbs.; (RT) 3,525 lbs.	(GS) 350 cid/190 hp	(GS 455) 455 cid/225 hp (Stage 1 V-8) 455 cid/275 hp	(GS 455 Stage 1) 5.8 seconds	(GS 455 Stage 1/automatic) 14.10 seconds @ 97 mph

MCFG **Says:** (HT) $30.2; (RT) $37K

He Says: A. B. Shuman said, "The amazing thing, considering all that's happened just in the area of emissions controls, is that a car that runs like the GS Stage 1 could still exist." Shuman called it, "The best example of the Supercar genre extant."

We Says: "A.B. said it as clear as A. B. C. and we have nothing to add about this great Buick muscle car."

1984-'87 GRAND NATIONAL

BUICK

1984-'87 GRAND NATIONAL

The mid-'84 Regal Grand National was a limited-production hi-po car. It displayed Buick turbo technology and gave the feeling of a NASCAR racer. It was a $1,282 option package. GNs included a 3.8L turbo V-6, fat black tires, a sport steering wheel, a tach, a boost gauge, and H.D. generator. They were black, with black bumpers, black rub strips, black guards, a black air dam, a black spoiler, black headlight bezels, turbo aluminum wheels with black paint and GN I.D. on the front fenders. The interior featured Lear Siegler front seats with the GN logo.

The '85 GN option featured the same stuff with new two-tone cloth bucket seats. With 200 hp, it went 0-to-60 in 8 seconds. This year 2,067 GNs were built, compared to 2,000 in '84.

Gray cloth bucket seats were used in '86 GNs. Buick advertised the turbocharged V-6 as "the most advanced hi-po engine offered in a Buick." Production increased to 5,512.

The '87 Regal GN package (code WE2) included the 3.8-litre turbo V-6 with intercooler, overdrive automatic, a 3.42 axle, a Gran Touring suspension, fast-ratio power steering and other cool stuff.

Factory MSRP	Wheelbase	Length	Shipping Weight	Base V-6	Engine Options	0-to-60 MPH	¼-Mile (automatic)
$15,136 *	108.1 in.	201 in.	3,580 lbs.	3.8L/245 hp	None	Low 6's	13.85 seconds @ 99.2 mph

* *($3,000 dealer mark-ups were seen)*

MCFG **Says:** ('84) $20K; ('85) $18K; ('86) $17K; ('87) $24K

They Says: The *GNRegistry.org* says, "Historically, Buick management did not have any reluctance or aversion to being known by the public as a maker of hi-po automobiles. This seems to have held true until just after the end of production of the Grand National in '87."

We Says: "Being automotive historians, we have to say we love Buick's olden-days hi-po attitude and we think the GN was one of the best expressions of it."

1987 GNX

Jerry Heasley

1987 GNX

To commemorate the end of Grand National production in '87, Buick planned the GNX, a car using the latest in electronics and turbocharging to create the *ultimate* modern musclecar.

The hot GN was being dropped in June-July '87. When enthusiasts realized these would be the last turbocharged, rear-wheel-drive Buicks they started buying them. The GN got an extension on life with 10,000 more assemblies scheduled, including 547 GNXs.

Chief engineer Dave Sharpe dreamed up the idea of a special car to mark the series' farewell. Mike Doble, of Advanced Concepts & Specialty Vehicles got the job and envisioned a modern GS-455/GSX Stage 1. The plan was to build the "quickest GM production supercar ever!"

ASC/McLaren (Automobile Specialty Co./McLaren Engines) helped. The heart of the car was a turbocharged, intercooled, blueprinted SFI V-6 with special bearings, shot-peened rods, and a high-rpm valve train.

The GNX got a "high-intensity" look with glossy paint, low-gloss Vaalex louvers, cast alloy wheels, flares, a hood power bulge and a deck lid airfoil.

Factory MSRP	Wheelbase	Length	Shipping Weight	Base V-6 (GNX)	Engine Options	0-to-60 MPH	¼-Mile (automatic)
$29,900	108.1 in.	200.6 in.	3,580 lbs.	3.8L/276 hp	None	5.5 seconds	13.43 seconds @ 104 mph

MCFG Says: $37K

He Says: GNX program manager Lou Infante said, "The net result is a mid-13 second GNX that's at home on the dragstrip, road course, and interstate."

We Says: "Dragstrip, road course, interstate? Heck, We'd be glad to drive a GNX slowly down our pot-holed township road—in fact, any excuse to drive one anywhere works for us!"

Jerry Heasley

1961 IMPALA SS

1961 IMPALA SS

The first SS was probably the purest "big" Chevy muscle car, since the '61 Impala was downsized. This option could be ordered for Impala coupes, sedans, and hardtops as a $54 dealer-installed extra. It included "SS" emblems, padded dash, spinner wheel covers, power steering/brakes, H.D. springs and shocks, sintered metallic brake linings, a 7,000-rpm tach, 8.00 x 14 whitewall tires, a dashboard grab bar, and a chrome four-speed shifter housing.

Two V-8s were available at prices in the $344 to $500 range. The 11:25 compression Turbo-Thrust 348 came in 340-hp (four-barrel) and 350-hp (Tri-Power) versions. A new 409-cid Turbo-Fire V-8 came in 360-hp (four-barrel), 380-hp (Tri-Power), or 409-hp (dual quad) versions. It had 11:1 compression. A four-speed close-ratio transmission was $188 extra.

Some experts warn that the '61 Impala SS is not the easiest car to restore. Only 456 Impalas were fitted with the "SS" package (including 142 with 409-cid engines), so parts are hard to find. But take heart, because a 409-cid '61 Chevy without SS equipment is also a desirable muscle car.

Factory ADP	Wheelbase	Length	Shipping Weight	Base V-8	Engine Options	0-to-60 MPH	¼-Mile
$3,273	119 in.	209.3 in.	3,480 lbs.	283 cid/ 170 hp	(Small block V-8) 283 cid/230 hp *	(HRM) 7 seconds	(HRM) 14.02 seconds @ 98.14 mph

* *(Big block V-8) 348 cid/340/350 hp; 409 cid 360/380/409 hp*

MCFG Says: (Impala sport coupe) $32.2 K

He Says: Ray Brock, in *Hot Rod*, said, "A car that is really a racing machine best describes Chevrolet's latest contribution to the hi-po field."

We Says: "We wish we could sing those famous lines, 'She's real fine . . . my 409!'"

1962 BEL AIR Z11 "BUBBLE TOP"

Jerry Heasley

1962 BEL AIR Z11 "BUBBLE TOP"

In '62, the 409 could be had in any big Chevy, even wagons. The 409 "Bubble-Top" Bel Air was the heart-stopping combination. This hardtop got its nickname from the vast sweeps of front and rear window glass and was a great drag car due to its lighter weight. Fit the 409 with a close-ratio four-speed and no one would come close in the stoplight drags (unless you missed a shift or your opponent had a Hemi-powered chopped Ford coupe). At the Saturday night drags the 409 would win you your car's value with impressive speeds like 115 mph in the quarter mile.

The first 409 Chevys with the lightweight Z11 drag racing package were constructed late in '62. They had an aluminum hood, aluminum inner fenders, and aluminum front fenders. The Bel Air "bubbletop" two-door sedan was the basis of most Chevrolet drag cars and weighed in at about 3,360 lbs. with Z11 equipment. Many sources indicate "about 100" Z11s were built (57 is given as the specific number made in '63). Hayden Profit's Z11 took AA/S Stock Eliminator honors at the U.S. Nationals in Indianapolis with a run of 12.83 seconds/113.92 mph in the quarter-mile.

Factory ADP	Wheelbase	Length	Shipping Weight	Base V-8°	Engine Options	0-to-60 MPH	¼-Mile
$2,668	119 in.	209.6 in.	3,360 lbs.	283 cid/170hp	327 cid/250 hp; 327 cid/300 hp; 409 cid/340 hp; 409 cid /380 hp*	(Z11) 6.3 seconds	(Z11) 12.2 seconds @ 103 mph

* Optional Z11 V-8; 409/409

MCFG Says: $75K.

They Says: "She's so fine my 409! Gonna save my pennies and save my dimes. Gonna buy me a 409, 409, 409."—*The Beach Boys*

We Says: "Our coin caddy is filled to the brim with pennies and dimes, but $32.75 won't even buy a 409 emblem these days!"

1963 CORVETTE STING RAY Z06

Jerry Heasley

1963 CORVETTE STING RAY Z06

Chevrolet's all-new '63 Sting Ray was hot. It had a glorious new body, broadened in scope with the first 'Vette coupe. It had an independent rear suspension, fuel injection, even knock-off wheels. And it had the Z06 racing option.

The Z06 kit bore the mark of Zora Arkus-Duntov, but not overtly. Duntov's intent was to keep the racing package nondescript, since Chevrolet was supposedly out of racing. Ready for sale in October of '62—and available strictly on the coupe—the Z06 option included a fuel-injected 327 and (sometimes) a 36.5-gallon fuel tank. This so-called "big tank" was used in only about 60 of the 199 Z06s made. The tank fit the back of the coupe body like a pea in a pod and helped make the 'Vette competitive in long-distance endurance racing.

The knock-off wheels, which became synonymous with the '63 Split-Window, had problems. They leaked air due to the porosity of the aluminum and poor sealing at the rims. No more than a dozen coupes and roadsters got them. Only one existing 'Vette with original knock-offs has been documented.

Factory ADP	Wheelbase	Length	Shipping Weight	Base V-8	Engine Options	0-to-60 MPH	¼-Mile
$6,732 *	98 in.	175.3 in.	N/A	(L84 coupe) 327 cid/360hp	None	(L84 coupe) 6.2 seconds	(L84 coupe) 14.6 seconds

* With mandatory options.

MCFG Says: $150,000
They Says: *The Standard Guide to American Muscle Cars* says, "In '63, no RPO option was hotter than Z06."
We Says: "Born to race!"

1963 IMPALA 427

1963 IMPALA Z11 AND IMPALA 427

Chevy built 25 new '63s with the Z11 option December 1,'62. On January 1, '63 came 25 more. Seven others were sold soon after. This lightweight drag kit was a $1,245 Impala sport coupe option. It now included an aluminum front bumper and stripped interior, plus the '62 content. The aluminum saved 112 lbs. Other tricks, such as no center bumper backing and bracing, also helped. By cutting another 121 lbs., the Impala dropped to about 3,340lbs.

A new 427-cid/430-hp big-block arrived in '63. It included a new dual four-barrel setup that isolated the intake runners from the engine valves. They had a separate valve cover. The cylinder heads had a new intake mating surface to match the manifold. There was a special cowl-induction air cleaner; a H.D. clutch, a four-speed, a Posi rear, semi-metallic brakes, and a tach.

Five Mark II NASCAR 427 "mystery engines" went to Daytona and won two 100-mile prelim races. They set a track stock car record. The rare engines were prototypes of the 396-427-454 family. They were closely related to the 409 and the Z11-optioned 427. GM's decision to adhere to the '63 AMA anti-racing ban put an end to these great engines.

Factory ADP	Wheelbase	Length	Shipping Weight	Base V-8	Engine Options	0-to-60 MPH	¼-Mile
(basic Z11) $4,031	119 in.	209.9 in.	(basic Z11) 3,340 lbs.	283 cid/195hp	327 cid/250 hp; 327 cid/300 hp; 409 cid/340 hp; 409 cid/400 hp*	6.3 seconds	12.2 seconds @ 103 mph

* Optional Z11 V-8 409/425; "Mystery" V-8 437/430

MCFG Says: ($75K)

They Says: www.Classiccar.com says, "The 409 passed the torch of fame and power to the 396 engine as the decade passed."

We Says: "Baseball great Reggie Jackson knows his muscle cars and the '63 Impala Z11 was a part of his outstanding collection."

Jerry Heasley

1964 CORVETTE STING RAY L84 "FUELIE"

1964 CORVETTE STING RAY L84 "FUELIE"

The '64 Sting Ray's styling was cleaned up a bit. The "Split Window" coupe was gone. The '63's fake hood vents were eliminated and the roof vents were restyled. A three-speed fan was available in the coupe to aid in ventilation.

A 327-cid V-8 with 10.5:1 compression, a single Carter WCFB four-barrel carb, and 250 hp was standard. The optional L75 ($54 extra) had a Carter aluminum Type AFB four-barrel carb. It developed 300 hp. Next came the L76 V-8 with mechanical valve lifters, a high-lift cam and a Holley four-barrel carb. It had 11:1 compression and developed 365 hp. Real muscle car fans wanted the L84, basically the L75 with Ram-Jet fuel injection.

Seven exterior colors were available for '64: Tuxedo Black, Ermine White, Riverside Red, Satin Silver, Silver Blue, Daytona Blue and Saddle Tan. All body colors were available with a choice of black, white or beige soft tops.

Chevrolet made 8,304 Sting Ray coupes and 13,925 Sting Ray ragtops.

Factory ADP	Wheelbase	Length	Shipping Weight	Base V-8	Engine Options	0-to-60 MPH	0-to-100 MPH
(L84) $4,790	108 in.	175.3 in.	(base coupe) 2,945 lbs.	327 cid/375hp	None	(L84) 6.3 seconds	(L84) 14.7 seconds

MCFG Says: $59.8K

He Says: "The professional road testers gave their stamp of approval to the 1964 Corvette," wrote Karl Lundvigsen in *Corvette: America's Star-Spangled Sports Car*."

We Says: "These were the days when the Corvette was trying to prove itself as a *real* world-class sports car and the mid-year 'fuelie' cars were proof positive that Chevy had made the grade with its fiberglass two-seater."

1965 CORVETTE STING RAY 396

Jerry Heasley

1965 CORVETTE STING RAY 396

If Sting Rays are the best 'Vettes, the '65 may be the best Sting Ray. Big news in '65 was the addition of four-wheel disc brakes as standard equipment. The small-block 'Vettes could always go. Now they could stop!

Performance enthusiast focused on the power train. Chevy's tried-and-true 250-hp Turbo-Fire 327 was standard. Next up was a 300-hp version of the 327, but new-for-'65 was a precursor to the famous LT1, a 350-hp 327 that combined "sizzle with calm, cool behavior." Then came the most powerful carbureted 327, putting out 365 ponies. The legendary Ram-Jet fuel injection made its final appearance in '65. At $538, it was expensive, but resulted in a 375-hp 327 world-class stormer—the ultimate small-block.

Bowing in April '65, a 396-cid big-block L78-coded V-8 marked the beginning of an exciting Vette era. Rated at 425 hp and priced at only $293, the 396 made the fuel-injected Vette seem superfluous in those days of cheap, high-octane gasoline. Big-blocks could be picked out by their slinky "power bulge" hood. Introduced at the same time was side-mounted exhausts.

Factory ADP	Wheelbase	Length	Shipping Weight	Base V-8	Engine Options	0-to-60 MPH	¼-Mile
(HT) $4,525; (RT) $4,315	98 in.	(HT) 175.3 in.; (RT) 175.3 in.	(HT) 2,975 lbs.; (RT) 4,022 lbs.	396 cid/425 hp	None	5.7 seconds	12.90 seconds @ 112 mph

MCFG Says: (HT) $76.8K; (RT) $84.8K

They Says: "Above all else, it's great fun to drive," said *Car Life* magazine.

We Says: "The 396 Turbo-Jet V-8 was awesome in big cars like the Impala and Caprice, even better in the SS 396 Chevelle, and a simply outrageous option in the Sting Ray."

1965 MALIBU Z16

Jerry Heasley

1965 MALIBU Z16

In February of '65, at the GM Proving Ground in Mesa, Arizona, Chevy debuted the Caprice's 396/325-hp V-8 and a 425-hp solid-lifter version for the 'Vette. The Chevelle lacked a big-block option, but one was actually offered via a "secret" program. "Malibu SS 396" was the official name of the hot 365-hp car. It was not promoted, since assemblies were extremely limited.

The reason? It was specially engineered at a high cost. On the surface, the Z16 looked like a Chevelle with a 396, but it went beyond that. It was more like a big car than a midsize car, and Chevy wasn't ready to mass produce it. The coupe had an H.D. ragtop frame, reinforced rear suspension, and two added body mounts. "Big-car" 11-inch power drums brakes were fitted, along with stiff springs and shocks.

The L37 V-8 had special left- and right-side exhausts. It was linked to a four-speed. An 8.875-inch ring gear was specified. Features unique to the Z16 included and air cleaner with metal crossed flags, "396 Turbo-jet" badges, a special taillight board with an SS emblem and a unique ribbed black molding. All Z16 Chevelles had a 160-mph speedo, an AM-FM Multiplex four-speaker stereo, and in-dash tach. Chevy made 201 of the Z16s.

Factory ADP	Wheelbase	Length	Shipping Weight	Base V-8	Engine Options	0-to-60 MPH	¼-Mile (automatic)
(Z16) $3,932	115 in	196.6 in.	(Malibu V-8 hardtop) 3,115 lbs	(Malibu) 283 cid/195 hp; 283 cid/220 hp	327 cid/250 hp; 327/300 * **	(Z11) 6.3 seconds	(Z11) 12.2 seconds @ 103 mph

* Optional V-8s (Malibue SS) 327/350; ** Optional Z16 V-8 396/375

MCFG Says: $54K

He Says: "A large part of the reason for the popularity of these cars is that Chevy sold lots of affordable cars in the '60s and many people remember and relate to them," Volo Auto Museum's Greg Grams says.

We Says: "Like a little cop car without the bubblegum machine!"

1966 CHEVELLE SS 396

Jerry Heasley

1966 CHEVELLE SS 396

The Chevelle's top option was no longer a Malibu SS, but simply a Chevelle SS 396. It had twin simulated hood air intakes, a black-out grille, wheelhouse moldings, ribbed and color-accented sill and lower rear fender moldings, a SS 396 grille badge, a SS 396 rear cove emblem, and "Super Sport" rear fender script. Specific mag-style wheel covers were included, as were five nylon red-stripe tires (white sidewall tires were a no-cost option). Chevelle interiors were all-vinyl, with a bench front seat standard. Many SS 396s had optional bucket seats.

The L34 version of the 396 shared its cylinder head and compression ratio with the base L35 version, but had a forged alloy crankshaft, dual exhausts, a higher-lift cam and chrome piston rings. The L78 engine, a midyear release, was probably installed in less than 100 cars. It had an 11.0:1 compression, fatter tailpipes, a solid-lifter cam and other go-fast goodies. Cars with this engine could do 0-to-60 mph in about 6.5 seconds.

All 396s could be ordered with a wide-ratio four-speed or close-ratio four-speed. Powerglide automatic was also available.

Factory ADP	Wheelbase	Length	Shipping Weight	Base V-8	Engine Options	0-to-60 MPH	¼-Mile
(HT) $2,276; (RT) $2,984	115 in.	197 in.	(HT) 3,375 lbs.; (RT) 3,470; lbs.	(L35) 396 cid/325 hp	(L34) 396 cid/360 hp; (L78) 396 cid/375 hp	(360 hp) 7.9 seconds	(360 hp) 14.66 seconds @ 99.88 mph

MCFG Says: (HT) $32K; (RT) $40K (add 10% 360 hp; 30% 375 hp)

They Says: "It handled very nicely and therefore was a ball to drive. Its engine, which is certainly one of the most advanced designs in the world, has great turbine-like smoothness with tremendous power (and probably more potential than the other cars by a wide margin) plus greater flexibility," said *Car and Driver*.

We Says: "This apple-pie-in-your-face midsized Chevy can burn rubber with the best of them!"

1966 CHEVY II NOVA SS 327

Jerry Heasley

1966 CHEVY II NOVA SS 327

In the early '60s, Ford's Falcon was hot-selling and Chevy's Nova was not selling. The boxy Chevy II needed a little pizzaz, so Chevy added an SS option for '63. The Nova SS featured a more complete instrument cluster, deluxe steering wheel, bucket seats, wheel covers, special interior/exterior trim and emblems. No big engine, though.

The Chevy II was significantly restyled for 1966 and the list of engines available for Nova SS models now included hot V-8s, namely the L79 version with a staggering 11.0:1 compression ratio. In essence, with this engine, the Nova became a "factory hot rod." Racecar tuner Bill Thomas built a similar Nova called "Bad Bascomb" two years earlier. The factory version did not have the same 'Vette independent rear suspension, but it was hot enough.

Car Life magazine (May 1966) tested the L79 Nova equipped in true muscle-car-era fashion with a four-speed manual gearbox, limited-slip differential, power steering and brakes, H.D. suspension, A/C, deluxe bucket seats, a console and full instrumentation. The 'Vette engine and other options raised the price from $2,480 to $3,662.

Factory ADP	Wheelbase	Length	Shipping Weight	Base V-8	Engine Options	0-to-60 MPH	¼-Mile (automatic)
(Nova SS base V-8) $2,536)	110 in.	183 in.	2,840	283 cid/ 195 hp	(Optional 283 V-8) 283 cid/220 hp (Optional 327 V-8) (L30) 327 cid/275 hp; (L79) 327 cid/350 hp	(L30) 8.6 seconds (L79) 7.2 seconds	(L30) 16.4 seconds @ 85.87 mph (L79) 15.1 seconds @ 93 mph

MCFG Says: (L30) $22K; (L79) $35.2K

They Says: *Car Life* (May 1966) said: "Unlike some samples from the supercar spectrum, it maintains a gentleness along with its fierce performance potential and who needs 400 inches for supercar status?"

We Says: "This is a car for the enthusiast who really appreciates a sleeper."

1966-1967 CORVETTE STING RAY 427

Jerry Heasley

1966-'67 CORVETTE STING RAY 427

The 427 'Vette, with its funnel-shaped hood, was introduced in 1966. The new V-8 was related to Chevy's 427-cid NASCAR "mystery" engine and the Turbo-Jet 396. The 'Vette 427 ragtop carried 7.7 lbs. per hp. Three four-speed gearboxes—wide-ratio, close-ratio and H.D. close-ratio—were optional. A desirable extra was side-mounted exhaust pipes.

For '67, the Vette got additional engine cooling vents and cars with 427s got a different power bulge hood and more horsepower when fitted with three two-barrel carbs The new hood had a large, forward-facing air scoop, usually with engine call-outs on both sides.

There are four versions of the 427 in '67. The L36 was about the same, the L68 had 400 hp and the L71 had Tri-Power with 435 hp. Extremely rare (only 20 built) was the aluminum-head L88. This powerhouse was officially rated at only 430 hp, but developed nearly 600 hp! In all, 9,707 big-blocks were built.

Factory ADP	Wheelbase	Length	Shipping Weight	Base V-8	Engine Options	0-to-60 MPH	¼-Mile
'66 (HT) $4,476; (RT) $4,265	98 in.	175.2 in.	(HT) 2,985 lbs.; (RT) 3,005 lbs.	(L36) 427 cid/390hp	427 cid (L30) 427 cid/425 hp	(L72) 5.7 seconds	14 seconds @ 102 mph
'67 (HT) $4,553; (RT) $4,341	98 in.	175.2 in.	N/A	(L36) 427 cid/390 hp	(L68) 400 hp; (L72) 425 hp; (L71) 435 hp; (L89) 435 hp; (L88) 560 hp	(L72) 5.7 seconds	14 seconds @ 102 mph

MCFG Says: (HT) $49-$51K; (RT) $54-$56K plus 20-70% for 427 options depending on horsepower rating

They Says: *Car Life* (August 1966) said, "It takes high-speed travel over a variety of roads and through a combination of curve radii to appropriately reveal the car's inner beauty."

We Says: "Gives you quite a launch-pad kick and quite a kick to drive as well."

1967 CAMARO SS

1967 CAMARO SS

"SS" meant hi-po in the Camaro's infancy. The initial offering for muscle car maniacs was a hot L48 295-hp/350-cid V-8 that came only with the SS 350. It had a raised, louvered hood, "bumblebee" striping, SS badges, red-stripe tires, and a stiff suspension.

An H.D. three-speed gearbox was standard in the SS. Options included a two-speed Powerglide, a four-speed gearbox, and rear axle ratios including 2.73:1, 3.07:1, 3.31:1, 3.55:1, 3.73:1, 4.10:1, 4.56:1, and 4.88:1. *Car and Driver* did 0-to-60 mph in 7.8 seconds and the quarter in 16.1 seconds at 86.5 mph. *Motor Trend* did 0-to-60 in 8 seconds and the quarter in 15.4 at 90 mph.

On November 26, 1966, Chevy released a pair of 396-cid big-block V-8 options: the $235 L35 produced 325 hp, while the $550 L78 produced an advertised 375 hp. *Motor Trend* tested an L35 SS 396 Camaro with four-speed gearbox at 6 seconds for 0-to-60 and a 14.5-second quarter mile at 95 mph. *Car Life* drove a similar car with automatic and registered a 6.8-second 0-to-60 time and 15.1 second quarter mile at 91.8 mph.

Since a total of 34,411 SSs were built and 29,270 were SS 350 models, that means 5,141 were SS 396s.

Factory ADP	Wheelbase	Length	Shipping Weight	Base 396 V-8	Engine Options	0-to-60 MPH	¼-Mile (automatic)
Base V-8 (HT) $2,572; (RT) $2,809	108.1 in.	184.7 in.	427 cid (HT) 2,920 lbs.; (RT) 3,180 lbs.	396 cid/325 hp	396 cid/350 hp; 396 cid/375 hp (limited sales)	*(Motor Trend)* 6 seconds	*(Motor Trend)* 14.5 seconds @ 95 mph

MCFG Says: (base V-8) (HT) $25K; (RT) $31K (add 15% for SS 396; add 40% for 375 hp)

They Says: *Car Life* said, "Fun to drive keynotes the Camaro. *C/L* testers can't remember when they've had cars with such a high fun content."

We Says: "The Camaro was merchandised as a be-what-you-want-it-to-be pony car, and the SS 396 was a be-what-you-want-it-to-be muscle car."

1967 CAMARO Z/28

1967 CAMARO Z/28

As every muscle car fan knows, racing helps sell cars. In 1967, the preferred racing venue for the Camaro was SCCA's Trans-Am series, where engine size was capped at 305 cid. Chevy's Vince Piggins decided the answer was a Camaro with a super-hot small-block V-8.

The Z/28 resulted. Z/28 was the code for a performance kit introduced November 26, 1966, during the American Road Race of Champions at California's Riverside Raceway. Chevrolet used a 283 V-8 in pilot versions of the Z/28, but it was too slow to be a winner. In the production car, Chevrolet combined the 327 block with the 283 crank and came up with a 302-cid V-8. By playing with other hi-po parts like a giant four-barrel carb, an aluminum high-rise intake, and L79 Vette heads, it got this motor to crank out about 350 hp and 320 lbs.-ft. of torque at 6200 rpm. However, to play it safe, less power was advertised.

The basic Z/28 package was $358, but other options were mandatory. The price included a heater, but not A/C. For those with serious racing in mind, even the heater could be deleted. The Z/28 performed very well and, since it was designed for competitive road racing, it had terrific handling and braking go with its impressive straight-line acceleration. Top speed was 124 mph!

Factory ADP	Wheelbase	Length	Shipping Weight	Base V-8 (Malibu)	Engine Options	0-to-60 MPH	¼-Mile
$4,200	108 in.	184.7 in.	3,520 lbs.	302 cid/290 hp	None	(360 hp) 6.7 seconds	(360 hp) 14.9 seconds @ 97 mph

MCFG Says: $47K

He Says: Dan Roulston, writing in *Car Craft* in '67 said, "It should run like a scalded cat on the strip."

We Says: "In retrospect, I can confirm that the Z/28 goes as fast as my girlfriend's cat whenever she (the cat) sees me coming."

1967 CHEVELLE SS 396

Jerry Heasley

1967 CHEVELLE SS 396

Twin fake hood air intakes, color-accented ribbed body sill and rear fender lower moldings, a black-out style grille and rear panel accents, "Super Sport" on the rear fenders, SS wheel covers, red-stripe tires, and an all-vinyl bench seat interior were SS 396 trademarks.

The 325-hp L35 version of the 396 was base engine, with the 350-hp L34 optional. The 375-hp L78 wasn't listed on Chevy spec sheets, but it was possible to purchase the hardware needed to "build" this option at your Chevy dealer's parts counter. The total cost of upgrading an L34 to an L78 was $475.80.

SS 396 buyers could get the 325-hp engine with a standard H.D. three-speed manual transmission, a four-speed manual gearbox, or Powerglide automatic (or later in the year, THM). There was a choice of nine axle ratios from 3.07:1 to 4.10:1, but specific options depended upon transmission choice. The 350-hp V-8 came with the H.D. three-speed manual, wide- or close-ratio four-speeds or Powerglide. There were eight rear axle ratios from 3.07:1 to 4.88:1, but you could not get all of them with every engine and transmission setup.

Annual production of Chevelle SS 396s fell a bit to 63,006.

Factory ADP	Wheelbase	Length	Shipping Weight	Base V-8	Engine Options	0-to-60 MPH	¼-Mile
(HT) $2,825; (RT) $3,033	115 in.	197 in.	(HT) 3,375 lbs.; (RT) 3,470 lbs.	396 cid/325 hp	396 cid/350 hp; 396 cid/375 hp (buildable)	6.5 seconds	14.66 seconds @ 99.88 mph

MCFG Says: (HT) $32K; (RT) $36K (add 10% for L34; add 30% for L78)

They Says: *Car and Driver* said that the SS 396, "scored very high with us because of its intrinsic balance. It handled nicely and was therefore a ball to drive."

We Says: "Chevelle sales set a record in '67 and its clear that the SS 396 was the muscular motivator of increased showroom activity."

Jerry Heasley

1967 IMPALA SS 427

1967 IMPALA SS 427

The Impala SS 427 was an "image" car. While the 427-cid V-8 was available in other Chevys, only the SS 427 came with a full assortment of muscle-car goodies, including badges and engine call-outs, a power dome hood, big wheels, a stiff suspension, and red-stripe tires.

SS equipment included vinyl-clad Strato bucket seats, a black-finished grille, wheelhouse moldings, black lower body and deck lid accents, SS badges, and specific wheel covers. The L36 option turned the SS into an SS 427. This $316 package included the SS 427 trim and a 385-hp 427 Turbo-Jet V-8.

Ordering this option required the buyer to add at least the H.D. M13 three-speed manual gearbox. For additional go-power, an M20 four-speed or THM could be specified, as could a more powerful 425-hp engine. Out of a total run of 76,055 Impala Super Sports, only 2,124 were SS 427s.

Viewing any SS 427 as a muscle car depends on one's definition of the species. The '67 was just slightly slower than a '70 SS 396 Chevelle with 350 hp, which isn't bad at all for a full-sized Chevy.

Factory ADP	Wheelbase	Length	Shipping Weight	Base four-barrel V-8	Engine Options	0-to-60 MPH	¼-Mile
(HT) $3,319; (RT) $3,570	119 in.	214 in.	(HT) 3,615 lbs.; (RT) 3,650 lbs.	427 cid/385 hp	421 HO Tri-Power V-8 427 cid/425 hp	8.4 seconds	15.8 seconds @ 88 mph

MCFG Says: (HT) $20K; (RT) $29K (add 40% for SS 427)

They Says: *Car Life*, May '67, said, "That's the SS 427—a family car for a swinging family, or possibly a good choice for a traveling swinger without a family."

We Says: "Here is a Chevrolet with the most advanced mobile creature comforts in combination with performance which was, usually, reserved for drag strip specials."

Jerry Heasley

1967 CHEVY II NOVA SS

1967 CHEVY II NOVA SS

Chevy made modest changes to the Nova's second-year "second-generation" styling. There was a new anodized aluminum grille with a distinct horizontal-bars motif and a Chevy II nameplate on the left side. The SS series was available as the top line in the Nova model range.

Appearance items included with the SS ranged from a special black-accented grille and specific SS wheel covers to body and wheelhouse moldings and SS badges. The interior featured all-vinyl front Strato bucket seats, a three-spoke steering wheel, and a floor shift trim plate.

Maximum output engine for the '67 Nova SS was the L79 350-hp 327 V-8. This four-barrel motor with 11.00:1 compression generated peak horsepower at 6000 rpm and put out 360 lbs.-ft. of torque at 3200 rpm. The Nova SS retained all of its 1966 gear selections and was surprisingly hot.

Factory ADP	Wheelbase	Length	Shipping Weight	Base V-8	Engine Options	0-to-60 MPH	¼-Mile
$2,487	110 in.	183 in.	2,690 lbs.	283 cid/195 hp	327 cid/275 hp; 327 cid/350 hp	(L79) 7.2 seconds	(L79) 15.10 seconds @ 93 mph

MCFG Says: $19.5K (add 60% for L79 SS 327/350)

He Says: LeRoi "Tex" Smith noted in *Motor Trend* in January '67, "The fattest parts catalog of all is authored by Chevrolet."

We Says: "While the base Nova SS used a relatively mild 275-hp version of the 327 (supposedly to keep it from robbing Camaro sales), the L79 was a hot package that turned the small Chevrolet into a factory hot rod.

Jerry Heasley

1968 CAMARO SS 396

1968 CAMARO SS 396

1968 Camaros had subtle frontal changes, ventless windows, Astro-Ventilation, rectangular parking lamps, new side-marker lamps and a silver grille. Front and rear spoilers were optional. Chevy grew Camaro SS options to five in '68. The SS 396 had a unique hood with four non-functional intake ports on either side.

The great-around-town L35, at $63, was the most popular option with 6,752 orders. Second in popularity was the hot L78 edition, which 4,889 buyers paid $316 to add to their car. The middle-of-the-road L34 version was $184 and went into 2,018 cars. Rarest was the all-out-hi-po L89 version with aluminum heads. Its output was rated the same as the L78s to fool the feds and the insurance salesmen. Due to a high $896 price tag, the L89 drew only 311 orders.

Other desirable Camaro SS 396 options included the M20 and M21 four-speeds, both for $195, the M22 H.D. four-speed gearbox for $322, ZL2 cowl-induction hood for $79, and JL8 four-wheel discs for $500.

Car Life magazine road tested a 375-hp SS 396 with cold-air induction and other muscle car hardware. Its top speed was 126 mph.

Factory ADP	Wheelbase	Length	Shipping Weight	Base 396 V-8	Engine Options	0-to-60 MPH	¼-Mile
(HT) $2,670; (RT) $2,908	108 in.	185 in.	(HT) 3,050 lbs.; (RT) 3,295 lbs.	396 cid/325 hp	396 cid/350 hp; 396 cid/375 hp; 396 cid/375 hp	6.6 seconds	15 seconds @ 94 mph

MCFG Says: (base V-8) (HT) $22K; (RT) $26K (add 25% for L35; 35% for L78; 40% for L89)

He Says: In *Chevrolet High-Performance*, Robert Ackerson said, "Production totals for '68 Camaros powered by 396 V-8s indicate increasing buyer interest in big-engined pony cars."

We Says: "The SS 396 Camaro virtually shouted the fact that this version of Chevy's pony car was the one to be seen in at the root beer stand or the Stoplight Grand Prix."

1968 CAMARO Z/28

1968 CAMARO Z/28

Even though it was made primarily for road racing and only 602 were built, the Z/28 had a strong impact on muscle car fans in '67. While it did not match Mustang sales, the Camaro was close in racing results and this fact rapidly enhanced the Z/28's appeal.

In Trans-Am racing, the Penske Camaros took checkered flags at Marlboro, Las Vegas, and Kent, Washington, earning driver Mark Donohue much-deserved recognition. The Z/28's image was mostly associated with this form of SCCA small-cubic-inch formula competition.

The '68 sport coupe-only Z/28 could not be ordered with air conditioning or automatic transmission. A four-speed gearbox and power-assisted front disc brakes were mandatory. Z/28s featured the same hot 302-cid small-block V-8 used in '67. It had an easy-to-remember 4.0 x 3.0-inch bore and stroke, a single 800-cfm Holley four-barrel carb, a special intake manifold and 11.0:1 compression. 290 was maximum horsepower at 5800 rpm and it generated 290 lbs.-ft. of torque at 4200 rpm.

In addition to the standard Muncie four-speed, a Muncie close-ratio four-speed was the only option. A 3.73:1 rear axle was standard; 3.07:1, 3.31:1, 3.55:1, 4.10:1, 4.56:1, and 4.88:1 were available. The Z/28 started to take off in sales this year and Chevy put together 7,199 examples of its Camaro road racer.

Factory ADP	Wheelbase	Length	Shipping Weight	Base V-8	Engine Options	0-to-60 MPH	¼-Mile
$3,297	108 in.	185 in.	(base V-8) 2,985 lbs.	302 cid/290 hp	None	7.4 seconds	14.85 seconds @ 101.4 mph

MCFG Says: $30K

They Says: *Car Life* (July '68) said, "A pint-size engine with the heart of a tiger gives it superior performance and sports car handling."

We Says: "Enthusiasts of the day didn't know that they were making history when they passed up those big-block muscle cars to purchase a Z/28."

Jerry Heasley

1968 CHEVY II SS "BIG BLOCK"

1968 CHEVY II SS "BIG BLOCK"

Chevy's senior-sized compact underwent a styling change in '68. The new body was longer and wider and featured a Chevelle-inspired semi-fastback roofline with wide, flaring sail panels. The new Chevy II was more of a five-passenger Camaro. Both cars shared the same platform, floor, forward subframe, front suspension, and rear suspension. All engines that fit in a Camaro could also be stuffed into a Chevy II.

When the Chevy II first arrived, it used an inline six as its basic (and most ordered) engine. But V-8s up to a 295-hp 350 were available. A midyear, the 325-hp 327 was added. Cars with this engine were capable of doing the quarter-mile in under 16 seconds at around 90 mph. Since this didn't quite cut the muscle car mustard, it wasn't long before the 396-cid Turbo-Jet V-8 with a choice of 350- or 375-hp was offered.

It didn't take long for drag racers like Dickie Harrell and hi-po dealers like Don Yenko Chevrolet and Nickey Chevrolet to realize that the Camaro-type engine bay could also accommodate a 427-cid Chevy big-block V-8, so a small number of such cars were constructed, mainly with drag racing in mind. 427 Novas were not factory issued, so it's hard to get information about cost, performance, or rarity.

Factory ADP	Wheelbase	Length	Shipping Weight	Base Big Block V-8	Engine Options	0-to-60 MPH	¼-Mile
(Big Block) (CPE) About $3,850	111 in.	187.7 in.	2,975 lbs.	396 cid/350 hp	396 cid/375 hp *	(estimated) 6.5 seconds	(estimated) 13.5 seconds @ 105 mph

* *(Non-factory) 427 cid/410 hp; 427 cid/450 hp*

MCFG Says: $62,000 for a Yenko 427

They Says: Chevrolet Motor Division advertised the 396-cid "big-block" Chevy II as "The toughest block on the block."

We Says: "These 'backyard big-blocks' were built only with drag racing in mind, whether the Christmas Tree was at the drag strip or next to the strip mall."

1968 CHEVELLE SS 396

1968 CHEVELLE SS 396

A new long-nose/short-deck body with a "wrap-over" front end characterized '68 Chevelles. GM mid-size cars now came in two wheelbases—the shorter for two-door models. Four-doors had a 4-inch-longer stance. The SS 396 was now a separate series. It included a sport coupe and a ragtop on the shorter wheelbase.

The SS 396 was more distinctive, thanks to matte black finish around lower body perimeter, except when the cars were finished in dark colors. Other SS features included F70 x 14 Wide-Oval red-stripe tires, accent stripes, a twin-domed hood with simulated air intakes, "SS" badges, vinyl upholstery and a H.D. three-speed transmission with floor shifter.

The standard engine was the L35 type 396. The L34 version was $105 extra and was the only option early in the year. When 375-hp Dodge Charger R/Ts and 445-hp Mercury Cyclones started stealing sales, Chevy re-released the L78 engine for just $237 more than a base V-8. About 57,600 Chevelle SS 396s were made. This total included 4,751 with the L78 engine and 4,082 with the L34 option.

Factory ADP	Wheelbase	Length	Shipping Weight	Base V-8	Engine Options	0-to-60 MPH	¼-Mile
(HT) $2,899; (RT) $3,102	112 in.	202 in.	(HT) 3,475 lbs.; (RT) 3,551 lbs.	(L35) 396 cid/325 hp	(L34) 396 cid/350 hp; (L78) 396 cid/375 hp	6.8 seconds	14.8 seconds @ 98.8 mph

MCFG Says: (HT) $28K; (RT) $35K (add 30% for L78)

They Says: *Car Life* said, "We are, of course, aware of the 12-second potential of the Chevelle SS 396 when fully prepared for strictly drag racing."

We Says: "A pretty car . . . pretty cool . . . pretty fast . . . pretty well perfect for just about any muscle car application."

John Kefalonitis

1968 CORVETTE 427

1968 CORVETTE 427

The 'Vette's first major restyling since '63 resulted in a more aerodynamic front end with vacuum-operated hidden headlights and disappearing wipers. Except for the rocker panels, the sides had no chrome. Push-button door handles were new. The blunt rear deck had four round taillights. The wraparound, wing-like rear bumper and license plate holder looked '67-ish. The fastback was replaced by a tunnel roof coupe with a removable back window and optional T-top. The ragtop's optional hardtop had a glass rear window.

Chevy's 427 big-block V-8 had a 4.251 x 3.76-inch bore and stroke and came in four versions. The least-powerful L36 had hydraulic valve lifters, 10:25:1 compression and a single Holley four-barrel carb. Then came the L68 with 10.25:1 compression and three Holley two-barrels. The L71 was a step up the performance ladder with its special solid-lifter cam, Tri-Power and 11.0:1 compression.

The L88 aluminum-head V-8 was the ultimate 427. This was a $947 option made primarily for racing. With a 3.36:1 rear axle, the L88 ragtop did the quarter-mile in 13.56 seconds at 111.10 mph.

Factory ADP	Wheelbase	Length	Shipping Weight	Base 427 V-8	Engine Options	0-to-60 MPH	¼-Mile
(CPE) $6,905; (RT) $6,562	98 in.	183 in.	(CPE) 3,055 lbs.; (RT) 3,068 lbs.	(L36) 427 cid/390 hp	(L71/L68/L88) 427 cid/400 hp; 427 cid/435 hp; 427 cid/560 hp	(L68) 7 seconds	(L68) 13.41 seconds @ 109.5 mph

MCFG Says: (CPE) $26K; (RT) $30K (add 50% for L71; 70% for L68; 100% for L88)

They Says: "The tall gear in back made 13.56 seconds at 111 mph seem respectable," said *Hot Rod* in '69. "But we know it's about two seconds from where it should be."

We Says: "The '68 Vette looked exciting just standing still; the addition of the 427 made it an exciting ride."

Jerry Heasley

1969 CAMARO RS/SS 396 INDY 500 PACE CAR

1969 CAMARO RS/SS 396 INDY 500 PACE CAR

Although not the hottest muscle Camaro of '69, (some 427-powered COPO cars were also built) the 396-powered Indy Pace Car is one of the most collected. After making a hit at the "Brickyard" in '67, Chevy was invited to bring the Camaro back.

The real Indy 500 Pace Cars were 375-hp SS 396 ragtops with Hugger Orange racing stripes, rear spoilers and Black-and-Orange hound's-tooth upholstery. About 100 official cars were built. Chevrolet then released the Indy Pace Car replica option (RPO Z11) and sold 3,674 copycat cars to the general public. The Z11 was actually just a $37 striping package for ragtops only. But other extras, such as the $296 SS option and the special interior, were also required. Buyers could order the pace car treatment on either RS/SS 350 or RS/SS 396 ragtops. The 350-powered versions are much more common. They had 300 hp.

To qualify as a collectible muscle car, an Indy Pace Car replica has to have the 396 big block, which came in four variations. These were the L35 ($63) with 325 hp, the L34 ($184) with 350 hp, the L78 ($316) with 375 hp and the L89 ($711) with aluminum heads and 375 hp. It isn't hard to guess which is rarest and most valuable.

Factory ADP	Wheelbase	Length	Shipping Weight	Base V-8	Engine Options	0-to-60 MPH	¼-Mile
$3,405	108 in.	186 in.	3,385 lbs.	350 cid/300 hp	396 cid/325 hp; 396 cid/350 hp; 396 cid/375 hp	6.8 seconds	14.77 seconds @ 98.72 mph

MCFG **Says:** $38K (add 25% for L78)

They Says: Chevrolet advertised, "A word or two to the competition—you lose" and an ad showing the Pace Car with Indy 500 cars read "The '69 Camaro SS keeps tough company."

We Says: "The '69 Camaro SS 396 was built to hug the road and cover the shortest distance between two points in the road fast. Pace Car duties reinforced the image."

1969 CAMARO Z/28

Jerry Heasley

1969 CAMARO Z/28

The restyled '69 Camaro had a squarish, race-car-like look. It was perfect for the Z/28's redesigned H.O. small-block. This 302-cid V-8 was created for Trans-Am racing. It featured big valve heads, a forged-steel crank, a new four-bolt-mains block with larger webbing, nodular iron main bearing caps, new pistons, a 30/30 solid-lifter cam, 11.0:1 compression and numerous other performance goodies.

The Z/28 was offered only as a coupe. Some say it came in a basic $458 version and a $758 version with dealer-installed headers. At least six variations exist. The basic package included the 302 V-8, dual exhausts with deep-tone mufflers, a H.D. suspension, rear bumper guards, a H.D. radiator, a temp-control fan, quick-ratio power steering, 15 x 7 Rally rims, E70 x 15 RWL tires, a 3.73:1 rear axle, and special hood and trunk stripes.

On October 18, bright engine accents and Z/28 emblems for the grille, front fenders and rear panel were added. Rally wheels were no longer specified, but wheel trim rings were. The price remained $458. On January 2, 1969, a tach or special instrumentation was made mandatory and the price rose to $474. On April 1, the specs were changed to read "dual exhausts" only and wheel center caps, front valance panel, and rear spoiler were specified. The price increased to $507. This year 20,302 Z/28s were made.

Factory ADP	Wheelbase	Length	Shipping Weight	Base V-8	Engine Options	0-to-60 MPH	¼-Mile
$3,588	108 in.	188 in.	(base V-8 coupe) 3,135 lbs.	302 cid/290 hp	None	7.4 seconds	15.1 seconds @ 95 mph

MCFG Says: $30K tops

He Says: Chevy GM Pete Estes said, "Boy, there are kids out there with money and when they hear how Mark Donahue cleans up in Trans Am racing with a Z/28, they've just got to have one for themselves. In '69, we plan to sell 27,000. Can you imagine, 27,000!"

We Says: "Estes' estimate was a little high, but the '69 Camaro Z/28 is such an awesome machine that it's a wonder Chevy didn't sell 27 million of them ... or at least 20 million."

Jerry Heasley

1969 CHEVELLE SS 396/SS 427

1969 CHEVELLE SS 396/SS 427

Except for how the SS 396 was merchandised, Chevy made no basic change in the design of its '69 mid-size muscle car. There was no separate SS 396 series this year. The SS equipment package became the Z25 option. It was ordered for 86,307 cars.

The popular option package included a big-block V-8, dual exhausts with oval tailpipes and bright tips, a black-painted grille, bright wheel opening and roof drip moldings, a black-painted cove, Malibu-style rear quarter end caps, taillights and taillight bezels, a twin power dome hood, special "SS 396" emblems on the grille, front fenders and rear deck lid and 14 x 7-inch SS wheels with F70 x 14 RWL tires. An extremely rare '69 engine was a 427-cid V-8 available on a special Central Office Production Order (COPO) basis from GM's Tonawanda, New York, factory.

Factory ADP	Wheelbase	Length	Shipping Weight	Base V-8	Engine Options	0-to-60 MPH	¼-Mile
(CPE) $2,680; (HT) $2,743 (Malibu HT) $2,822; (RT) $3,021	112 in.	197 in.	(CPE) 3,165 lbs.; (HT) 3,205/3,230 lbs.; (RT) 3,300 lbs.	396 cid/ 325 hp	396 cid/350 hp; 396 cid/375 hp; 396 cid/375 hp	(375-hp) 5.8 seconds	(375-hp) 14.41 seconds @ 97.35 mph

MCFG **Says:** (Malibu SS 396) (HT) $25K; (RT) $31K

They Says: *Motor Trend* said, "It has the mellowest roar we've heard since our last flat-head Ford with dual Smithies and that was a few years ago."

We Says: "The Chevelle SS 396 has evolved into a 'poster boy' for the muscle car movement and its value has risen proportionately."

1969 CORVETTE STINGRAY 427

Jerry Heasley

1969 CORVETTE STINGRAY 427

After a year's absence, the Stingray name (now spelled as one word) re-appeared on the front fenders. The back-up lights were integrated into the center taillights. The ignition was now on the steering column and the door depression button used in '68 was eliminated. (A key lock was put in its place.) Front and rear disc brakes, headlight washers, a center console, wheel trim rings, carpeting and all-vinyl upholstery were now standard 'Vette equipment.

The 390-hp 427 V-8 was again the starting-point engine for muscle car enthusiasts. Then came RPO L68 for $327 extra. It was the same 10.25:1 compression V-8 fitted with three two-barrel carbs, which upped its output to 400 hp. The 435-hp L71 427 Tri-Power engine also returned in much the same form as '68. Its price tag was $437.

Three ultra-high-performing options began with the L88. It included a "power blister" hood. This year the basic package was $1,032. There was also the L89 V-8 for $832. The ultimate 1969 power option was the all-aluminum ZL1 V-8. Only two ZL1s were made and the specs are a secret.

Factory ADP	Wheelbase	Length	Shipping Weight	Base 427 V-8	Engine Options	0-to-60 MPH	¼-Mile
(HT) $4,781; (RT) $4,438	98 in.	183 in.	(HT) 3,140 lbs.; (RT) 3,145 lbs.	427 cid/390 hp	427 cid/400 hp; 427 cid/435 hp *	6.5 seconds	(L88) 14.10 seconds @ 106.89 mph

Ultra Hi-Po options: (L71/L89) 427 cid/435 hp; (L88) 427 cid/560 hp

MCFG Says: (HT) $26K; (RT) $30K (add 40% for L68; add 20% for L71/L89; add 40% for L89)

They Says: *Car Life* said, "With this one beautiful exception, there is no such thing as a true American sports car."

We Says: "Awesome … just awesome. The L71 made the trip down the quarter-mile in 13.94 seconds at 105.63 mph and the L88 had a top speed of 151 mph."

1970 CAMARO RS/SS 396

Jerry Heasley

1970 CAMARO RS/SS 396

Sales of the third "Hugger" were slow. Chevy dealers continued to sell leftover '69 Camaros until they ran out. The '70 model (a.k.a. "'70 1/2 Camaro") went on sale February 26, '70. It was completely revamped with high-intensity headlights, a semi-fastback roof, a snout-style egg-crate grille, and a smoother looking rear. Only a coupe was offered. Standard equipment included GM safety features, Strato-Bucket vinyl seats, carpets, Astro-Ventilation, a left outside rearview mirror, side marker lights, and E78-14 tires. The base engine was a 307-cid small-block V-8.

The SS package included a 300-hp 350, bright engine accents, power brakes, special ornaments, hood insulation, F70-14 RWL tires, 14 x 7 wheels, a black grille, Hide-Away wipers, and SS emblems for $290. RS equipment included a black grille with a rubber-tipped vertical center bar and resilient body-color frame, among other things.

The SS 396 substituted a 396-cid V-8 with a 4.126 x 3.76-inch bore and stroke. It actually displaced 402 cubic inches, although Chevy promoted it as a "396." It had a 10.25:1 compression ratio and a single four-barrel carb. Advertised horsepower was 350 at 5200 rpm.

Factory ADP	Wheelbase	Length	Shipping Weight	Base V-8	Engine Options	0-to-60 MPH	¼-Mile
$3,724	108 in.	186 in.	3,275 lbs.	350 cid/300 hp	396 cid/350 hp; 396 cid/375 hp	(L78) 6.8 seconds	(L78) 13 seconds @ 108 mph

MCFG Says: (HT) $24K

They Says: Chevrolet advertised, "The new Camaro—one look says a lot—one drive says it all."

We Says: "The Camaro got a redesign that brought a sleeker, more refined look for '70."

Jerry Heasley

1970 CAMARO Z28

1970 CAMARO Z28

Styling, engineering, performance, and quality in the '70 Z28 were high. But, its production total of 8,733 was low enough to make owning one an uncommon treat.

A good indication of the Z28's exceptional nature was winning *Car Life* magazine's first "Showroom Trans-Am Championship" pitting four American sports compacts against each other in acceleration, braking, and cornering. The performance of each was rated by a point system such as the SCCA uses. The cars were then run over a challenging road course to see which could cover it quickest.

A Mustang, Firebird, AMX, and Camaro were compared. The Z28, with its new 350 V-8, was quickest on the drag pad. It did the quarter-mile in 14.50 seconds with a 100.22 mph terminal speed. This gave the Camaro five championship points. It came in second in braking, earning four more points. With its neutral cornering, the Mustang won the handling test, but the Camaro was a close second. The Camaro's average course speed—1:02.6—was also good for second place in the so-called "main event." In all, the Z28 garnered 17 points and was declared the winner.

Factory ADP	Wheelbase	Length	Shipping Weight	Base V-8	Engine Options	0-to-60 MPH	¼-Mile
$3,794	108 in.	186 in.	3,172 lbs.	350 cid/360 hp	None	5.8 seconds	14.2 seconds @ 100.3 mph

MCFG Says: $22K

They Says: "The winner is the Camaro Z28 with 17 points," *Car Life* concluded. "One first, three seconds. The fastest car, and the more consistent."

We Says: "After the screaming orange stripe jobs of the late-'60s, some people didn't appreciate how fast the sophisticated-looking '70 Z28 really was, but the numbers tell the story."

1970 CHEVELLE SS 396

Jerry Heasley

1970 CHEVELLE SS 396

Chevelles had a fatter, more sculptured appearance for 1970. A horizontally split grille with "blended" dual headlights was new. The SS 396 returned, but shortly after production started, the bore size of the big-block V-8 was increased from 4.094-inches to 4.125 inches. This bumped actual displacement to 402 cubic inches, but Chevy kept calling the engine the "Turbo-Jet 396."

Thirteen items made up the SS 396 package: a 350-hp 396 L34 V-8, bright engine accents, power front disc brakes, dual exhausts with bright tips, a black-accented grille, wheel opening moldings, a black resilient rear bumper panel, a special domed hood, the F41 H.D. suspension, special chassis features, SS I.D. including SS emblems on the grille, fenders, rear bumper, steering wheel and door trim, 17 x 7-inch rally wheels and F70 x 14 RWL tires. The optional L78 V-8 had 375 hp at 5600 rpm and 415 lbs.-ft. of torque at 3600 rpm. The aluminum-head L78/L89 version also carried a (conservative) 375 advertised horsepower rating.

Factory ADP	Wheelbase	Length	Shipping Weight	Base SS 396 V-8	Engine Options	0-to-60 MPH	¼-Mile
$4,926*	112 in.	197.2 in.	4,310 lbs.*	(L34) 402 cid/350 hp	(L78) 402 cid/375 hp; (L78/L89) 402 cid/375 hp	(L34) 8.1 seconds	15.5 seconds @ 90.42 mph

* (Sport coupe as tested)

MCFG Says (sport coupe) $27K (add 30% for 375 hp); (convertible) $32K (add 30% for 375 hp)

They Says: "The SS 396 is a complete bill of fare," *Car Life* pointed out. "Order the dinner and you get the salad and the vegetables."

We Says: "Performs like the best muscle cars with handling improved to rival the best sports cars."

1970 CHEVELLE SS 454

Jerry Heasley

1970 CHEVELLE SS 454

By 1970, the SS 396 was no longer the fastest muscle car in town. It was a snappy performer, but muscular newcomers of other brands were faster. To swing the pendulum back, Chevy released a new SS 454. Many conside it the ultimate development of the hot Chevelle SS.

The 454 had a 4.250 x 4.00-inch bore and stroke. It came in two versions. The LS5 featured a 10.25:1 compression ratio and a 750-cfm Rochester Qudrajet carb. This engine was included in the SS 454 option for $503. The hotter LS6 version was $263 additional.

The LS6 was a super-hi-po engine featuring things like four-bolt main bearings, nodular iron bearing caps, H.D. connecting rods, big-diameter exhaust valves and a solid-lifter cam. A test car powered by the LS6 engine moved from 0-to-60 mph in 5.4 seconds and did the standing-start quarter mile in 13.81 seconds at 103.8 mph. That was with THM and a 3.77:1 rear axle. You could also order either 454-cid engine with one of three available four-speeds. Only 3,773 of the SS sport coupes and ragtops built in '70 had one of the 454-cid V-8s and only a relative handful were LS6 editions.

Factory ADP	Wheelbase	Length	Shipping Weight	Base 454 V-8	Engine Options	0-to-60 MPH	¼-Mile
*(HT) $4,470; (RT) $4,670	112 in.	197.2 in.	(HT) 3,307 lbs.; (RT) 3,352 lbs.	(LS5) 454 cid/360 hp	(LS6) 454 cid/450 hp	(LS6/ *Motor Trend*) 7 seconds	(LS6/*Motor Trend*) 13.8 seconds @ 97.4 mph

* As tested price.

MCFG Says: (HT) $31K; (RT) $36K (add 50% for LS6)
He Says: In *Motor Trend* (December '69), A.B. Shuman said, "The massive 450-hp engine in the Chevelle had to come out as top dog in our forays on the 1/4-mile."
We Says: "It's one of those muscle cars that made the insurance company guys turn pale as a ghost when they checked the spec sheet."

Mike Lange

1970 CORVETTE

1970 CORVETTE

The '70 'Vette featured refinements on the basic styling used since '68. There was a new ice-cube-tray grille and matching side fender louvers, rectangular amber front signal lights, fender flares, and square exhausts. The bucket seats and safety belt retractor containers were improved.

A new 454 V-8 featured a 4.251 x 4.00-inch bore and stroke. The LS5 had an advertised 390 hp at 4800 rpm and 500 lbs.-ft. of torque at 3400 rpm. Another hot option was the LT1 V-8, based on the 350 small-block V-8. It was good for 370 hp at 6000 rpm and 380 foot-pounds of torque at 4000 rpm.

A 465-hp LS7 454 V-8 was listed in some early '70 sales literature, but never made it to the showroom. Only one car with the LS7 engine was ever built. *Sports Car Graphic* editor Paul Van Valkenburgh drove it 2,500 miles and raved about it. The car did the quarter-mile in 13.8 seconds at 108 mph. GM's policies against ultra-hi-po cars at this time led to the option being dropped. With the LT1 around, 'Vette lovers didn't miss it much.

Factory ADP	Wheelbase	Length	Shipping Weight	Base V-8	Engine Options	0-to-60 MPH	¼-Mile
(LT1 *Car Life* test car) $6,316	98 in.	182.5 in.	(LR1 *Car Life* test car) 3,710 lbs.	(ZQ3) 350 cid/300 hp	(Small block) (L46) 350 cid/350 hp; (LT1) 350 cid/370 hp*	(LT1) 5.7 seconds	(LT1) 14.7 seconds @ 102.15 mph

* Big Block V-8 Options: (LS5) 454 cid/390 hp; (LS7) 454 cid/465 hp

MCFG Says: (CPE) $25K; (RT) $29K (add 70% for LT1; add 30% for LS5)

They Says: *Car Life* magazine said of the LT1, "It is, at this writing, the best of all possible Corvettes."

We Says: "This shiny-bumper shark feels pretty much at home on the street or on the racetrack."

1970 MONTE CARLO SS 454

Jerry Heasley

1970 MONTE CARLO SS 454

Based on the 116-inch-wheelbase Chevelle sedan, the Monte Carlo hardtop had its own longer frame to accommodate a classic-looking 6-foot-long hood, but it still shared many parts with Chevy's intermediate. Big-block V-8s fit easily in the new car's engine bay.

Monte Carlos had different weight distribution, so Chevy beefed up the springs and shocks and installed heavier stabilizers. The SS 454 Monte Carlo came an auto-leveling system with rear shocks that had pressurized air bags.

Standard equipment included all features found on Chevelle Malibus, plus power front disc brakes and G78-15B tires. Chevrolet's new 454 Turbo-Jet V-8 was available with the SS 454 package only. It had a 4.251 x 4.00-inch bore and stroke, 10.25:1 compression and a single four-barrel carb.

With only 2.6 percent of the '70 Monte Carlos built with the SS 454 option, total production for the year was a mere 3,823 copies of the muscle car version. That's one reason why a '70 SS 454 Monte Carlo is now worth its weight in gold.

Factory ADP	Wheelbase	Length	Shipping Weight	Base V-8 (SS 454)	Engine Options	0-to-60 MPH	¼-Mile
(as tested) $5,139	116 in.	205.8 in.	4,420 lbs.	454 cid/360 hp	None	(SS 454) 7 seconds	(LT1) 14.9 seconds @ 92 mph

MCFG Says: $20.5K (add 20% for SS)

They Says: *Car Life* said of the Monte Carlo SS 454, "Chevrolet's new personal car becomes a gentleman's bomb!"

We Says: "*Car Life's* test car did 0-to-60 in 7.2 seconds and the quarter-mile in 16.2 seconds at 90.1 mph, which we would call realistic, but not slow by any means."

Jerry Heasley

1970 NOVA SS 350/396

1970 NOVA SS 350/396

The '70 Nova had a new grille insert with squarer openings than the previous year's model. The "Coke bottle"-shaped body had the popular long hood/short rear deck look. Variable-ratio power steering was a new extra. This was also the era of GM's in-the-windshield antenna that helped youthful Nova owners tune in their favorite music while cruising on Friday night.

Chevy dealers had plenty of extra-cost options to pump up the out-the-door price of the coupe, which sold for $2,503 with a base V-8. Muscle car fans skipped the base 307 V-8 for the Z26 Nova SS package. Its included a 300-hp 350 V-8, dual exhausts, power front disc brakes, a simulated hood air intake, simulated fender louvers, bright accents, a black-finished grille, a black rear end panel, 14 x 7-inch wheels, E70 x 14 white-stripe tires, hood insulation and "SS" emblems. A four-speed or THM was mandatory with the $291 SS option.

Two optional Turbo-Jet V-8s were available for those who wanted to compete in the "stoplight grand prix" either at a drag strip or the downtown cruising strip. The first L34 big-block came with the 350-hp 396 (actually 402) V-8 and cost $184. The L78 package included the 375-hp 396 V-8 for $316 above the cost of the base 350. Nova SS packages were added to 19,558 cars in '70, of which 1,947 had the L34 V-8 and 5,262 had the L78.

Factory ADP	Wheelbase	Length	Shipping Weight	Base V-8	Engine Options	0-to-60 MPH	¼-Mile
(as tested) $3,807	111 in.	189.4 in.	3,094 lbs.	350 cid/300 hp	396 (402) cid/ 350 hp; 396 (402) cid/ 375 hp	(350) 9.3 seconds	(350 cid) 16.5 seconds @ 85 mph

MCFG **Says:** $20.5K (add 20% for SS)

They Says: *Car Life* said, "Here's a trim package, Nova, a special suspension, and a rapid-firing engine."

We Says: "The SS 350 was an interesting package aimed at the young buyer who wanted to go just a little fast for just a little extra money."

1971 CAMARO RS/SS 396

Jerry Heasley

1971 CAMARO RS/SS 396

The easiest way to spot a '71 Camaro is to look for high-back buckets with integral headrests. Otherwise, little was changed. All GM safety features, power front discs, steel door guardrails, vinyl seats, bucket-style rear seats, carpeting, a cigar lighter, Astro-Ventilation, E78-14 tires, and a three-speed with floor shift were standard. The base V-8 was a 307-cid small block.

The SS included a 270-hp 350 V-8, dual exhausts, bright engine accents, special ornamentation, hood insulation, F70-14 RWL tires, 14 x 7-inch wheels, a black grille and Hide-Away wipers. The RS added a black-finished grille with a rubber-tipped vertical center bar and resilient body-color frame, independent left and right front bumpers, a license plate bracket below the right front bumper, parking lights with bright accents molded on the grille panel, Hide-Away headlights, bright moldings, and other stuff.

The 396 (actually 402 cubic inches) had a high-lift cam, hydraulic lifters, dual exhausts, 8.5:1 compression and a Rochester four-barrel carb. An M20 wide-ratio four-speed with floor shifter was standard with the 396 and could be hooked to 3.73:1 or 4.10:1 rear axles. An M21 close-ratio four-speed was available. A three-speed M40 THM came with either column or floor shift.

Factory ADP	Wheelbase	Length	Shipping Weight	Base "396" V-8	Engine Options	0-to-60 MPH	¼-Mile
$3,222	108 in.	188 in.	3,218 lbs.	396 (402) cid/ 300 hp	None	N/A	N/A

MCFG Says: $18K (add 10% for SS; 20% for RS/SS; 20% for 396)

They Says: *Motor Trend* (December 1970) said, "If the pony car concept wanes in the next decade, the latest Camaros will be remembered as the zenith of development of that particular genre."

We Says: "The RS/SS 396 was recommended by *Motor Trend* for 'effortless cruising' and proved that Chevy 'had it all together' as far as the sports-compact muscle car niche went."

Jerry Heasley

1971 CHEVELLE "HEAVY CHEVY"

1971 CHEVELLE "HEAVY CHEVY"

The Heavy Chevy package was a midyear option for any '71 Chevelle sport coupe with V-8 power that didn't have the optional SS equipment package. It had a dealer cost of $113 and retailed for $142.

Contents of this VF3 package included a black-accented grille, special body side striping, "Heavy Chevy" decals for the hood, front fenders and rear deck, a special domed hood with locking pins, and other goodies.

Like Plymouth's Road Runner, Pontiac's "Judge" and Ford's Falcon Torino, the Heavy Chevy was aimed at budget-priced buyers. Although it looked like a real muscle car, its 350-cid 200-hp base engine did not command the same insurance premiums as larger big-block V-8s.

Only 6,727 cars were fitted with this package, but it is not known if all the cars were of one series, or if both Chevelle and Malibu versions were ordered. The list below shows the base prices of the sport coupe in both series, with the retail price of the YF3 package added. The Heavy Chevy was also available with 245-, 270- and 300-hp V-8s.

Factory ADP	Wheelbase	Length	Shipping Weight	Base V-8	Engine Options	0-to-60 MPH	¼-Mile
(Chevelle) $2,804; (Malibu) $2,951	97 in.	178 in.	(Chevelle) 3,300 lbs.; (Malibu) 3,327 lbs.	350 cid/200 hp	350 cid/245 hp; 350 cid/270 hp; 400 cid/400 hp	(270 hp) 10.1 seconds	16.9 seconds @ 82 mph

MCFG Says: (Chevelle) $23K; (Malibu) $25K

They Says: www.chevelle.com says, "Choosing is what the Heavy Chevy is all about. Settle for its looks or make it a **h-e-a-v-y Heavy Chevy** with options."

We Says: "Not the fastest muscle car, but it has 'the look' and the name is catchy, so the collector prices seem to be climbing accordingly."

Jerry Heasley

1971 CHEVELLE SS 454

1971 CHEVELLE SS 454

Chevelles had frontal changes in '71. A new twin-level grille was divided by a bright horizontal bar. The front parking lights were moved to the fenders. Muscle car madness was in decline and this was an era of "lick-'em-stick-'em" muscle with the decals, but not the big-cube engines, of the recent past. Chevy let buyers order all SS goodies on any '71 Malibu sport coupe or ragtop as long as it had a 350-, 400- or 454-cid V-8. The SS 454 was the *real* musclecar.

The RPO Z15 SS package sold for $357. It included power brakes with discs up front, a black-accented grille, a special suspension, a special domed hood with functional hood lock pins, SS identification for the hood and rear deck and fenders, a driver's side remote-control sports mirror, gray-finished 15 x 7-inch five-spoke Sport wheels, F60 x 14 RWL tires, a black-accented steering column and a steering wheel with SS nameplate.

If you wanted a '71 SS 454 you had to order one of the two big-block engines as an add-on option. Both came with the choice of a four-speed or a three-speed THM. Chevy put together an estimated 80,000 cars that carried the SS option this year. Of those units, 19,292 were equipped with 454-cid V-8s.

Factory ADP	Wheelbase	Length	Shipping Weight	Base V-8	Engine Options	0-to-60 MPH	¼-Mile
(LS5) (HT) $3,443; (RT) $3,645	112 in.	197.5 in.	(LS5) (HT) 3,407 lbs.; (RT) 3,452 lbs.	(LS5) 454 cid/365 hp; (LS6) 454 cid/425 hp	None	(LS5) 6 seconds	(LS5) 13.77 seconds @ 100 mph

MCFG **Says:** (HT) $26K; (RT) $32K

They Says: "There's still an SS 454," Chevy advised. "Any car that was named the best of its kind in *Car and Driver's* reader's choice (the '70 Chevelle SS 454) is sure to stay around."

We Says: "If the muscle car era was singing its swan song, the SS 454 at least let it go out carrying a tune."

Jerry Heasley

1987 CAMARO 5.7-LITER IROC-Z

1987 CAMARO 5.7-LITER IROC-Z

The 5.7-liter IROC-Z arrived in '87. Chevy advertised it as "a mean hombre in '87 with the arrival of the 5.7-liter TPI V-8 power plant roaring under the hood of the hot IROC-Z."

With the earlier 5.0-liter IROC-Z already accounting for nearly 25 percent of Camaro Z28 sales (which in turn represented 47 percent of all Camaros sold) the 5.7-liter version was expected to up overall business. A potential impediment, the unavailability of air conditioning on the 5.7-liter IROC-Z, was temporary, since it was slated for availability starting in October '86.

Except for its Camaro LB9 drive belts, exhaust system and electronic control module, the new L98 IROC-Z V-8 was identical to the Vette 5.7-liter TPI engine. With the big engine, a number of extra-cost options were mandatory. They included a special MX4 version of the four-speed 700R4 automatic transmission with an upgraded torque converter, a limited-slip differential, four-wheel disc brakes and an engine oil cooler. Also available in limited numbers as an '87 model was an IROC-Z Camaro ragtop conversion done by the American Sunroof Corporation (ASC) of Livonia, Mich.

Factory ADP	Wheelbase	Length	Shipping Weight	Base V-8	Engine Options	0-to-60 MPH	¼-Mile
(CPE) $15,412; (RT) $19,841	101 in.	188 in.	(CPE) 3,121 lbs.; (RT) 3,350 lbs.	350 cid/190 hp	350 cid/225 hp	6.2 seconds	14.5 seconds @ 96 mph

MCFG **Says:** (CPE) $10.2K; (RT) $20K

They Says: *Hot Rod* magazine, in its January 1987 issue, suggested that "it could be the closest facsimile to a full-bore road racing car you'll ever drive."

We Says: "These cars are really fast with the 350 stuffed under the hood. Prices are climbing fast, too."

Jerry Heasley

1990 CORVETTE ZR1

1990 CORVETTE ZR1

Could it be that Chevy decided to launch an effort to compete in the space race? The '90 Vette ZR1 was a rocketship that might give that impression. Another impression that the ZR1 imparted was that this built-for-speed bowtie creation would become an instant collecter car.

ZR1 collectibility went beyond initial demand for the car. Subtle styling changes set it apart from the '90 Vette coupe, as did its low production. Estimates from Chevrolet had only 2,000 ZR1 'Vettes being produced for 1990. In the end, 3,049 were built.

The ZR1, at first glance, looked like a 'Vette coupe, but it was stretched 1 inch and was 3 inches wider to accommodate an increased rear tread width. The ZR1's telltale was its rectangular taillights. The ZR1 also had a unique drive train. Its all-aluminum LT5 V-8 produced enough thrust to send a ZR1 into orbit. The LT5 was constructed by boat-engine specialists at Mercury Marine. An AZF six-speed was mated to the LT5. The ZR1 did not come with automatic.

Factory ADP	Wheelbase	Length	Shipping Weight	Base V-8	Engine Options	0-to-60 MPH	¼-Mile
$62,675	96.2 in.	177.4 in.	3,465 lbs.	350 cid/375 hp	None	4.3 seconds	14.5 seconds

MCFG **Says:** $49K

He Says: "The ZR1 is head and shoulders above the Ferraris and Lamborghinis," Glenn Ross said. "It drives like it's on silk."

We Says: "The ZR1 took forever to get here, but once it arrived, it didn't take long to go away—very fast!"

1993 CAMARO Z-28

1993 CAMARO Z-28

The fourth-generation Camaro was introduced a few months into the '93 model run. It featured an all-new body, a reworked chassis and a Z28 that came only one way—fast. Performance, handling, and even comfort were improved over Gen III models.

Only the coupe was offered in '93. The body, while sleeker than the old style, featured a 68-degree raked windshield and a steel structure to which composite (plastic) panels were attached. Optional glass roof panels retailed for $895.

The engine was an aluminum head 350-cid LT-1 V-8. You also got a standard B-W T-56 six-speed, four-wheel antilock disc brakes, 16 x 8-inch aluminum wheels, and Goodyear GA P235/55R16 tires. Z-rated GS-C Goodyears were optional at $144. The Z-rated tires raised top speed from 108 mph to 150 mph. Optional on the Z28 at $595 was the THM 4L60. Like the LT1 V-8, this automatic transmission had seen service on the Vette.

The no-excuses Z28 was an immediate hit with the car magazines. *Car and Driver* pitted it against the Ford Mustang Cobra and declared the Z28 the fastest.

Factory ADP	Wheelbase	Length	Shipping Weight	Base V-8	Engine Options	0-to-60 MPH	¼-Mile
$17,269	101.1 in.	193.2 in.	3,373 lbs.	350 cid/275 hp	None	5.3 seconds	14 seconds @ 100 mph

MCFG **Says:** $13,500 (add 10% for Indy Pace Car)

They Says: *Motor Trend* tested several performance cars and noted that the Camaro—with a top speed of 151 mph—represented the "biggest bang for the buck" of the bunch.

We Says: "These Camaros were good-looking machines that caught your eye at a traffic light—and they could go as fast as they looked."

1999 CAMARO Z28 SS

CHEVROLET
1999 CAMARO Z28 SS

The '99 Camaro Z28 SS was top dog in a *Car and Driver* comparison test in August '99. The face off pitted the ragtop version of Chevy's muscular pony car against counterpart ragtops wearing Pontiac Firebird Trans Am and Ford SVT Cobra Mustang badges.

Powering the Z28 SS was a 346-cid 16-valve LS1 V-8 with an aluminum block and heads. It had GM's engine-control system with port fuel injection. This system generated 320 hp at 5200 rpm and 335 lbs.-ft. of torque at 4000 rpm. With this engine, the Z28 SS was not the fastest car in the test, but it was right up there. Available factory transmission options included a six-speed manual gearbox or a four-speed automatic.

The '99 Camaro Z28 SS really excelled when it came to roadability and handling. It had a tight suspension, excellent steering, and great brakes. The Camaro Z28 SS ragtop used in the test did 0-to-100 mph in 12.8 seconds and 0-to-130 mph in 24.6 seconds. The car's top speed was recorded as 160 mph.

Factory ADP	Wheelbase	Length	Shipping Weight	Base V-8	Engine Options	0-to-60 MPH	¼-Mile
(HT) $24,370; (RT) $31,350	101.1 in.	193.2 in.	(HT) 3,446 lbs.; (RT) 3,565 lbs.	346 cid/320 hp	None	5.3 seconds	13.9 seconds @ 103 mph

MCFG **Says:** (HT) $13K; (RT) $16K

They Says: *Car and Driver* said, "The Camaro Z28 SS is the best car to drive on an every-day basis; ABS braking and traction control are important considerations when it comes to driving in such a machine daily."

We Says: "On a good day you can grab a good example of the '99 SS on eBay for $13K or so and you'll feel good about doing it."

1963 POLARA 500

Doug Mitchel

DODGE

1963 POLARA 500

It is hard to think of the '63 Dodge Polara 500 ragtop as a muscle car, until you see the results that Jim Wright recorded when he test drove such a car for *Motor Trend* magazine. He noted that the car's times through various speeds and the quarter-mile were "very impressive," especially considering that it used a 3.23.0:1 rear axle.

With its 4.25 x 3.38-inch bore and stroke, Chrysler's 383 big-block was one of the best engines for performance driving. It used 10.0:1 aluminum pistons and the four-barrel version was a deep-breathing V-8 that could rev to a 5,500-rpm red line, above its 4,600-rpm horsepower peak. The torque output was a strong 425 lbs.-ft. at 2,800 rpm. Wright's car had a B-W T-10 four-speed with a 2.20.0:1 low gear, which didn't hurt its drag strip performance one bit.

The '63 Polara was considered the top trim level "Dodge" back in '63, when the even fancier Custom 880 was thought of as, well, a Custom 880 instead of a Dodge. The basic Polara 500 ragtop (which included four bucket seats) listed for $3,196 and weighed 3,546 lbs.

Factory ATP	Wheelbase	Length	Curb Weight	Base V-8	Engine Options	0-to-60 MPH	¼-Mile
(convertible) $4,266	119 in.	208.1 in.	(convertible, as tested) 3,985 lbs.	318 cid/ 230 hp	383 cid/305 hp; 383 cid/330 hp	7.7 seconds	15.8 seconds @ 92 mph

MCFG Says: $25K

He Says: "Barring the all-out drag-strip engines, there aren't many that can stay with the 330-hp "383" in acceleration," said Jim Wright in *Motor Trend*.

We Says: "Some muscle can punch a hole in a wall and other muscle can move mountains. The '63 Polara with the right engine/trans/axle combo falls into the latter category."

Jerry Heasley

1966 CORONET 500 HEMI

1966 CORONET 500 HEMI

Introduced in '65, the mid-sized Coronet became the centerpiece of Dodge muscle car history. An ad that ran that year asked "Why not drop a Hemi in the new Coronet 500?" But, the '65s came only with the Race Hemi, which created more of a drag machine than a muscle car. This was corrected by making the 425-hp Street Hemi available in 1966. Displacement-wise and power-wise, it matched the race version, but the big difference was a hydraulic lifter cam and a 10.5:1 compression ratio. It was the most powerful production car engine ever built, but was still suited to street use. In addition, the optional Hemi engine was a good deal, for under $500.

The Coronet was restyled in 1966. The top-of-the-line Coronet 500 model had Charger-like bucket seats with a choice of all-vinyl or vinyl-and-fabric upholstery. Dodge offered a selection of 15 exterior colors in acrylic enamel finish.

A "500" designation on the car indicated the model, but not the engine. In fact, you really had to open the hood to see if there was a Hemi lurking underneath. Only 340 Coronet 500 hardtops (204 of them four-speeds) got the Hemi, along with just 21 ragtops (12 with four-speeds). Another 379 of the other Coronets also had this engine added.

Factory ADP	Wheelbase	Length	Shipping Weight	Base Hemi V-8	Engine Options	0-to-60 MPH	¼-Mile
(HT) $3,205; (RT) $3,421	117 in.	203 in.	(HT) 3,275 lbs.; (RT) 3,345 lbs.	426 cid/425 hp	None	6.1 seconds	14.5 seconds @ 97 mph

MCFG Says: (HT) $15.5K; (RT) $25K (add 100% for Hemi)

They Says: *Car Review* (April 1966) said, "To put it simply, these sleepers are wide-awake performers."

We Says: "Buying a Hemi Coronet was like getting an atomic bomb in a plain brown paper wrapper."

Jerry Heasley

1966 HEMI CHARGER

1966 HEMI CHARGER

Fastbacks were in vogue in the mid-'60s. Based on a silver show car, the Charger was a super-streamlined Coronet with a rich interior. Enthusiast mags rushed to do tests and usually drove cars with the 325-hp 383 V-8 that were actually quite fast. *Car and Driver* registered a 7.8-second 0-to-60 time and did the quarter-mile in 16.2 seconds at 88 mph. With the same engine and tranny, *Motor Trend* reported an 8.9-second 0-to-60-mph time and 16.3 seconds for the quarter mile at 85 mph. The Hemi could shave roughly two seconds or more off both times.

The availability of the 425-hp 426 Hemi made the large, lush Charger a contender in the muscle car market. The Hemi featured dual four-barrel carbs, extra-wide dual exhausts and all sorts of H.D. performance hardware. The use of either a four-speed or a TorqueFlite was mandatory.

Total production of 1966 Chargers hit 37,300 cars. Of these, only 468 had Hemis and 218 featured TorqueFlite. NASCAR drivers thought the fastback would enhance the Charger's aerodynamics in stock car racing, but it actually tended to lift at the rear. After spoilers were added, the Chargers won 18 races.

Factory ADP	Wheelbase	Length	Shipping Weight	Base V-8	Engine Options	0-to-60 MPH	¼-Mile
$3,146	117 in.	203 in.	3,499 lbs.	318 cid/230hp	361 cid/265 hp; 383 cid/325 hp; 426 cid/425 hp	6.4 seconds.	14.16 seconds @ 96.20 mph

MCFG Says: (Hemi Charger) $65K

They Says: *Car Life* (January 1966) said, "Return with us now to those thrilling days of yesteryear … when out of the past comes the thundering hoof beats of the great horse Silver."

We Says: "Sounds like C/L was a little hung up on the silver show car, but the Hemi Charger was definitely *precious metal*—and still is today."

1967 HEMI CORONET

1967 HEMI CORONET

In '66, the new Street Hemi came in the 1966 Coronet 500, the Dodge 440, and base models, but pre-production photos showed '67 Coronet 500 hardtops with "426 Hemi" badges, creating confusion. Press kits said the Hemi came only as a limited-production option for the top-line Coronet R/T and Charger. Production totals (283 Coronet R/Ts and 118 Chargers) bear out limited production and indicate you couldn't get a Street Hemi in other Coronets, but that's wrong.

The Coronet 440 two-door hardtop was being built to meet NHRA SS/B rules. The WO23 cars—as they are known—were part of the Mopar tradition of special lightweight models built for drag racing.

WO23s had standard sheet metal and the big hood scoop used on earlier S/S Dodges. Sound deadeners and body sealers were deleted, the battery was trunk mounted, and the front sway bar was axed (quick cornering not required). There were two versions. One had a modified TorqueFlite and a 4.86:1 MoPar Sure-Grip axle. The second had a four-speed, Hurst linkage, and other racing stuff. To meet NHRA rules, Dodge had to build at least 50, but 55 went out the door. Plymouth also built 55 similar Plymouth Belvedere II two-door hardtops.

Factory ADP	Wheelbase	Length	Shipping Weight	Base V-8	Engine Options	0-to-60 MPH	¼-Mile
$3,494	117 in.	203 in.	3,686 lbs.	426 cid/425 hp	None	4.8 seconds	13.5 seconds @ 105 mph

MCFG **Says:** $65K

He Says: "If you ordered a Hemi in your Coronet, you certainly had a sleeper on your hands," wrote Anthony Young in *Mighty Mopars 1960-1974*. "Short of popping the hood, there was little to tell the guy waiting in the next lane at the stoplight that you had a Hemi."

We Says: "With the hood-scooped R/T making hot sheet headlines in '67, the regular Coronet with Hemi power was a true wolf in sheep's clothing."

1967 CORONET R/T

Jerry Heasley

1967 CORONET R/T

Many muscle cars were weekend racers in the '60s. R/T badges underlined this road-and-track image. A Charger grille distinguished the hot mid-size Coronet R/T, though it lacked the fastback's retractable headlights. Other features included simulated rear fender air vents and non-functional hood scoops. The package also included a stiff suspension, H.D. brakes and 7.75 x 14 Red Streak tires. Production amounted to 10,181 cars, including 628 ragtops.

Standard under the hood was the Magnum 440 linked to a four-speed or TorqueFlite. This V-8 had a 4.32 x 3.75-inch bore and stroke, 10.1:1 compression and a single four-barrel carb. It developed 375 hp at 4600 rpm and 480 lbs.-ft. of torque at 3200 rpm. One 440-powered R/T did 0-to-60 mph in 7.2 seconds and the quarter-mile in 15.4 at 94 mph. *Motor Trend* drove the same car with racing slicks and did the 0-to-60-mph test in 6.5 seconds. The fat-tired car required 14.7 seconds flat for the quarter mile.

The Hemi was available, on special order, for $908. A total of 238 Coronet R/T coupes and ragtops carried the Hemi engine option in '67 and 121 also had four-speed manual gearboxes.

Factory ADP	Wheelbase	Length	Shipping Weight	Base V-8	Engine Options	0-to-60 MPH	0-to-100 MPH
(HT) $3,199; (RT) $3,438	117 in.	203 in.	(HT) 3,545 lbs.; (RT) 3,640 lbs.	440 cid/ 375 hp	426 cid/425 hp (Hemi)	(Stock tires) 6.8 seconds; (Slicks) 6.6 secs.	(Stock tires) 15 seconds @ 96 mph; (Slicks) 14.8 seconds @ 99 mph

MCFG Says: (440-cid) (HT) $22K; (RT) $30K (Hemi $65K for hardtop)

They Says: Dodge ads said, "Sweet as it can be on the road. Hot as you want it on the track."

We Says: "Speaks softly, but carries a big kick!"

1967 HEMI CHARGER

Phil Kunz

1967 HEMI CHARGER

The little-changed '67 Dodge Charger was aimed at the sporty-car buyer who didn't want to give up room and comfort. With its slant towards competition in NASCAR and USAC, Dodge wanted the Charger to reflect its racing image and again offered it with a nice selection of V-8s. The base engine was a 230-hp 318. The next step up was a 326-hp big-block 383. There was also the 375-hp 440 good for 0-to-60 in 8 seconds and a 15.5-second quarter mile at 93 mph. But, the top dog was the Hemi.

The Hemi was an $878 option in the Charger. With either the 440 or the Hemi, the three-speed TorqueFlite came with a high-upshift speed governor. If you ordered a four-speed, a Sure-Grip rear axle was mandatory. A good idea for the Hemi Charger was 11-inch front disc brakes that slowed the car from 60 mph in an amazing 133 feet.

1967 Chargers are rarer than '66s—only 15,788 were built. This included 118 cars with Hemi, of which half had a four-speed. If you're considering buying a '67 Hemi Charger, you might appreciate knowing that it got 11.7 mpg in city driving and about 14.4 mpg on the open highway. Don't tell that to the people who set CAFE standards. One of them might have a heart attack!

Factory ADP	Wheelbase	Length	Shipping Weight	Base V-8	Engine Options	0-to-60 MPH	¼-Mile
(Hemi) $4,006	117 in.	203.6 in.	3,475 lbs.	318 cid/230 hp	383 cid/326 hp; 440 cid/375 hp; 426 cid/425 hp	6.4 seconds	14.16 seconds @ 96.15 mph

MCFG Says: (Recent asking price $67,500)

They Says: "The knowledge that the car is king at the stoplight, but making no arrogant display of this monarchy is the one-upmanship of the Hemi Charger," said *Car Life*.

We Says: We remember the great Hemi Charger ads, like the one that read, "Even Custer couldn't muster a stampede like this."

1968 CORONET R/T

1968 CORONET R/T

The Coronet R/T was completely restyled for '68, when 10,456 coupes and ragtops combined were made. Equipment included bucket seats, dual exhausts, H.D. suspension, H.D. brakes and other goodies, including a 150-mph speedo and TorqueFlite. Bumblebee stripes (or no cost optional body side stripes) set off the exterior. Coronet R/Ts used the same interior as Coronet 500s, but had a special "power bulge" hood with simulated air vents.

In a *Motor Trend* comparison of eight '68 super cars (Road Runner, Charger R/T, GTO, GS 400, Chevelle SS 396, 4-4-2, Torino, and Coronet R/T) the Coronet was said to have a "good engine" and to be "easily the best in comfort and in room." It's quality of construction was rated "surprisingly good" and the magazine liked its comfort, roominess, good assembly quality, engine and boulevard ride.

This season, the optional Street Hemi V-8 cost $605. It was put in 94 Coronet R/Ts with four-speeds and 136 with TorqueFlite. Experts believe that one stick shift car and eight automatics were ragtops. Hemi cars came with a special H.D., but air conditioning couldn't be ordered.

Factory ADP	Wheelbase	Length	Shipping Weight	Base V-8	Engine Options	0-to-60 MPH	¼-Mile (automatic)
(HT) $3,379; (RT) $3,613	117 in.	207 in.	(HT) 3,565 lbs.; (RT) 3,640 lbs.	400 cid/375 hp	426 cid/425 hp (Hemi)	6.9 seconds	15.1 seconds @ 94 mph

MCFG Says: (440-cid) (HT) $22K; (RT) $30K ($65K for Hemi)

They Says: *Car Life* (April 1968) tested the 440 version of the Coronet R/T and stated, "The 440 roared."

We Says: "The only think to complain about with the Coronet R/T is the fact that Dodge didn't sell more of them."

1968 SUPER BEE

1968 SUPER BEE

Budget-priced muscle cars were a late-'60s Chrysler innovation. Dodge's entry was the Coronet Super Bee, introduced in February 1968 with a price tag in the $3,395 range. It was based on the Coronet 440 two-door sedan, because a "post" coupe was needed to accommodate the non-lowering rear windows that swung open on hinges mounted to the center pillar.

Base engine was the big-block 383 V-8 in 335-hp format linked to a H.D. four-speed with Hurst's "Competition-Plus" floor shifter. Monster dual exhausts, fat F40 x 14 tires and an H.D. suspension with fat torsion bar were included. Everything was fat except the price tag.

Also part of the Super Bee look was a dummy "power bulge" on the hood, a bench seat interior, wide wheels and rear bumblebee striping with a bee inside a circular decal emblem. You couldn't get a vinyl roof, but for $712, you could add the Hemi. A total of 166 Hemi Super Bees were produced. Ninety-two had four-speeds and 74 had TorqueFlite.

Factory ADP	Wheelbase	Length	Shipping Weight	Base V-8	Engine Options	0-to-60 MPH	¼-Mile
(CPE) $3,076; (HT) $3,138	117 in.	207 in.	(CPE) 3,440 lbs.; (HT) 3,470; lbs.	383 cid/335 hp	440 cid/375 hp; 426 cid/425 hp	(Hemi) 6.8 seconds	14.60 seconds @ 99 mph

MCFG Says: (CPE) $30K; (HT) $34K (add 100% for Hemi)

They Says: *Car Review* (April 1986) said, "Dodge liked to call the Super Bee a 'real super car' and to back that up, they diddled with the 383 to dial in more power and torque."

We Says: "This hot Dodge was tops at buzzing down the quarter-mile or stinging its rivals in a stoplight grand prix."

Phil Kunz

1968 DART GTS

1968 DART GTS

GTS stood for GT Sport, but the new mini muscle car was more than a sporty compact. Two hefty V-8s were available. A small-block 340 was standard. It was derived from the 273-318 engine family and had 10.5:1 compression ratio and a single four-barrel carb. The 340 cranked out 275 hp at 5000 rpm and 340 lbs.-ft. of torque at 3200 rpm.

A 300-hp 383 big-block V-8 with a four-barrel carb was optional. The 383 added 89 lbs. with a four-speed and 136 lbs. with automatic. A 3.23:1 rear axle was supplied, but 3.55:1 and 3.91:1 were optional.

Technical enhancements included chrome-tipped low-restriction exhausts, a Rallye suspension, 14 x 5.5-inch wheels and E70-14 Red Streak tires. A column-shifted three-speed was standard, but most GTS' had a four-speed with a Hurst shifter or a competition-type TorqueFlite. Identifying the GTS were hood power bulges with air vents, racing stripes, special GTS emblems and simulated mag wheel covers. A rear end bumblebee stripe was a no-cost option. Vinyl bucket seats were standard in the hardtop and optional in the ragtop.

Factory ADP	Wheelbase	Length	Shipping Weight	Base V-8	Engine Options	0-to-60 MPH	¼-Mile (automatic)
(HT) $2,611; (RT) $3,383	111 in.	196 in.	(HT) 3,375 lbs.; (RT) 3,470 lbs.	340 cid/275hp	383 cid/300 hp	(340) 6 seconds	(340) 14.38 seconds @ 97 mph

MCFG Says: (340) (HT) $20K; (RT) $29K; (383) (HT) $22K; (RT) $30K

He Says: "Not to take the edge off Road Runner, GTS might be a more sensible package," said *Hot Rod's* Steve Kelly. "The base price is higher, but you get carpet on the floor, fat tires, buckets, and a other niceties that can make Saturday night roaming more comfortable."

We Says: "The smaller engine in the Dodge Dart GTS V-8 was an advantage in some drag racing classes."

1968 HEMI CHARGER R/T

1968 HEMI CHARGER R/T

The Charger underwent a vast amount of change in 1968. Dodge stylists did a great job of adopting the "Coke bottle" look to the more smoothly rounded body. Neat details included an integral rear spoiler and a competition-type gas filler cap.

Equal suitability for street performance and drag racing was what Dodge's R/T designation implied. *Motor Trend* summed up the R/T look as a Charger with a set of mags, Wide-Ovals, and a bumblebee stripe around its rear. Name badges, H.D. underpinnings, and a 375-hp 440 Magnum V-8 with 10.1:1 compression and a four-barrel carb rounded out the image.

This was the only '68 Charger you could get with a Hemi. The engine cost $605 LBJ dollars, which may explain why only 475 such cars were built. 211 had the four-speed, a no-cost extra. Other available options included a limited-slip differential for $42, a tach for $49, custom wheels for $97, a console for $53, power brakes for $42 and front disc brakes for $73. Bucket seats and hi-po tires were standard.

Factory ADP	Wheelbase	Length	Shipping Weight	Base V-8	Engine Options	0-to-60 MPH	¼-Mile
(Hemi Charger) $4,110	117 in.	208 in.	3,575 lbs.	(base Charger R/T) 440 cid/375 hp	(Hemi Charger) 426 cid/425 hp	(Hemi Charger) 6 seconds	(Hemi Charger) 13.54 seconds @ 101 mph

MCFG **Says:** (426 Hemi) $35K

They Says: *Car Life* (April 1968) said, "Let's hope the Scat Pack doesn't get too much faster. The cars might just make it past the striper the next time."

We Says: "Steve McQueen's '68 'Bullitt' was probably the best-known Charger R/T and every car nut in America wanted to be a flying detective or a jumpin' Hazard boy."

1969 CHARGER 500

1969 CHARGER 500

The '68 Charger's new styling boosted its sales to 96,100. Wind tunnel testing showed the good-looking body's recessed grille and tunneled rear window created turbulence on NASCAR superspeedways. Dodge figured out that a flush grille and flush glass could reduce wind resistance. Some say the prototype with these changes was really a 1968 Charger.

The production 1969 Charger 500 was a special model based on that prototype. It was released to the public September 1, 1968, as a '69 model. Chrysler said it was offered specifically for hi-po racing tracks and available only to qualified race drivers. This was a good promotion and muscle car lovers flocked to Dodge dealers to buy one of the cars. The body modifications were done by Creative Industries, in Detroit. A minimum of 500 cars had to be sold to authorize the changes and make the 500 legal for racing under NASCAR rules.

Some books say Hemis were standard, but 392 of these cars have been researched and about 9 percent had a Hemi. Officially, 32 Hemi-powered cars were built, though experts have tracked down serial numbers for 35 such vehicles.

Factory ADP	Wheelbase	Length	Shipping Weight	Base 396 V-8	Engine Options	0-to-60 MPH	¼-Mile (automatic)
$3,993	117 in.	208 in.	3,710 lbs.	440 cid/375 hp	426 cid/ 425 hp	(4S) 5.7 seconds; (AT) 5.7 seconds	*(Motor Trend)* (4S) 13.68 seconds @ 104.8 mph; (AT) 13.92 seconds @ 104.5 mph

MCFG Says: (HT) $38K (add 100% for Hemi)

They Says: A four-speed Dodge Hemi Charger 500 takes the title of quickest test car; the automatic version wasn't far behind," said *Car Life* in April '69.

We Says: "This is probably one on the neatest-looking setups you will find on any muscle car. It's smooth and slippery looking."

1969 CHARGER DAYTONA

1969 CHARGER DAYTONA

The '69 Daytona was designed to return the NASCAR championship to Dodge. A fiberglass "nose cone," front fender-top scoops (for tire clearance), and a massive rear spoiler distinguished Dodge's new rocketship racing car. A company named Creative Industries received the contract to build 500 Daytonas to legalize the 200-mph body modifications for stock car competition.

Daytonas swept the first four places in the race they were named after—the Daytona 500—that season. At the Bonneville Salt Flats in Utah, Bobby Isaac also set an unlimited class speed record of 217 mph.

Experts say that total production of Daytonas was 503 units. Officially, 433 cars with base 375-hp 440 Magnum V-8s were built for the streets and 70 were turned out with Hemi V-8s under their snout. The breakout as to how many of the Hemi Daytonas had four-speed manual or automatic transmissions was 22 and 48, respectively. One yellow Daytona, with 5,000 original miles, has been documented to be a car with a dealer-installed 440 Six-Pack V-8. Dodge did not, however, offer this setup as a factory option.

Factory ADP	Wheelbase	Length	Shipping Weight	Base V-8 (Malibu)	Engine Options	0-to-60 MPH	¼-Mile
$4,000	117 in.	208 in.	3,694 lbs.	440 cid/375 hp	426 cid/426 hp	(Hemi) 6.6 seconds	(Hemi) 13.92 seconds @ 104.10 mph

MCFG Says: $64K (add 50% for Hemi)

He Says: In *Motor Trend*, Eric Dahlquist stated, "The wind slick Daytona Charger, from Dodge City, reaffirms the daring of the men in the white hats."

We Says: "The muscle-car mate to '59 Caddy tail fins and quickly becoming THE automotive icon of the '60s."

1969 CHARGER R/T

Don Bowser

1969 CHARGER R/T

The Charger didn't change much. The '69 grille was divided into two sections and the taillights were modified a bit. However, the fastback was basically the same good-looking beast on the outside. The interior, including the well-designed dash, also had very few mods. There was a large-faced tach and the gauges were done in white on black to make them stand out.

The R/T was the hi-po version and came only as a hardtop coupe. The R/T was the only Charger available with the Hemi. The 425-hp 426 powerhouse had a $648 price tag.

Charger R/T production leaped from the '68 total of 17,582 units up to 20,057 units. A new option for Chargers (also available on the R/T) was the SE (Special Edition) interior with leather bucket seats, lots of extra lights, and wood-grained trim pieces. Sinking in popularity to 400 production units was the Hemi Charger R/T. Around 192 of the Hemi-powered cars had four-speeds.

DODGE

Factory ADP	Wheelbase	Length	Shipping Weight	Base V-8	Engine Options	0-to-60 MPH	¼-Mile
$3,592	117 in.	208 in.	3,646 lbs.	440 cid/375 hp	383 cid/330 hp; 426 cid/425 hp	6 seconds	13.9 seconds @ 101.4 mph

MCFG Says: $34K: (add 40% for 440; add 100% for Hemi)

They Says: As *Motor Trend* magazine put it, "That brute Charger styling, that symbol of masculine virility, was still intact."

We Says: "Hey, we know a few 'goils' who love their Six-Packs as much as any macho man—and we're not talking about beer cans."

1969 CORONET R/T

1969 CORONET R/T

DODGE

In '69, the Coronet R/T continued as the high-po model. It included all Coronet 500 features, plus a 440 Magnum V-8, TorqueFlite, a light group option, body sill moldings and R/T bumblebee stripes across the trunk lid and down the fender sides. Two simulated hood scoops located on the rear fenders, were optional.

A "Six-Pack" of carbs was the big news for the '69 Coronet R/T. A fiberglass performance hood covered the three two-barrel carbs. A Ramcharger fresh-air induction system (standard on Hemis) was optional. It had twin hood scoops that fed cold air into a fiberglass plenum bolted under the hood. There was also a wider choice of rear axle ratios. Dodge put added emphasis on the "Track" portion of the Road/Track model designation by adding more muscle to Coronets. The previous front fender medallion became a large decal that appeared as part of the rear bumblebee stripe. The four-barrel 440 was standard.

The Hemi was a $418 option for '69 Coronet R/Ts. Model-year production totaled 7,238 hardtops and ragtops combined. This included 97 two-door hardtops (58 with a four-speed) and 10 ragtops (six with TorqueFlite) fitted with 426 Hemis.

Factory ADP	Wheelbase	Length	Shipping Weight	Base V-8	Engine Options	0-to-60 MPH	¼-Mile
(HT) $3,442; (RT) $3,660	117 in.	207 in.	(HT) 3,601 lbs.; (RT) 3,721 lbs.	440 cid/375 hp	440 cid/390 hp; 426 cid/425 hp	(440 Six-Pack) 6.6 seconds	(440 Six-Pack) 13.65 seconds @ 105.14 mph

MCFG Says: (HT) $34K; (RT) $40K (add 40% for 440 Six-Pack; add 100% for Hemi)

He Says: In *Mighty Mopars 1960-1974* Anthony Young said, "The Coronet R/T and the Super Bee finished out the '60s as two of Dodge's most formidable and most affordable muscle cars."

We Says: "The call letters 'R/T' stood for road-and-track and the Coronet was just an awesome muscle car in both enviroments."

1969 DART GTS

1969 DART GTS

The GTS or GT Sport was one of nine different Dart models that Dodge buyers could select in '69. It combined a dressy look and assortment of upscale equipment with a 340-cid base engine and a powerful new big-block option. Bucket seats were optional in the GTS ragtop.

The '69 version of the GTS sported a new black grille with a bright horizontal center bar. There was also a new blacked-out rear body panel. Also included were E70-14 redline tires, TorqueFlite, a three-spoke steering wheel, dual exhausts, carpeting, and an engine dress-up kit.

The '69 GTS 383 was a kind of "sleeper" in muscle car circles because the optional 383-cid V-8 was up-rated. New for the GTS was a rear bumblebee stripe with a separate lower section and the GT Sport name written on it.

As in '68, the production of '69 Dart GTS models was a part of the total of 20,900 GT series V-8s produced, but hardtops and ragtops together came to 6,700 cars with the GTS goodies.

Factory ADP	Wheelbase	Length	Shipping Weight	Base V-8	Engine Options	0-to-60 MPH	¼-Mile
(HT) $3,226; (RT) $3,49	111 in.	196 in.	(HT) 3,105 lbs.; (RT) 3,210 lbs.	340 cid/275 hp	318 cid/230 hp; 383 cid/330 hp	(383) 6.0 seconds	(383) 14.40 seconds @ 99 mph

MCFG **Says:** (340) (HT) $20K; (RT) $29K; (383) (HT) $22K; (RT) $30K

They Says: *Car Life* said, "All-around performance that outdoes its bigger cousins and most other rivals."

We Says: "The GTS always had that Spanky McFarland-like 'I'm-a-tough-little-guy-and-you'd-better-not-try-it' look as it came rolling into Mel's Drive-In."

1969 DART SWINGER 340

DeWayne Behnke

1969 DART SWINGER 340

Another member of the Dodge "Scat Pack" that proudly wore its bumblebee stripes was the '69 Dodge Dart Swinger 340. Designed to give muscle car fans more bang for the buck by emphasizing performance over luxury, the Swinger fit right into the same "budget muscle car" trend that produced the Road Runner and GTO Judge. It was a small-scale counterpart to such models.

In addition to the hot drivetrain, Swinger goodies included a three-spoke steering wheel with padded hub, a H.D. Rallye suspension, bumblebee stripes, D70 x 14 wide-tread tires, dual exhausts, a performance hood with die-cast louvers, and fat 14-inch wheels. Seven colors were available for the car and four colors for vinyl roofs. All-vinyl upholstery (with full-carpeting on four-speed cars only) was included. Two axle options—a 3.55:1 and a 3.91:1—gave better drag strip performance.

A total of 20,000 were built. Even today, muscle car collectors can find bargains in the Swinger 340 market. These cars don't look as flashy as a GTS, although they are equally as fast.

Factory ADP	Wheelbase	Length	Shipping Weight	Base V-8	Engine Options	0-to-60 MPH	¼-Mile
$2,836	111 in.	196 in.	3,097 lbs.	340 cid/275 hp	None	6.9 seconds	14.8 seconds @ 96 mph

MCFG **Says:** $20.5K

They Says: *Car Life* (January '69) said, "The Swinger 340 isn't a supercar, it's just faster than a Swinger. For once, the ad men picked the right name; the Swinger does."

We Says: "A small car doesn't need a big-block to go fast. The Swinger is a muscle car bargain and if you shop well, you can probably 'swing' a good deal on one of these."

Don Bowser

1969 SUPER BEE

1969 SUPER BEE

Only a few changes were made in the '69 Coronet Super Bee. They included a single, wider rear bumblebee stripe, "Scat Pack" badges on the grille and trunk, and front fender engine call-outs. Three two-barrel Holley carbs on an Edelbrock aluminum manifold created a new "Six-Pack" option with 390 hp and 490 lbs.-ft. of torque. The Six-Pack included a flat black fiberglass hood that locked in place with four chrome pins. The hood was entirely removable. The Six-Pack came with a four-speed or TorqueFlite and a 9 3/4-inch Dana 60 Sure-Grip 4.10:1 axle.

A Ramcharger cold-air induction system was new and standard with the Street Hemi. It had two large hood-mounted air scoops, an underhood air plenum, and a warm/cold air switch. Among the Super Bee options were a 3.55:1 limited-slip differential ($102), power disc brakes ($93), head restraints ($26), foam-padded seats ($9), automatic transmission ($40), a remote-adjustable mirror ($10), rear quarter air scoops ($36), a tach and clock ($50), and cold air induction ($73).

A total of 27,800 Super Bees were built. This included 166 Hemi-powered cars, 92 of them with four-speeds.

Factory ADP	Wheelbase	Length	Shipping Weight	Base V-8	Engine Options	0-to-60 MPH	¼-Mile
(CPE) $3,076; (HT) $3,138	117 in.	207 in.	(CPE) 3,440 lbs.; (HT) 3,470 lbs.	383 cid/335 hp	440 cid/375 hp; 426 cid/425 hp	(383) 6.6 seconds	(383) 14.73 seconds @ 95.6 mph

MCFG Says: (CPE) $31K; (HT) $32K (add 75% for Six-Pack; add 100% for Hemi)

They Says: *Car Life* said, "Right out of the box the Super Bee lives up to its decals and it's a honey of a low-budget super car."

We Says: "If you described the Coronet Super Bee as 'low-bills no-frills thrills' you'd be right on the money."

Jerry Heasley

1970 CHALLENGER R/T

1970 CHALLENGER R/T

The Challenger was Dodge's late-breaking answer to the Mustang and Camaro. In '70, it came as a beautifully styled hardtop, a ragtop, and a Special Edition (SE) formal-roofed hardtop.

All three Challenger body styles were offered in the high-po, V-8-only R/T series. R/Ts included a 383 base V-8 engine and a four-barrel carb. Buyers could add a 375-hp Magnum 440 V-8 to the R/T for $131 or get a 390-hp version for $250 more. A ragtop with the 390-hp 440 was tested by *Car Life* magazine. *C/L* must have got a good buy. They said it cost $3,222 as tested. The car weighed 3900 lbs. The Street Hemi V-8 was also available for $779. The high price held down orders, so Hemi R/Ts are rarest today.

Dodge built 14,889 Challenger R/T hardtops in model-year '70. The ragtop had a 3,979-unit production run. Rarity buffs might be interested in one of the 1,070 Challenger SEs that left the factory. Hemi production included 287 hardtops (137 with four-speeds), 60 SE hardtops (23 with four-speeds) and nine ragtops (five with four-speeds). All Hemi Challengers were R/Ts. They could do the quarter-mile in 14 seconds at 104 mph.

Factory ADP	Wheelbase	Length	Shipping Weight	Base V-8	Engine Options	0-to-60 MPH	¼-Mile
(383) (HT) $3,266; (RT) $3,535; (FT) $3,437	110 in.	191.3 in.	(383) (HT) 3,402 lbs.; (RT) 3,467 lbs.; (FT) 3,437 lbs.	383 cid/ 335 hp	(440 V-8) 440 cid/375 hp; 440 cid/390 hp (Hemi V-8) 426 cid/425 hp	(440 ragtop) 7.1 seconds	14.64 seconds @ 97.82 mph

MCFG **Says:** (HT) $27K; (RT) $33K; (FT) $28K (add 40% for 440; add 100% for Hemi)

They Says: *Car Life* said, "What do you call a car with a 440 Six-Pack, four on the floor, purple metallic paint and an urge to challenge the world? Genghis Grape!"

We Says: "Went to an Elton John concert in one of these cars and felt like a pinball wizard by the end of the night."

Jerry Heasley

1970 CHALLENGER T/A

1970 CHALLENGER T/A

"Wild and woolly" is a good way to describe the '70 Dodge Challenger T/A. Dodge scheduled production of 2,500 to make its new pony car eligible for SCCA Trans-Am racing. Chrysler's Pete Hutchinson used a de-stroked 340 V-8 as the basis for a competition coupe with only 305 cid, but 440 hp. Ray Caldwell—who worked for Autodynamics—built the Challenger T/A that Sam Posey drove to fourth place in SCCA standings.

Street T/As had the same snorkel hood scoop, side-exit exhausts, and pinned-down flat-black hood. They had differences under the hood, where special goodies included a 340-cid Six-Pack V-8 and a TorqueFlite or four-speed. A ducktail rear deck spoiler was part of the package, along with H.D. underpinnings. The package included a Sure-Grip differential, performance axles, semi-metallic front disc and rear drum brakes, a specific black body side tape stripe and mixed size tires (E60-15 front/G60-15 rear). To provide clearance for the exhaust pipes with fatter rear tires, the T/As were "jacked-up" in the rear with increased rear spring camber.

Factory ADP	Wheelbase	Length	Shipping Weight	Base V-8	Engine Options	0-to-60 MPH	¼-Mile
(HT) $3,818	110 in.	191.3 in.	(HT) 3,585 lbs.	340 cid/290 hp	None	5.8 seconds	14.1 seconds @ 103.2 mph

MCFG **Says:** (HT) $42K

They Says: *Car and Driver* said, "Lavish execution with little or no thought towards practical application."

We Says: "Kissin' cousin to the AAR 'Cuda, the Challenger T/A was good for 0-to-60 mph in a flat 6 seconds It could hit the century mark in 14 seconds and cover the quarter-mile in 14.5."

B.J. Ingargiola

1970 CHARGER 500 383

1970 CHARGER 500 383

The NASCAR-racing Charger 500 of '69 had a new "personality" for '70. It was what we call a "de-contented" car today. It did not have a racing-inspired flush grille or flush rear window for better aerodynamics. And it was available with a 145-hp Slant Six or a 230-hp small-block 318 V-8. Naturally, prices started at about $700 lower than in '69.

No longer did "Charger 500" automatically mean "muscle car." It could provide a little street muscle, however, if the right engine options were added. The options included three versions of the big-block 383 V-8, the hottest one pirated from the new Challenger.

The 440 Six-Pack and Hemi V-8s were not regular production options for the Charger 500. The 383-cid V-8 came in a two-barrel version for $70 and a pair of four-barrel versions that added at least $138 to the price. The 383-cid four-barrel V-8 was offered with 330-hp or 335-hp and the higher-horsepower was significantly different than the lower. The 335-ponies version used the 375-hp 440 engine with Dodge's hot "Magnum" cam and freer-flowing heads.

Factory ADP	Wheelbase	Length	Shipping Weight	Base big-block V-8	Optional big-block V-8s	0-to-60 MPH	¼-Mile
$3,246	117 in.	208 in.	3,363 lbs.	383 cid/290 hp	383 cid/330 hp; 383 cid/335 hp	(383/300) 7.2 seconds	14.59 seconds @ 96 mph

***MCFG* Says:** $20K

They Says: Writing in *Motor Trend* (December '70), A.B. Shuman said, "the engine is flexible, the transmission easy to work."

We Says: "This is a great 'everyday' muscle car that combines above-average performance with an affordable price and fairly decent road manners."

1970 CHARGER 440 R/T

Jerry Heasley

1970 CHARGER 440 R/T

The '70 Charger used the '69 body with minor trim changes. The R/T was a hi-po version. It had a new grille, a new loop-style front bumper, two hood scoops near the outside of the hood, big bolt-on scoops with R/T badges on the rear quarter panels, a choice of longitudinal or bumblebee racing stripes, a new interior and wild exterior colors.

The Magnum 440 V-8 was standard, along with TorqueFlite, a H.D. 70-amp/hour battery, H.D. automatic-adjusting drum brakes, H.D. shocks, an extra-heavy-duty suspension, three-speed windshield wipers, all-vinyl front bucket seats, carpeting, a cigar lighter and F70-14 fiberglass-belted whitewall tires or black RWL tires. "R/T" was on the center of the rear panel.

A hefty jump to $3,711 was seen in the base price of the 440-powered Charger R/T. Total production this year dropped to 10,337 units, which included a mere 42 cars with 426 Hemis.

Factory ADP	Wheelbase	Length	Shipping Weight	Base V-8	Engine Options	0-to-60 MPH	¼-Mile
(as tested) $5,546	117 in.	208 in.	(as tested) 4,545 lbs.	440 cid/375 hp	440 cid/390 hp; 426 cid/425 hp	(440/ *Car Life*) 7.2 seconds	(440/*Car Life*) 14.71 seconds @ 96.67 mph

MCFG Says: $37K (add 120 percent for Hemi)

They Says: *Car Life* said, "They keep making the Charger go like stink and handle better than a lot of so-called sportsters."

We Says: "For a big car the Charger packed a big wallop when it came to high-speed performance."

Jerry Heasley

1970 CORONET SUPER BEE

1970 CORONET SUPER BEE

Restyled along the lines of the R/T, the Super Bee did not get dummy rear fender scoops as standard equipment. It also had horizontally divided taillights. New options included a hood tach and spoiler. Buyers could get the R/T-type bumblebee stripe or pipe-shaped upper and lower rear fender stripes with a circular Super Bee decal between them. The car's wild character was suggested in paint colors such as Plum Crazy, Sublime and Go-Mango, and extras such as the "Kruncher" and "Bee-Liever" performance options.

Still standard ingredients were the 383-cid magnum V-8, an H.D. torsion-bar suspension and a three-speed manual transmission (last year's four-speed manual gear box was optional.) Despite the price reduction, production dropped to 11,540 hardtops and 3,966 coupes. Hemis went into only 32 hardtops (21 with four-speed) and four coupes (all four-speeds). Wouldn't you love to own one today?

Factory ADP	Wheelbase	Length	Shipping Weight	Base V-8	Engine Options	0-to-60 MPH	¼-Mile
(CPE) $3,012; (HT) $3,074	117 in.	210 in.	(CPE) 3,528 lbs.; (HT) 3,563 lbs.	383 cid/335 hp	440 cid/390 hp; 426 cid/425 hp	(383) 7.1 seconds	(383) 15 seconds @ 96 mph

MCFG Says: (CPE) $28K; (HT) $30K (add 40% for 440; add 100% for Hemi)

They Says: "Dodge introduces a new model Super Bee at a new lower price. $3,074," said Dodge ads for the '70 Coronet Super Bee."

We Says: "If bees drove Dodges, they'd find plenty to buzz about in the Dodge Super Bee."

Jerry Heasley

1970 DART SWINGER 340

1970 DART SWINGER 340

Another member of the Dodge "Scat Pack" returning in '69 was the Swinger 340 hardtop. It had revised front and rear cosmetics and a slightly lower price tag. A three-speed was on the standard equipment list. Instead of small power vents, the mini Mopar muscle machine now carried two long, narrow hood scoops.

Other standard Swinger 340 features included a 3.23:1 rear axle ratio, Firm Ride shocks, a Rallye suspension, and front discs.

Despite the introduction of the Challenger, the Swinger 340 remained popular enough to generate 13,785 assemblies. One reason for its popularity was that insurance companies considered it a "compact" car and charged lower premiums than other muscle cars required. Of course, it was also as fast as—or even slightly faster than—the 340 powered Dart GT Sport. Even today, muscle car collectors can find bargains in the Swinger 340 market, since these cars don't look as flashy as a GTS, although they are equally fast.

Factory ADP	Wheelbase	Length	Shipping Weight	Base V-8	Engine Options	0-to-60 MPH	¼-Mile
$2,808	97 in.	178 in.	3,179 lbs.	340 cid/275 hp	N/A	6.5 seconds	14.5 seconds @ 98 mph

MCFG Says: $17.6

He Says: Writing in *Car Review* (January '86) Jerry Heasley said, "If the Road Runner was the first econo-supercar, then the Dart was very much its counterpart in the compact lineup. Nobody built this type of car better than the 'Good Guys' in the white hats from Dodge."

We Says: "For '70, the Dodge Dart Swinger 340 was the newest member of the 'Scat Pack' and the 'Good Guys' advertised it as '6000 rpm for under $3,000.'"

1971 HEMI CHALLENGER

1971 HEMI CHALLENGER

Dodge scored a hit with its first pony car, the '70 Challenger. It succeeded so well that it outsold the Barracuda 83,000 to 55,000 units in its first year. With the Challenger, Dodge was selling performance, so it's not surprising that 93 percent of the '71s had a V-8 instead of the Slant Six. Nearly 17 percent had optional engines, including the 425-hp Hemi.

The Street Hemi was a $790 option. It had a 4.25 x 3.75 inch bore and stroke, 10.25:1 compression, hydraulic lifters and dual four-barrel Carter AFB carbs. This was the last year for the Hemi, as emissions, safety and insurance concerns put the horsepower race under a caution flag.

On Hemi Challengers, a flat-black air scoop was mounted to the carbs and poked through a hole in the hood. This "shaker" hood let you could watch the torque twist the engine. Some cars also had chrome NASCAR-style hood hold-down pins.

Factory ADP	Wheelbase	Length	Shipping Weight	Base Hemi V-8	Engine Options	0-to-60 MPH	¼-Mile
(Hemi w/ common extras) (CPE) $5,353; (HT) $5,450; (RT) $5,707	110 in.	192 in.	(CPE) 3,080 lbs.; (HT) 3,120 lbs.; (RT) 3,210 lbs.	318 cid/230 hp	318 cid/230 hp; 383 cid/335 hp; 383 cid/330 hp; 340 cid/275 hp; 440 cid/375 hp; 440 cid/390 hp	5.8 seconds	12.95 seconds @ 106.5 mph

MCFG **Says:** (CPE) $45K; (HT) $50K; (RT) $58K

They Says: *Road Test* said, "For the street racer who doesn't mind sticking close to 6 grand in his toy, the 440 Six-Pack or 426 Hemi will be very hard to beat in the stoplight grand prix."

We Says: "There wasn't anything on the market that could rival the go-power of the Hemi if all you wanted to do was go fast in a straight line."

Jerry Heasley

1971 CHARGER R/T "440 SIX-PACK"

1971 CHARGER R/T "440 SIX-PACK"

The Charger started life in 1966 as a specialty car, but it caught on and grew to become an important parts of Dodge's line. In '69, over 70,000 Chargers were sold. For '71, management decided that it was time to give the Charger an image of its own—separate from that of the mid-sized Coronet. The Charger name was applied to two-door hardtops, while the Coronet name was used on Dodge's longer-wheelbase four-door sedans.

The re-sized Charger was 2 inches shorter in wheelbase than the '70 model and more than 3 inches shorter. However, it had nearly 3 more inches of front overhang and 3 1/2 inches more width. This made it the perfect size for a sporty performance car. Charger's R/T was the quintessential muscle car. It was actually a sub-series of the middle-priced Charger 500 series. It included all of the many features of the Charger 500, plus hot stuff like H.D. underpinnings and the 440 Magnum V-8.

The 440 Six-Pack V-8 was a $262 option. When it was added, the R/T price climbed above $4,000. In that era, typical options added about $1,700 to the cost of most Chargers, so a well-equipped R/T probably went out the door for around $5,500.

Factory ATP	Wheelbase	Length	Shipping Weight	Base 440 V-8	Engine Options	0-to-60 MPH	¼-Mile
Approx. $5,500	97 in.	178 in.	3,945 lbs.	440 cid/370 hp	440 cid/385 hp; 426 cid/425 hp	6.9 seconds	14.74 seconds @ 97.3 mph

MCFG Says: $29K (add 50% for 440 Six-Pack)

They Says: *Motor Trend* (December '70) said, "It was evident after the initial success of the '68-'70 Chargers, the Dodge stylists would have to burn some midnight oil to create a fresh approach that would again make Charger something unique in an industry where very little is unique. As far as the *Motor Trend* staff is concerned, they succeeded."

We Says: "Dodge said 'this car was designed strictly for adults' and it was, especially when compared to the lick'em-stick'em psuedo-muscle cars that kids were buying in '71-'72."

1971 CHARGER SUPER BEE HEMI

Jerry Heasley

1971 CHARGER SUPER BEE HEMI

Dodge's one-year-only Charger Super Bee used the same body as other Chargers. It represented a low-cost, hi-po package. Base priced at $3,271, the Super Bee included a standard 383-cid 300-hp Magnum V-8, four-barrel carb, three-speed floor shift, "power bulge" hood with flat black finish, tape stripes, bumblebee decals and an interior similar to that of the Charger 500, but substituting a standard bench seat. Rallye suspension components were used.

Available V-8s included the 440 Six-Pack or the 426-cid Street Hemi. Unlike the 8.7:1 compression base engine, these muscle "mills" had high-test hardware and continued to offer 385 or 425 hp.

The 440 Six-Pack Super Bee was advertised at 485 hp. It did 0-60 mph in 6.9 seconds and the quarter-mile took 14.7. With a Hemi, this 3,640-lb. machine moved into the same bracket as the original Charger 500. Not too many '71 Hemi Super Bees were built. The total was 22 cars, of which nine had four-speeds and 13 came with TorqueFlite.

Factory ATP	Wheelbase	Length	Curb Weight	Base Hemi V-8	Engine Options	0-to-60 MPH	¼-Mile
(HEmi) $4,966	115 in.	205.4 in.	(Hemi) 4,083 lbs.	426 cid/425 hp	None	5.7 seconds	13.73 seconds @ 104 mph

MCFG **Says:** $27K (add 100% for Hemi)

He Says: Writing in *Motor Trend* (December '70) A.B. Shuman said, "If the Super Bee SE was interesting, the Hemi car was remarkable. It was a Hemi and you knew it!"

We Says: "You've heard of 'killer bees?' Dodge's '71 Hemi Super Bee may have been the first of the killer variety to hit America."

1971 DEMON 340

Jerry Heasley

1971 DEMON 340

After its success as the '70 Plymouth Duster, Dodge couldn't wait to get MoPar's 108-inch wheelbase coupe for its compact Dart line. That chance came in the fall of '70, when the Demon was added to the '71 lineup. It was the first Dart with an under-110-inch wheelbase.

Like the Duster, the Demon came in two models. The Demon 340, which cost just $18 more than the base six, came with a well-balanced small-block V-8, a floor-shifted three-speed, a Rallye instrument cluster, H.D. suspension, E70-14 tires, stripes and dual exhaust.

Playing the option list was the name of the game and the 340 had interesting extras including a dual-scoop hood with hood pins, a rear spoiler and a "Tuff" steering wheel. You could also order a four-speed gearbox or TorqueFlite and an upgraded interior.

The 340 was a card-carrying member of the '71 Dodge "Scat Pack." The Demon was a success, with 69,861 base models and 10,098 Demon 340s built.

Factory ATP	Wheelbase	Length	Shipping Weight	Base V-8	Engine Options	0-to-60 MPH	¼-Mile
$3,396	108 in.	192.5 in.	3,353 lbs .	340 cid/275 hp	N/A	7.8 seconds	14.56 seconds @ 96 mph

MCFG **Says:** $14K

He Says: Tony Gray, in *Road Test*, said, "Anyone in the market for a low-priced performance car ought to look over the Dodge Demon 340 with considerable care."

We Says: "In a *Motor Trend* 'comparo' test against the Nova SS 350 and AMC Hornet SC 360, the '71 Demon 340 had the smallest motor and the biggest performance numbers."

1971 HEMI CHARGER R/T

Jerry Heasley

1971 HEMI CHARGER R/T

The '71 Dodge Charger was completely restyled. The aim was to make it distinct from the Coronet. A new 115-inch wheelbase was used to carry semi-fastback coupe and hardtop bodies. All models featured rear quarter windows that swept up from the fender to meet the sloping upper rear window frame. A full-width bumper/grille was split by a large vertical divider and the rear end was set off with a small "lip" on the trunk lid that formed a short spoiler.

The base Charger was offered with the choice of a 225-cid Slant Six engine for $2,707 or a 318-cid small-block V-8 for $2,802. The hotter Charger 500 series—which included the $3,271 Super Bee model and the $3,422 SE (special edition) model—came standard with a 383-cid "big-block" V-8. There was also a one-car R/T series.

The Charger R/T listed for $3,777 and included a 70-amp-hour battery, H.D. brakes, H.D. shock absorbers, a pedal dress-up kit, an extra-heavy-duty Rallye suspension, TorqueFlite (or a four-speed), a 440-cid Magnum V-8 and R/T identification. The 426-cid Hemi V-8 was available in Charger R/Ts for $707 extra. According to Mopar authority Galen V. Govier, Hemi Charger production was 22 Super Bees and 63 R/Ts.

Factory ADP	Wheelbase	Length	Shipping Weight	Base V-8	Engine Options	0-to-60 MPH	¼-Mile
$4,484	115 in.	206 in.	3,685 lbs.	426 cid/425 hp	454 V-8 440 cid/370 hp; 440 cid/385 hp	(Hemi) 5.7 seconds	(Hemi) 13.73 seconds @ 104 mph

MCFG **Says:** $29K (add 100% for Hemi)

He Says: Writing in the July '87 issue of *Musclecar Review*, Paul Zazarine said, "The Charger R/T offered a fresh look and a new attitude in mid-sized performance."

We Says: "With the Hemi stuffed under the hood, the Charger R/T quickly developed a 'bad attitude,' especially when GM and FoMoCo muscle rolled by."

Joe Maggio

1972 DEMON 340

1972 DEMON 340

The Demon was essentially a repainted and striped Plymouth Duster with a bit more styling flair and tougher quality control. *Motor Trend* writer Jim Brokaw described the first Demon 340 as a "reasonable alternative" for buyers who wanted an insurable muscle car with just enough spice to make it interesting. Its 340-cid V-8 had a 4.04 x 3.31-inch bore and stroke. It developed 275 hp at 5000 rpm and 340 lbs.-ft. of torque at 3200 rpm. The Demon 340 had a four-barrel carb and 10.0:1 compression. A three-speed stick shift was standard.

Options included a four-speed and an automatic. A 3.91:1 rear axle was used along with E70-14 tires.

For '72, the Demon received just minor trim and taillight changes. It remained on the same wheelbase utilized the year before. It was 71.6 inches wide and 52.8 inches high. Dodge used a 57.5-inch front track and a 55.5-inch rear track. If you ordered a '72 Demon 340, Dodge would add H.D. shock absorbers front and rear, a front sway bar and H.D. torsion bars. The '72 version of the 340-cid engine had a lower 8.5:1 compression ratio.

Factory ADP	Wheelbase	Length	Shipping Weight	Base V-8	Engine Options	0-to-60 MPH	¼-Mile
$3,297	108 in.	192.5 in.	3,360 lbs.	340 cid/275 hp	None	8 seconds	14.80 seconds @ 95 mph

MCFG **Says:** $14K

They Says: *Musclecar Review* (June '89) said, "Even with a shipping weight of less than 3,200 lbs., the 340 Demon was not to be taken lightly."

We Says: "Don't let the 240 net hp rating fool you—with 275 gross hp and its light weight, the Demon was a devil of a mini muscle car."

1992 VIPER RT/10

Doug Mitchel

1992 VIPER RT/10

It all started in a brainstorming session by Chrysler's president Bob Lutz, design VP Tom Gale, engineering VP Francois Castaing and Carroll Shelby. They envisioned a successor to the great American sports cars of the '60s. Shelby's famous Cobra was used as the benchmark.

The Viper's shape recalled the roadsters of the mid-'60s and featured an integrated sport bar and side-exhaust pipes. Recreating the Cobra's driving attributes and making them "perfect" for the modern world was Castaing's job. "The Viper had to evoke all the emotions of driving the '60s muscle car, but it had to be refined to today's engineering standards," he said. "The engine had to be powerful—and sound like it—but much more drivable and durable than yesterday's muscle car engines." An aluminum V-10 that produced 400 hp and 450 lbs.-ft. of torque was used.

A Viper prototype paced the '92 Indy 500 and 285 Viper RT/10 were made that first year.

Factory ADP	Wheelbase	Length	Shipping Weight	Base V-10	Engine Options	0-to-60 MPH	¼-Mile
$53,300 (w/gas guzzler tax)	96.2 in.	175.1 in.	3,300 lbs.	488 cid/400 hp	None	4.6 seconds	12.9 seconds @ 113.8 mph

MCFG **Says:** $45K

He Says: "In our minds' eye, the Cobra was perfect, so, we had to design Viper as we remembered Cobra," said Viper designer Tom Gale.

We Says: "When Carroll Shelby showed us the prototype at the SEMA show, we couldn't believe Dodge had the guts to make it for production—but they did."

Jerry Heasley

1996 VIPER GTS COUPE

1996 VIPER GTS COUPE

Like the RT/10, the GTS stole hearts as a concept car. It was intro'ed at the '93 Detroit Auto Show. The GTS program was green lighted in May '93 and 34 months later the first GTS started was made. In August '95, Dodge displayed a prototype at a Dodge Viper Owner Invitational in Monterey, California and offered current owners a voucher for the first GTSs made. More than three-quarters of the '96 calendar year production of 1,700 was instantly spoken for.

The GTS continued the original look, but more than 90 percent of the car was new. There was a new body, new interior and a modified V-10 with less weight and more power. Enclosing the Viper necessitated a new weatherstrip system, a more powerful air conditioner, dropped glass in the doors and an innovative electronic entry system. An adjustable pedal system allowed the driver to move the clutch, brake and accelerator pedals up to four inches via one knob.

Even with the addition of the roof, backlight and roll-up windows, the weight of the GTS was actually 60 lbs. lighter than that of the roadster.

Factory ADP	Wheelbase	Length	Shipping Weight	Base V-10	Engine Options	0-to-60 MPH	¼-Mile
$73,000 (w/luxury and guzzler taxes)	96.2 in.	176.7 in.	3,445 lbs.	488 cid/450 hp	None	4 seconds	12.4 seconds @ 118 mph

MCFG **Says:** $55K (add 10% for Indy Pace Car; GTS-R $200K)

He Says: "From the beginning, developing the GTS coupe was a more difficult task than the roadster because the car evolved with a broader character," said Roy Sjoberg, Team Viper executive engineer.

We Says: "If the RT/10 was akin to Carroll Shelby's Cobra, the GTS was akin to Enzo Ferrarri's 'prancing horse' cars."

1960 GALAXIE SPECIAL 360

Jerry Heasley

1960 GALAXIE SPECIAL 360

As full-sized '60 cars began appearing in showrooms, at drag strips and on tracks, it was obvious that "performance options" was no longer the dirty term it had been since '57. Cubic inches, ram induction, multi-carbs and different combos of each were made widely available.

An exception at the start of the model year was the full-sized Ford. Its hottest option was the 300-hp 352 V-8 that dated back to '58. But if Ford got a late start in the new performance sweepstakes, by the end of '59 things started to change with the 360-hp Thunderbird Super V-8. Based on the 352, this "Interceptor" or "Super Interceptor" motor carried an "R" code. At first, the 360 came only with a B-W T-85 three-speed (with or without overdrive), and other go-fast stuff. *Motor Life* magazine got hold of a pre-production example that did 0-to-60 mph in 7.5 seconds. Top speed was 152 mph.

At the top of the line was the sleek Starliner two-door hardtop and its ragtop counterpart the Sunliner. Technically, they were in a Galaxie Special series. The most desirable combination for the 360-hp 352 is with either of these models.

Factory ADP	Wheelbase	Length	Shipping Weight	Opt. Super Intercep. V-8	Engine Options	0-to-60 MPH	¼-Mile
(HT) $2,485; (RT) $2,717	119 in.	213.7 in.	(HT) 3,667 lbs.; (RT) 3,841 lbs.	352 cid/ 360 hp	None	(360 hp) 7.5 seconds	(HRM) 14.02 seconds @ 98.14 mph

*Note: **Motor Trend** (February '60) tested a 352-cid/300-hp Galaxie. 0-60 took 11.7 seconds. The 1/4-mile took 20.7 seconds at 80 mph.*

MCFG Says: (HT) $23K; (RT) $31K

He Says: In *Hot Rod* (December '59) Ray Brock wrote, "We like the way it looks, rides, corners, stops and especially how it goes when equipped with the 360-horsepower engine."

We Says: "Back in the '60s, this was the performer that people had been waiting for, with a Tri-Power engine capable of pushing a stock-bodied coupe over the 150-mph mark."

Jerry Heasley

1961 GALAXIE STARLINER 390

1961 GALAXIE STARLINER 390

In '60, Ford had advised the AMA that it was suspending its support of the trade organization's four-year-old ban on stock car racing. Ford showed up at Daytona with a 360-engined Starliner that ran 40 laps at an average of 142 mph. By fall, similar cars were in the hands of racecar drivers.

Inspired by the "win-on-Sunday-sell-on-Monday" mentality, Ford released a 390 V-8 at the start of the year and a four-speed near the end of the season. Both performance add-ons were hot options for the steamy Starliner hardtop.

The new-for-'61 Starliner was smaller, but had a bigger engine. Three versions of the 390 were offered. The standard rating was 300 hp. A police car variant was rated for 330 hp. Tops on the list was the 375-hp Thunderbird Super edition with a four-barrel carb. At midyear, when Tri-Power was released, it pushed the big engine up to 401 hp and Fords dominated drag racing.

Starliner production—including sixes and smaller V-8s—was 29,669 units. However, the number of 401-hp and 375-hp 390-powered cars built was smaller.

Factory ADP	Wheelbase	Length	Shipping Weight	Base 390 V-8	Engine Options	0-to-60 MPH	¼-Mile
$2,713	119 in.	209.9 in.	3,615 lbs.	390 cid/300 hp	390 cid/330 hp; 390/375 hp	7.0 seconds	15 seconds

MCFG Says: $21K (add 20% for 390 T-Bird Special)

They Says: *Car Review* (December '85) said, "In base form the 390 was nothing to write Henry about, having just 300 hp, but by using some components from the earlier 352 Interceptor, Ford came up with the 375-hp 390 Thunderbird Special. Put that in your Galaxie and smoke the tires."

We Says: "Despite its spaceship name and looks, the Galaxie had the underhood stuff to make a drag strip competitor feel like a tricycler with a CHP cruiser on his tail."

1962 GALAXIE 500XL 406

1962 GALAXIE 500XL 406

The '62 Fords stood out as one of the best examples of Ford's competence in design. They were large, but their clean lines—totally free of fins and GM—gave them a handsome appearance. Ford got back into performance in '60-'61. The results included the debut of the triple-carb 401-hp 390 V-8 and a B-W four-speed for 390-powered Fords.

Early in '62, Ford intro'ed a new 406 V-8. This "T-Bird Special 406" carried over the triple carbs, special cam, valve gear, ignition, bearings and exhausts of the 401-hp 390. Despite a similarity to previous V-8s, there were changes in the engine that reflected Ford's expertise in developing modern, hi-po cars.

Included in the $380 price tag of the 406 (one of which was Ford's 30 millionth V-8) was a comprehensive performance package. Its big feature was a B-W 4-speed with ratios of 2.36:1, 1.78:1, 1.41:1 and 1.0:1. Less apparent—until the 406-powered Ford got going—were its 20 percent stiffer springs and shocks. Ford had no sintered metallic brakes, but 3-inch brake drums fitted with hard linings slowed Fords from top speeds near 140 mph.

Factory ADP (406)	Wheelbase	Length	Shipping Weight	Base V-8	Engine Options	0-to-60 MPH	¼-Mile
(HT) $3,648; (RT) $3,898	119 in.	209.3 in.	(HT) 3,672 lbs. (RT) 3,831 lbs.	406 cid/405 hp	None	7 seconds	15.5 seconds @ 92 mph

MCFG **Says:** (406) (HT) $24.7K; (RT) $31.2K

They Says: In *Hot Rod*, Ray Brock wrote, "Anyway you look at it, this is a bargain priced hi-po automobile. Ford should have no trouble selling 10,000 of these items."

We Says: "Give me a 406-motivated '62 Galaxie ragtop with a double-heart rear window and I'll be back in High School Seventh Heaven."

1963 GALAXIE 427

Jerry Heasley

1963 GALAXIE 427

Ford needed a drag racing program if it wanted to compete in the muscle car market. The first sign was the late '62 release of two 406-cid V-8s. Ford got its act in gear around mid-'63. Its first step was the release of the good-looking '63 1/2 Galaxie fastback. Then came a new 427-cid V-8 with massive muscle for the street, the drag strip, and the NASCAR superspeedways.

To promote the 427-powered '63 Galaxie, Ford manufactured 50 "factory lightweights" at its factory in Atlanta, Georgia. Made for going down the quarter-mile faster than the competition, the bare-bones cars had fiberglass doors, hoods, trunks and front-end components. The bumpers and other parts were aluminum.

In addition to the just-for-racing cars, FoMoCo produced 4,978 big Fords with one of two versions of its big V-8. One was a 425-hp 427 tuned for the street. The second street engine was a 427 with a single four-barrel carb. It produced 410 hp. Both of the big engines were available in Galaxie or Galaxie 500 XL two-door hardtops. The dual-quad engine was a $462 option.

Factory ADP	Wheelbase	Length	Shipping Weight	Base V-8	Engine Options	0-to-60 MPH	¼-Mile
(427/425) (Galaxie 500) $3,245; (Galaxie 500 XL) $3,730	119 in.	209.9 in.	(Galaxie 500) 3,769 lbs.; (Galaxie 500 XL) 3,825 lbs.	(Q-Code) 427 cid/410 hp; (R-Code) 427 cid/425 hp	None	6.9 seconds	14.9 seconds @ 96 mph

MCFG **Says:** (Galaxie 500) $21K; (Galaxie 500 XL) $22K (add 40% for 427)

He Says: Brock Yates said, "The Chevrolets were fast, but frail, the Pontiacs were strong, but not strong enough, and when the flag fell on the fifth annual Daytona 500, there they were, five Ford fastbacks rumbling across the line in a hot, noisy formation."

We Says: "A 427 just doesn't take no for an answer and Ford proved it at Daytona in '63."

1964 FAIRLANE "THUNDERBOLT"

Jerry Heasley

1964 FAIRLANE "THUNDERBOLT"

Ford's Total Performance program pitted factory lightweight 427 Galaxies against S-D Pontiacs and Dodge Ramchargers. The Fords couldn't lose weight like the unibody Mopars and often ran second. In '62, racers started dropping big-blocks in Fairlanes. The next year Tasca Ford campaigned an A/FX '63 Fairlane with a glass body and 427, dubbing it the "Thunderbolt."

Late in '63, NHRA adopted minimum weight rules for stock-class drag cars, squeezing the Galaxies out of the drag racing picture. Ford teamed up with Andy Hotten to build 57 Fairlane 427-powered racecars weighing about 3,203 lbs. They had fiberglass fenders, teardrop hood blisters, Plexiglas windows, lightweight buckets, cold-air-induction, 8000-rpm Rotunda tachs, modified front suspensions (to accommodate a 427) and many equipment deletions and special competition features. The 425-hp big-block V-8 actually cranked out some 500 hp.

These special drag cars soon adopted the Thunderbolt name and became known as "T-Bolts." Due to demand, a second batch of all-white cars was made. The first 11 cars were painted maroon and 10 had four-speeds. The 100 additional cars were painted white and 89 had four-speeds. Soon, the new Mustang took over and the short history of T-Bolts halted.

Factory ADP	Wheelbase	Length	Shipping Weight	Base T-Bolt V-8	Engine Options	0-to-60 MPH	0-to-100 MPH
NA (modified)	NA (modified)	NA (modified)	3,203 lbs.	427 cid/425 hp	None	N/A	11.76 seconds @ 122.7 mph

MCFG Says: Not listed, but last we heard six figures.

He Says: Allen Hunt of *Car Life* magazine (May '64) said, "Obviously it's a racing car ... and one calculated to put Ford right back in the front row on the drag strips this summer."

We Says: "We watched in awe as restored T-Bolts blasted down the strip during the Muscle Car Showdowns at Quaker State Dragway."

Jerry Heasley

1964 GALAXIE 427

1964 GALAXIE 427

Despite their best-ever-for-Ford performances on drag strips, the '63 Galaxie lightweights didn't dominate quarter-mile competition the way Ford hoped. They competed with Pontiac's powerful 421 SD V-8 and Chrysler's Hemi. To keep up with the Joneses, Ford created Fairlane-based T-Bolts that could run a drag strip in less than 12 seconds at close to 125 mph.

Still, full-sized 427-powered Fords were the hot ticket in stock car racing. To get them NASCAR sanctioned, Ford kept making big muscle cars and a full-size lightweight drag package, too. In '64, a Galaxie A/Stock dragster package was offered for two-doors. Also available was a B/Stock Dragster package that added a low-riser manifold for the 427. The cars came in white with red interiors. Body sealer, insulation and heaters were deleted. Added were lightweight seats and a fiberglass "power bubble" hood. The grille had fiberglass air-induction vents.

FORD

Factory ADP	Wheelbase	Length	Shipping Weight	Base 427 V-8	Engine Options	0-to-60 MPH	¼-Mile
* (HT) $3,200; (RT) $3,462; ** (HT) $3,256; (RT) $3,518	119 in.	210 in.	(Galaxie 500XL) (HT) 3,582 lbs.; (RT) 3,757 lbs.	427 cid/410 hp	427 cid/425 hp	(Galaxie 500XL) Just over 6 seconds	(Galaxie 500XL) Under 15 seconds

* *(Galaxie 500XL - 410 hp)*

** *(Galaxie 500XL - 425 hp)*

MCFG **Says:** (Galaxie 500 hardtop) $21K (add 40% for 427 V-8)

They Says: Said *Car Life,* "With performance a byword at Ford these days, it's not surprising that that plant's '64s look as though they should go places quickly."

We Says: "After five fastback Fords rumbled across the line in order in '63, the Galaxie 427 became a legend in muscle car land."

1965 GALAXIE 427

Jerry Heasley

1965 GALAXIE 427

The '65 full-sized Fords were billed as "the newest since 1949." Clean, sharp, square lines characterized fresh new styling set off by a radiator grille with thin, horizontal bars and dual headlights stacked on top of each other. There was a slight "Coke bottle" shape to the rear.

With a move towards selling luxury and comfort, it might seem strange that Ford continued offering the 427 V-8 for the big cars, but remember that this engine had to be NASCAR-certified to help maintain Ford's "Total Performance" image. After NASCAR kicked the Chrysler Hemi out of stock car racing, the 427 was king and took a record 48 Grand National wins. The big-block didn't fit into Falcons, Mustangs and Fairlanes without extensive modifications, so it was up to the Galaxie to keep the engine a "production option."

It's likely that the majority of full-sized Ford fitted with the 427 (except for all-out race cars) were Galaxie 500XL models. A Galaxie 500XL two-door hardtop with the 425-hp 427 "Thunderbird Super High-Performance" V-8 could be purchased for as little as $3,233 in '65.

Factory ADP	Wheelbase	Length	Shipping Weight	Q-Code V-8	R-Code V-8	0-to-60 MPH	¼-Mile (automatic)
$3,233	119 in.	210 in.	3,507 lbs.	427 cid/410 hp	427 cid/425 hp	4.8 seconds	14.9 seconds @ 96 mph

MCFG Says: (Galaxie 500) $16K; (Galaxie 500 XL) $17K (add 50% for 427)

They Says: *Car Life* said, "This one has more muscle than the Olympic Games."

We Says: "Ford didn't lie in its ad when it said, 'Don't let the look of cool elegance give you any false ideas about the character of these '65 Fords; that sculptured metal covers the hottest road missile you can find in any U.S. showroom.'"

Jerry Heasley

1965 MUSTANG GT

1965 MUSTANG GT

It is not often that a car creates its own market segment, but the Mustang—introduced April 17, 1964—did. Purists debate whether Mustangs produced prior to September '64 are '64 1/2 or '65 models. When it comes to the GT equipment group, there can be no question, as it was unveiled for the first anniversary of the Mustang on April 17, 1965.

The Mustang had the popular long hood/short deck look and bucket seats. At first it came as a sport coupe and a ragtop. In the fall of '64, a fastback called the 2+2 was added. A long options list was important in marketing Mustangs. Buyers could add lots of appearance and convenience extras, plus some bolt-on hi-po hardware.

Combining mechanical upgrades with new visual pieces made the GT package special. First, the buyer had to order an optional V-8, which at the time included the 225-hp Challenger Special 289 at $157 or the Hi-Po 271-hp 289-cid engine for $430. The GT option included quick-ratio steering, disc front brakes, and other flashy stuff.

Factory ADP	Wheel-base	Length	Shipping Weight	Base V-8	Engine Options	0-to-60 MPH	¼-Mile
(Base V-8) (HT) $2,427; (FB) $2,639; (RT) $2,663	108 in.	181.6 in.	(HT) 2,720 lbs.; (FB) 2,770 lbs.; (RT) 2,904; lbs.	289 cid/200 hp	289 cid/225 hp; 289 cid/271 hp	(289 cid/ 271 hp) 7.5 seconds	(289 cid/ 271 hp) 15.7 seconds @ 89 mph

MCFG Says: (base V-8) (HT) $23.5K; (FB) $$28K; (RT) $33K (add 10% for GT; add 30% for Hi-Po)

They Says: *Car Life* said, "Ford started a round-up of its state-of-the-Total-Performance-art to produce the Mustang."

We Says: "Though it was far from the fastest car of the '60s, the Mustang GT played a big role in building enthusiasm for muscle cars and rarely gets full credit for this."

1965 SHELBY COBRA 289

Jerry Heasley

1965 SHELBY COBRA 289

Cobra is the ultimate American road warrior because it brought the USA its first and only World Manufacturer's Championship. The year was '65 and the car was the 289 Cobra roadster. Despite the British origins of its chassis—beefed-up to accept American V-8 power—the Cobra was a unique marque. It was built by Shelby-American of Los Angeles. Carroll Shelby contracted with AC of England for the chassis and body and put the dream together using Ford engines.

The small-block Cobra weighed slightly over 2,000 lbs. and topped 150 mph. It was quicker than any other sports car. Shelby's idea was to sell a street version of the racecar to finance the track cars, although any final accounting showed that Ford backed the Shelby racing program to benefit from the on-track publicity associated with its new small-block V-8.

Shelby accomplished his goal with the Cobra, beating Ferrari for the World Manufacturer's Championship. At the end of the run of the small-block roadster, Shelby-American built about 30 cars with automatic transmissions. Sadly, most of the automatics were changed over to four-speeds, but a few do exist today, including CSH 2549.

Factory ADP	Wheelbase	Length	Shipping Weight	Base V-8	Engine Options	0-to-60 MPH	¼-Mile (automatic)
$5,995	108 in.	181.6 in.	2,550 lbs.	289 cid/271 hp	None	4.5 seconds	12.20 seconds @ 118 mph

MCFG **Says:** $125,000-$150,000

They Says: "When the Cobra is certified for production sports racing, a fox will have been dropped among the chickens," said *Car Life*.

We Says: "We don't know about feathers, but fiberglass was flying all around the hen house after Cobra arrived."

Jerry Heasley

1965 SHELBY-MUSTANG GT-350/ GT-350R

1965 SHELBY-MUSTANG GT-350/GT-350 R

Ford wanted a higher-performance, specialty-type Mustang—a car that could compete with Chevy's 'Vette. This suggested a two-seat car. Higher performance meant hopping up the 289, since Ford big-blocks wouldn't fit and small-blocks worked best in road racing. Both jobs were turned over to Shelby-American, which built a street version the Mustang GT that Carroll Shelby named the GT-350. With racing victories a major goal, Shelby-American also built a race-ready competition model that was not meant for street use called the GT-350R.

To satisfy SCCA regs at least 100 race and street cars had to be built. Therefore, 110 white fastbacks—each fitted with 289-cid hi-po K-code V-8s with solid valve lifters and 271 hp—were lifted off an assembly line in San Jose, California.

The R came with all GT-350 features, plus lots of racing stuff, like a fiberglass front panel, engine oil cooler, big radiator, brake cooling assemblies, a 34-gallon gas tank, a quick-fill gas cap, an electric fuel pump, a performance exhaust system, 7.15-inch mag wheels, revised wheel openings, a roll bar, a shoulder harness, a fire extinguisher, a flame-resistant interior, a plastic rear window, and sliding plastic side windows.

Factory ADP	Wheelbase	Length	Shipping Weight	K-code V-8	Engine Options	0-to-60 MPH	¼-Mile
(GT-350) $4,547; (GT-350R) $5,950	108 in.	181.6 in.	(stock GT) 2,515 lbs.	(GT-350) 289 cid/306 hp; (GT-350R) 289 cid/325 350 hp	None	(GT-350) 6.5 seconds	(GT-350) 14.90 seconds @ 95 mph

MCFG Says: (GT-350): $63K

He Says: "The differences and the superiority of the GT-350 over the standard Mustang or even the HP Mustang must be sampled to be fully appreciated," said Jim Wright in *Car Life*. "The GT-350 is all that most of us wanted the Mustang to be in the first place."

We Says: "Fast fastback on the fast track when it comes to muscle car pricing."

1966 FAIRLANE GT/GTA

Jerry Heasley

1966 FAIRLANE GT/GTA

The totally redesigned '66 was the first *production* Fairlane to carry a big-block V-8. The outside size didn't change much, but underhood dimensions grew, allowing the Fairlane to become FoMoCo's "factory hot rod" when monster V-8s were ordered. The big-engined Fairlane competed head-to-head with the GTO.

A 315-hp 390 V-8 was *standard* in the Fairlane GT. The GTA had lots of performance parts and a 335-hp engine. A limited number of Fairlanes were sold with "side-oiler" 427-cid wedge V-8s. Some of them even hit NASCAR ovals. The 427-powered Fairlanes were characterized by a big air scoop that gulped cold air at the front of the hood. Only about 60 Fairlanes with 427s were produced.

Both Fairlane GTs were part of the 500/XL line. Ford built 33,015 two-door hardtops and 4,327 ragtops. The GT package included badges, a special hood, striping, engine dress-up parts, a H.D. suspension, front discs, bucket seats, a center console and a sport steering wheel. The 315-hp V-8 featured a hot cam, special manifolds and a single 4-barrel carb. The '66 Fairlane GTA hardtop ("A" meant automatic) with the 335 hp V-8 had only 10.5 lbs. per horsepower.

Factory ADP	Wheelbase	Length	Shipping Weight	Base V-8	Engine Options	0-to-60 MPH	¼-Mile (automatic)
(HT) $2,843; (RT) $3,068	116 in.	198.8 in.	(HT) 3,375 lbs.; (RT) 3,470 lbs.	390 cid/315 hp	390 cid/335 hp	6.8 seconds	15.2 seconds

MCFG Says: (HT) $17K; (RT) $24K (add 50% for 427-cid V-8)

He Says: *Car Life's* Gene Booth said, "The GTA (do you suppose it will be called the 'GeeTAw?') plants Ford firmly in the performance market."

We Says: "Little GTA, you really give a thrill, four-barrel and a Sport shift and a 390 mill … wind 'em up, wind 'em out, you wound up like the GTO."

Jerry Heasley

1967 FAIRLANE 427

1967 FAIRLANE 427

The '67 Fairlane continued to use the '66 body with minor trim changes. The grille was a single aluminum stamping and the taillights were divided horizontally by the back-up light.

The 427-cid "side-oiler" V-8 was again on the Fairlane options list. The '67 edition of *Car Fax* indicates it came in non-GT club coupes and sport coupes. A notation indicates that prices for the two 427 options were not available in late '66, but prices for the 410-hp 427 in Galaxies without the 7-Liter package was $975, which is likely in the ballpark of the Fairlane option.

The milder 410-hp version with one four-barrel-carb was first choice. A hairier 425-hp version with twin Holley four-barrels was optional. Both included transistorized ignition, H.D. battery, H.D. suspension, extra-cooling package and four-speed.

Racing versions of the 427 were offered with a new "eight-barrel" induction system that put about 30 extra ponies on tap.

Factory ADP	Wheelbase	Length	Shipping Weight	Base 427 V-8	Engine Options	0-to-60 MPH	¼-Mile
(approx. w/427) (500 CPE) $3,400; (500 HT) $3,550	116 in.	197 in.	(base V-8) (500 CPE) 2,938 lbs.; (500 HT) 3,061 lbs.	427 cid/410 hp	427 cid/425 hp	6.5 seconds	14.66 seconds @ 99.88 mph

MCFG Says: (CPE) $7.1K; (HT) $11.5K (add 50% for 427)

They Says: Ford advertisements said, "The 427 Fairlane is also available without numbers."

We Says: "There was nothing middle-of-the-road about Ford's midsized muscle machine."

Jerry Heasley

1967 MUSTANG 390

1967 MUSTANG 390

The '67 Mustang got a jazzy new body, a wider tread, and more engines. Option choices were widened and now included a Tilt-Away steering wheel, a built-in heater and air conditioner, an overhead console, a Stereo-Sonic tape system, and other stuff inside and out.

Outside, the '67 Mustang was heftier and more full fendered. Especially low and sleek was the new 2+2, featuring all-new sheet metal. The roofline had a clean, unbroken sweep to a distinctive, concave rear panel. Functional air louvers in the roof rear quarters were thinner than previously.

Mustangs had bigger engine bays and a new 315-hp 390 "big-block." This small bore-long stroke engine was related to the Ford FE block introduced in '58. It provided a good street-performance option with a low $264 price tag and "mucho" low-end performance and torque. All '66 engines were carried over, along with a new 200-hp two-barrel "Challenger 289" V-8. This motor was standard in GTs. GTA was the new designation for cars with automatic transmission.

Factory ADP	Wheelbase	Length	Shipping Weight	Big Block V-8	Engine Options	0-to-60 MPH	¼-Mile
(FB V-8) $2,698; (HT V-8) $2,567; (RT V-8) $2,814	108 in.	183.6 in.	(FB V-8) 2,830 lbs.; (HT V-8) 2,803 lbs.; (RT V-8) 2,957 lbs.	390 cid/335 hp	None	(390 cid) 7.8 seconds	(390 cid) 15.5 seconds @ 91.4 mph

MCFG Says: (FB) $24.5K; (HT) $21.5K; (RT) $30K (add 10% for 390 V-8)

They Says: *Car Life* magazine said, "Mustangs, like hamburgers, have become an American institution."

We Says: "A bigger, better, more beastly Mustang was Dearborn's best 'better idea' yet."

Jerry Heasley

1968 FORD MUSTANG CJ 428/SCJ 428

1968 FORD MUSTANG CJ 428/SCJ 428

Ford introduced the 428CJ V-8 on April 1, 1968. Production of the engine continued through '70. Rated conservatively for 335 hp at 5200 rpm, the '68 Mustang CJ 428 put out more like 375 to 400 gross hp. It was hot competition for the SS 396 from Chevy, the 400 HO from Pontiac, the 440 Magnum from Mopar and literally any car on the street in '68.

A hi-po variant of the basic 428, the main features of the CJ were heads similar to the Ford 427 "low-riser"-type (with bigger ports), a cam from the 390-cid GT engine, a cast-iron copy of the 428 Police Interceptor intake manifold, and a 735-cfm Holley four-barrel carb.

For '68 1/2, all Cobra Jets were coded "R" in the fifth digit of the vehicle identification number (VIN) and all were Ram-Air cars (featuring an air cleaner and flapper assembly mounted underneath the hood). A small scoop sat atop the hood to admit cold air to the Holley four-barrel.

The 428 SCJs were built with drag strip duty in mind, which is why Ford beefed up the bottom end and added an engine oil cooler, but left the top end alone.

Factory ADP	Wheelbase	Length	Shipping Weight	Base V-8	Engine Options	0-to-60 MPH	¼-Mile
(base V-8) (HT) $2,707; (FB) $2,818; (RT) $2,920	108 in.	183.6 in.	(base V-8) (HT) 2,861 lbs.; (FB) 2,885 lbs.; (RT) 2,971 lbs.	289 cid/ 195 hp	302 cid/230/hp; 390 cid/280 hp; 390 cid/325 hp Optional CJ 428 428 cid/335 hp	(CJ 428) 6.9 seconds	(CJ 428) 14.57 seconds @ 99.5 mph

MCFG **Says:** (HT) $21.5K; (FB) $24.5K; (RT) $30K: (add 30% for CJ 428; add 40% for SCJ 428)

They Says: After a drag strip test, *Hot Rod* magazine declared the Mustang's 428 CJ to be "the fastest running pure stock in the history of man."

We Says: "140 mph probably isn't enough. These cars are really fast with the 390 stuffed under the hood. Prices are climbing fast, too."

1968 MUSTANG GT/GTA & "CALIFORNIA SPECIAL"

Jerry Heasley

1968 MUSTANG GT/GTA & "CALIFORNIA SPECIAL"

Subtle changes were made to '68 Mustangs. Bucket seats, a floor-mounted stick, a Sport steering wheel, and carpeting remained standard. Minor updates included a front Mustang emblem "floating" in the grille, script-style Mustang body side nameplates and cleaner-looking bright metal trim on the cove. There was a new "2-tone" hood.

The $147 GT option included stripes, ether rocker panel type or a reflecting "C" stripe. Other goodies included fog lights, a GT gas cap and GT wheel covers. A total of 17,458 GTs were made in '68. A GT-390 is a desirable collector's car.

New engine options were offered in '68. The 302 V-8 was also offered in a 220-hp version with a two-barrel carb. Big-block options included two "FE" V-8s, the 390 and the 427. The 427 was used in only a handful of cars, then phased out in December '67. Starting in April '68, a new 428-cid Cobra-Jet V-8 was put into about 2,817 Mustangs. Ram Air induction was available on 428s.

About 5,000 GT/CS "California Specials" were made. They had a Shelby-type deck lid spoiler, sequential taillights and black-out grille, but no Mustang grille emblem.

FORD

Factory ADP	Wheelbase	Length	Shipping Weight	Base V-8	Engine Options	0-to-60 MPH	¼-Mile
(base 289 V-8 Models) (HT) $2,707; (FB) $2,818; (RT) $2,920	108 in.	184 in.	(HT) 2,861 lbs.; (FB) 2,885 lbs.; (RT) 2,971 lbs.	289 cid/195 hp	302 cid/230 hp; 390 cid/320 hp; 427 cid/390 hp; 428 cid/335 hp	(428 SCJ) 5.4 seconds	(428 SCJ) 13.90 seconds @ 102 mph

MCFG Says: (HT) $21.5K (FB) $$24.5K; (RT) $30K (add 10% for GT; 10% for GT 390; 50% for 427; 30% for 428)

They Said: "Turn yourself on, switch your style and show a new face in the most exciting car on the American road," said one Ford advertisement.

We Says: "We have a cruise every Wednesday night and when one of the '68 Mustang GT big-blocks turns up, it's time to remember why the good old days were so great."

Jerry Heasley

1968 SHELBY-MUSTANG GT 500KR

1968 SHELBY-MUSTANG GT 500KR

Someone stole the Shelby GT 500KR that *Car Life* was going to test. You couldn't blame them. With its 428-CJ V-8, it was a big temptation to any cat burglar.

Everyone knew what Cobra meant and "GT 500" was well understood by '68. As for "KR," the folks at Ford and Shelby said it stood for "King of the Road." Under the hood was a CJ-428 with a 4.13 x 3.98-inch bore and stroke, 10.6:1 compression, special hydraulic lifters, dual branched headers, and one extra-big Holley four-barrel. Its true output was 435-500 hp.

The Shelby KR package included a fiberglass hood and front panels, functional air scoops, hot air extractors, a big speedo and tach, gauges on the console, vinyl buckets, thick carpeting, a wood-look dash trim, suspension upgrades (including staggered shocks), E70-15 Goodyear Polyglas tires, a limited-slip differential, engine dress-up items, and special stripes.

Although not the fastest car ever made, the GT 500KR was the fastest Shelby-Mustang made up to its time. Production included 1,053 fastbacks and 518 ragtops.

Factory ADP	Wheelbase	Length	Shipping Weight	Base V-8	Engine Options	0-to-60 MPH	¼-Mile
(HT) $4,472; (RT) $4,594	108 in.	184 in.	(HT) 3,175 lbs.; (RT) 3,270 lbs.	428 cid/335 hp	None	6.9 seconds	14.57 seconds @ 99.55 mph

MCFG Says: (HT) $53K; (RT) $76K (add 30% for "KR")

They Says: *Car Life* said, "The King of the Road will wow the neighbors, cover ground, and make drivers of ordinary Mustangs eat their hearts out."

We Says: "The GT 500KR wasn't the undisputed king of drag racing, but, there's more to life than the quarter-mile."

1969 FAIRLANE 428-CJ/SCJ

Jerry Heasley

1969 FAIRLANE 428-CJ/SCJ

The hit of the season in Ford's mid-sized line for '69 was a low-buck muscle car called the Torino Cobra. Designed to steal sales away from Plymouth's Road Runner, the Torino Cobra was offered in notchback and fastback models with the 428-CJ V-8. Also standard was a four-speed gearbox, an H.D. suspension, and cartoon decals of the coiled-snake Cobra emblem.

The idea of a "stripper" car at a budget price had great appeal to many people, but there were those who liked their muscle cars with a bit more spit and polish, so Ford also offered the same goodies, as optional equipment, in all '69 Fairlanes—not just the Fairlane Torino models.

Few, if any, such engines made their way into base Fairlanes, since this series did not offer the fastback style. This model was merchandised in the Fairlane 500. Of course, you could also get a 428-CJ in the regular hardtop, if you wanted a "sleeper" type muscle car. One of the buff books tested a '69 Fairlane Cobra two-door hardtop with the 335-hp 428 V-8. It gave the price of the car as $3,139. The hot Fairlane moved from 0-to-60 in 6.3 seconds and did the quarter mile in 14.5 seconds.

Factory ADP	Wheelbase	Length	Shipping Weight	Base 428 Cobra-Jet V-8	Optional 428 Super Cobra-Jet V-8	0-to-60 MPH	¼-Mile
(FB) $3,139	116 in.	202 in.	3,208 lbs.	428 cid/325 hp	428 cid/335 hp	7.8 seconds	14.9 seconds @ 95.2 mph

MCFG Says: (FB) $22K (add 40% for 428)

They Says: *Car Life* said, "The Cobra may not eat all birds for breakfast, but when it does, it doesn't chew with its mouth full."

We Says: "When you add up the numbers to get Total Performance, the '69 Fairlane 428-CJ/SCJ is what you wind up with."

1969 MUSTANG BOSS 302

Jerry Heasley

1969 MUSTANG BOSS 302

The Boss 302 was Ford's Z/28. It had a beefed-up four-bolt-mains 302, a stronger crank, and redesigned "Cleveland" cylinder heads that promoted better breathing. A stock Boss 302 could do 0-to-60 in under 9 seconds and nudge the century mark in the quarter-mile.

While a Boss 302 in the hands of a collector is likely to be driven a little more gingerly than the paces original owners put these cars through, Ford built an rpm limiter to keep lead-footed types from blowing up the engine. Basically, the limiter worked by counting ignition impulses and not allowing the engine to exceed 6,000 rpm.

The Boss can be recognized by matte black paint on its hood and trunk, Boss 302 names on its sides, a front spoiler and styled steel wheels. Its equipment includes front disc brakes and a four-speed. The optional rear spoiler was obviously decorative.

Unlike other performance cars, the Boss 302 had exceptionally good street manners—although the firm suspension did broadcast tar strips and other pavement irregularities. Open the door and the Boss is just a Mustang. The interior is attractive, but it features the infamous "park bench" rear seat. That's okay, though, the fastback wasn't really designed to be a four-seater.

Factory ADP	Wheelbase	Length	Shipping Weight	Base V-8	Engine Options	0-to-60 MPH	¼-Mile
$4,025	108 in.	188 in.	3,253 lbs.	302 cid/290 hp	None	6.9 seconds	14.9 seconds @ 96 mph

MCFG Says: $42K

They Says: Ford advertisements said, "The nearest thing to a Trans-Am Mustang you can bolt a license plate onto."

We Says: "With a thoroughbred engine and thoroughbred styling by Larry Shinoda, the Boss 302 was a winner from the start."

Jerry Heasley

1969 MUSTANG BOSS 429

1969 MUSTANG BOSS 429

Late in '69, Ford boss Bunkie Knudson decided to stuff the 429 H.O. NASCAR V-8 into the Mustang. The ex-Pontiac chief became Ford's president in the summer of '68. He had made his reputation turning Pontiacs into go-fast machines. Dearborn wanted to make the 429 H.O. legal in stock car racing. Knudson suggested dropping it into the Mustang, instead of the Galaxie.

Boss 429 production started in January '69. The stock NASCAR 429 V-8 was used. The cars were put together on an aftermarket basis by Kar-Kraft of Brighton, Michigan. Each Boss 429 was hand built. Production ran from January through July. A total of 859 units was produced, including two Boss Cougars.

All Boss 429s went through final inspection for equipment verification and certification prior to shipment. Each had a specific KK 429 NASCAR serial number from KK-1201 to KK-2558.

Factory ADP	Wheelbase	Length	Shipping Weight	Base V-8	Engine Options	0-to-60 MPH	¼-Mile
$4,932	108 in.	188 in.	3,375 lbs.	429 cid/375 hp	None	7.1 seconds	14.09 seconds @ 102 mph

MCFG Says: (HT) $64K

He Says: Brad Bowling (*Standard Catalog of Mustang 1964-2001*) noted, "Ford was delighted to give birth to a set of twins in 1969—the ready-to-race Boss 302 and 429 were both built around state-of-the-art, high-performance power plants."

We Says: "Whoever had a hand in making the Boss 429 would be prosecuted under the Patriot Act today—for terrorizing other muscle cars."

1969 MUSTANG MACH 1

Jerry Heasley

1969 MUSTANG MACH 1

The '69 Mustang got a major restyling. The larger new body kept the Mustang image. The fastback, formerly known as the 2+2, was now called the SportsRoof. The Mach 1 was based on this body style. "Mustang Mach 1—holder of 295 land speed records," said Ford's *1969 Performance Buyer's Digest*. "This is the one that Mickey Thompson started with. From its Wide-Oval, belted tires to its wind tunnel designed SportsRoof, the word is 'go.'" The production car had the same wind-splitting sheet metal as the modified Mach 1 that screamed around Bonneville at over 155 mph, hour after hour, breaking 295 USAC speed and endurance records.

Standard features included a matte black hood, a simulated hood scoop, and exposed NASCAR-style hood lock pins (which could be deleted). A reflective side stripe and rear stripes carried a "Mach 1" designation just behind the front wheel arches and above the chrome pop-up gas cap. Chrome styled steel wheels and chrome exhausts tips (with optional four-barrel carbs) were other bright touches. Dual color-keyed racing mirrors and a handling suspension were used.

Mach 1's had the Mustang's fanciest interior with high-back bucket seats, black carpets, a rim-blow steering wheel, a center console, a clock, sound deadening insulation and teakwood-grained trim on the doors, dash and console.

Factory ADP	Wheelbase	Length	Shipping Weight	Base V-8	Engine Options	0-to-60 MPH	¼-Mile
$3,122	108 in.	188 in.	3,253 lbs.	351 cid/250 hp	351 cid/290 hp; 390 cid/320 hp; 428 cid/335 hp	(428) 5.5 seconds	(428) 13.90 seconds @ 103.32 mph

MCFG Says: $28K (add 30% for 428-CJ; add 40% for 428-SCJ)

They Says: *Car Life* (March '69) said, "Greatness makes its own demands. An enthusiast will find the Mach 1 a rewarding car. Best Mustang yet and quickest ever."

We Says: "The Mach 1 was Dearborn's budget-basement version of the race car that Carroll Shelby whipped up on the Left Coast."

1969 TORINO COBRA

Jerry Heasley

1969 TORINO COBRA

This Torino Cobra line included just two body types: formal hardtop and Sports roof. The emphasis was on performance when you went Cobra shopping, and the standard equipment included a 335-hp 428 Cobra-Jet V-8, a four-speed manual transmission, a competition suspension, Wide-Oval tires, and 6-inch-wide wheels with hub caps.

The base Cobra V-8 featured a 4.13 x 3.98-inch bore and stroke, a 10.6:1 compression ratio, 335 hp at 5200 rpm and 440 foot-pounds of torque at 2600 rpm. You could get an optional 290-hp 351 V-8 if you wanted to save on gas. Also optional was the 428 "Ram Air" V-8, which carried the same 335-hp rating, but achieved it at a higher 5600 rpm peak. Its torque output was 445 lbs.-ft. at 3400 rpm and it had a 10.7:1 compression ratio. The Ram Air engine featured a functional hood scoop to "ram" cold air into the Holley four-barrel. This set up was $133 extra.

If you did not want to shift for yourself, a SelectShift was optional for $37 and it came with a floor shift and optional center console.

Factory ADP	Wheelbase	Length	Shipping Weight	Base V-8	Engine Options	0-to-60 MPH	¼-Mile
(HT) $3,206; (FB) $3,181	116 in.	202 in.	(HT) 3,546 lbs.; (FB) 3,588 lbs.	428 cid/335 hp	351 cid/290 hp; (Ram Air) 428 cid/335 hp	(Ram Air) 6.3 seconds	(Ram Air) 14.5 seconds @ 100 mph

MCFG Says: (both) $25K

They Says: "Torque gives rubber big bite for fast acceleration," *Motor Trend* summarized. "Four-speed helps. Ford has many hop-up parts for 428."

We Says: "Ford's sexy-looking Torino had an Italian name that meant 'fast' in any language."

Jerry Heasley

1969 TORINO TALLADEGA

1969 TORINO TALLADEGA

Named after an Alabama town where a new 2.66-mile superspeedway was opened, the Talladega had an extended nose and flush grille. A revised Torino rear bumper was used up front and the rocker panels were reworked. The result was a car 6 inches longer and 1 inch lower than a stock Torino fastback. NASCAR teams started from stock and enhanced their Talladegas.

In stock format, power came from a 335-hp CJ-428 available only with Cruise-O-Matic. Ford wanted stock car drivers, not street racers, to create the Torino's performance image. They did. David Pearson won his second straight championship driving for Holman & Moody.

Early race cars ran the 427. Beginning in March, they got the new "semi-hemi" 429. The 429s were *not* put in showroom cars, since Boss 429 Mustangs satisfied race-sanctioning requirements for that motor. The '69 Talladegas were fast, but their '70 replacements were five mph slower on the big tracks. As a result, factory teams ran year-old models at many tracks during the '70 season. Counting prototypes, Talladega production easily passed 500 and hit 754. The cars came in Wimbleton White, Royal Maroon, or Presidential Blue with black bench seats.

Factory ADP	Wheelbase	Length	Shipping Weight	Base V-8	Race V-8	0-to-60 MPH	¼-Mile
$3,297	116 in.	202 in.	3,558 lbs.	(showroom) 428 cid/335 hp	429 cid/375+ hp	(428 CJ) 7.1 seconds	(428 CJ) 14.70 seconds @ 96 mph

MCFG Says: $20K (add 40% for 428)

They Says: www.musclecarplanet says, "Though this car was a bit heavier, the 428 CJ still pushed it to mid-14-second quarter-miles, though it was better suited to left turns on the oval."

We Says: "The perfect quarter-mile machine for the Ford fan who wants to go drag racing against Starsky & Hutch rather than Gas Rhonda."

Brad Bolwing

1970 MUSTANG BOSS 429

1970 MUSTANG BOSS 429

The awesome Boss 429 Mustang returned in '70, again powered by the company's NASCAR-spec 429 V-8 and again hand assembled by Kar-Kraft in Brighton, Michigan. Production of '70 versions kicked off in August '69 and ended that December. A total of 500 cars were put together, including two "Quarter-Horse" Mustangs. Total two-year production was 1,359 units, which included a pair of '69 Boss 429 Cougars.

All vehicles, except for a handful of prototypes and a couple of factory drag cars, were completely assembled and fully dressed with thermactor pollution equipment, power steering, and special exhaust manifolds. The '70s were painted one of five colors: Grabber Blue, Grabber Green, Grabber Orange, Calypso Coral, or Pastel Blue. They had black or white upholstery.

In April '70, *Motor Trend* got its hands on a car set up for B-Stock drag racing. It belonged to Chuck Foulger, former head of FoMoCo drag racing, who operated a performance dealership in the magazine's back yard. Writer A.B. Shuman found the car had too much power. "It was a good ride, but still over half a second away from the B/Stock record," he said. "As they're now made, a stock Boss 429 should run high 13s in the quarter as delivered."

Factory ADP	Wheelbase	Length	Shipping Weight	Base V-8	Engine Options	0-to-60 MPH	¼-Mile
(M/T car) N/A	108 in.	188 in.	3,400 lbs.	429 cid/375 hp	None	5.3 seconds	12.3 seconds @ 112 mph

MCFG Says: (HT) $64K

He Says: A. B. Shuman said, " The guys who put them together have insisted all along that it isn't a drag racing car, but the people who buy them want respectable performance."

We Says: *Motor Trend* made the drag-racing Boss 429 stand up on its drag slicks like the stallion that it was."

Jerry Heasley

1970 MUSTANG MACH 1 CJ 428/SCJ 428

1970 MUSTANG CJ 428/SCJ 428

The '70 Mustang had some distinctions from the '69. The biggest change was a return to single headlights. They were located inside a larger new grille opening. Simulated air intakes replaced the outboard headlights on the '69 models. The rear end was also slightly restyled.

Standard equipment included carpeting, bucket seats, bias-ply tires, a locking steering column, a full-synchronized stick shift with a floor-mounted lever, and a rear deck lid spoiler on SportsRoof models. Among many muscle car options were power front discs, a functional hood scoop, louvered rear window Sport Slats, a Hurst shifter, a tach, and a Drag Pack.

In addition to the base hardtop and ragtop, models included the hot Mach 1 fastback, the luxurious Grande hardtop, and the race-bred Boss 302 fastback. With engine options, you could change the Boss 302 into a Boss 351 or a Boss 429. Mustang offered nine engines to pick from. While "Boss" models were a hit with enthusiast mags, the CJ 428/SCJ 428 both returned.

FORD

Factory ADP	Wheelbase	Length	Shipping Weight	Base V-8	Engine Options	0-to-60 MPH	¼-Mile
(base w/428) (HT) $3,400; (FB) $3,450; (RT) $3,704	108 in.	187.4 in.	(HT) 3,145 lbs.; (FB) 3,112 lbs.; (RT) 3,267 lbs.	428 cid/ 335 hp	None	5.5 seconds	13.9 seconds @ 103.32 mph

MCFG Says: (HT) $30K; (FB) $35K; (RT) $40K

He Says: In his book *Fast Mustangs*, Alex Gabbard noted, "The 428 Cobra Jet engine was called 'the fastest running pure stock in the history of man.'"

We Says: "The 428 CJ.SCJ Mustangs are famous for grabbing the Stock Eliminator title at the '70 NHRA Winternationals."

Jerry Heasley

1970 MUSTANG MACH 1

"Five years ago, Mustang started a whole new idea in sporty cars," said one ad. "And Mustang's been first ever since." The ad listed "sporty facts" that made the Mustang tops in its market segment: (1) Six great models (Mach 1, Grande, Boss 302, hardtop, convertible and SportsRoof); (2) Nine engines to pick from (including 351 Windsor, 351 Cleveland and two 428s); (3) Loaded with sporty features and (4) You can design it yourself with more options than ever.

The '70 Mach 1 featured the year's new front-end styling and had its taillights recessed in a flat panel with honeycomb trim between them. Ribbed aluminum rocker panel moldings with big Mach 1 call-outs and a cleaner upper rear quarter treatment without simulated air scoops at the end of the main feature line were seen. A black-striped hood with a standard fake scoop replaced the completely matte-black hood. New twist-in hood pins held the hood down. You could get now a shaker hood scoop on Mach 1's with the standard 351-cid V-8. A redesigned steering wheel was the big interior change.

Factory ADP	Wheelbase	Length	Shipping Weight	Base 427 V-8	Optional V-8	0-to-60 MPH	¼-Mile
$3,271	108 in.	187.4 in.	3,169 lbs.	351W cid/ 250 hp	351C cid/300 hp; 428 cid/335 hp; 428 cid/360 hp	(351 Cleveland four-barrel) 8.2 seconds	(351 Cleveland four-barrel) 16 seconds @ 86.2 mph

MCFG **Says:** $28K (add 40% for 428 CJ-R)

He Says: A.B. Shuman, writing in *Motor Trend* (April '70) said, "It was painted 'Ticket-Grabber-Yellow' (I think that's what they call it) with flat black tape stripes, a combination that elicits such man-on-the-street comments as, 'Is that a production car?'"

We Says: "With the 352, this was a 'put-it-in-context' muscle car that you could drive every day (and still grab a few tickets), but for strip action, the 428 was the option to add. The somewhat heavier Cougar 428 CJ-R clone did the quarter in 13.91 seconds at 103.9 mph."

1970 TORINO COBRA

Jerry Heasley

1970 TORINO COBRA

Thirty-four years ago, Ford had its intermediate cars on a two-year styling cycle. As a result, a styling change was due for '70. No matter how good the '68-'69 Fairlane fastbacks looked or how fast they ran in stock car races, it was time for a new sheet metal. Wheelbase and length increased and weights went up, too.

A full line of models was again available, topped by the Torino Cobra. Its new standard power plant was the 385 series 429-cid big-block V-8. Cobras also came with Ford's top-loader four-speed, a Hurst shifter, a competition suspension (with staggered rear shocks), 7-inch-wide steel wheels, F70-14 Wide-Oval tires, a black hood with locking devices, black-out trim and Cobra badges. Bench seats were standard.

Engine options included CJ and SCJ versions of the 429. For $155 you could get Traction-Lok differential. For $207, a 4.30:1 Detroit Locker rear axle was available.

Production was 7,675. The Torino Cobra was supposed to be the car of record for NASCAR Grand National racers, but turned out to be slower than the '69 Talladega. This forced the race teams to run year-old cars.

FORD

Factory ATP	Wheelbase	Length	Shipping Weight	Base V-8	Engine Options	0-to-60 MPH	¼-Mile
$4,318	117 in.	206.1 in.	4,002 lbs.	(CJ) 429 cid/370 hp	(SCJ) 429 cid/370 hp	6.4 seconds	14.5 seconds @ 99 mph

MCFG Says: $25K

He Says: A.B. Shuman, writing in *Motor Trend* magazine, said, "Maybe this shaped-for-the-wind thing is for real."

We Says: "Though conceived of as the answer to the winged Dodge Charger Daytona and Plymouth Superbird, the Torino Cobra was more of a street muscle car."

Jerry Heasley

1971 MUSTANG BOSS 351

1971 MUSTANG BOSS 351

Mustangs grew to their all-time largest for the '71. Wheelbase was up an inch, length increased 2.1 inches, and width grew 2.4 inches (to 74.1). The latter was accompanied by a tread increase that permitted the big-block 429 V-8 to fit in the engine compartment with ease. Although the 429-powered cars were most muscular, the Boss 351 was perhaps the most interesting.

The Boss 429 was dropped early in '70 and new racing rules eliminated the need for the Boss 302. The Boss 351's purpose was just to tap into what was left of the declining hi-po market. Like its predecessors, the Boss 351 was based on the SportsRoof. It was considered an option package. The heart of the new Boss 351 package was the "Cleveland" V-8 with four-bolt mains, solid lifters, and a four-barrel carb. The '71s were the last high-compression Ford engines and the last using gross advertised horsepower numbers.

Boss 351 features included a four-speed "top-loader" transmission with a Hurst gear shifter, a competition-type suspension, power front disc brakes, 3.91:1 Traction-Lok gearing, dual exhausts with non-exposed tips, a (infamous) rev limiter, side and rear identification decals, a matte black hood with functional scoops and locks, and body side stripes.

Only about 1,800 Boss 351s were made, which adds up to rarity today.

Factory ATP	Wheelbase	Length	Shipping Weight	Base SS 396 V-8	Engine Options	0-to-60 MPH	¼-Mile
$4,817	109 in.	189.5 in.	3,345 lbs.	351 cid/330 hp	None	5.9 seconds	13.98 seconds @ 104 mph

MCFG **Says:** $42K

They Says: *Road Test* (March '71) said, "The sophisticated Mustang. The '71 Boss is 40 hp bossier than last year's 302; still gives fine handling coupled to straightaway performance."

We Says: "When you were working for the man back in '71, a car like this could make you look forward to the weekend—especially your trip to the drag strip on Sunday afternoon."

1971 MUSTANG MACH 1

Jerry Heasley

1971 MUSTANG MACH 1

The Mach 1 returned for '71. It included color-keyed mirrors, a honeycomb grille, color-keyed bumpers, sport lamps, a new gas cap, decals, tape stripes and black or Argent Silver lower body finish. A hood with NASA-style air scoops was a no-cost option with the 302 V-8 and standard otherwise. Available for the last time was the big-block 429. It came in CJ and SCJ Ram-Air versions. Ford put together 1,255 of the CJ-R equipped Mach 1's and 610 of the SCJ-R's.

Basically a de-stroked T-bird/Lincoln 460, the 429 had a wedge combustion chambers derived from up-to-date performance technology. The CJ-R utilized large valves, a hydraulic cam, 4-bolt mains, re-worked porting and a 700-cfm Quadrajet carb (sourced from GM). A Ram-Air induction system was included. A Drag Pack option, with either a 3.91:1 Traction-Lok differential or a 4.11:1 Detroit Locker axle, was mandatory. This option also included an oil cooler for when things really got hot at the drag strip. Other 429 SCJ-R performance features included solid valve lifters, adjustable rocker arms, drop-forged pistons, and a 780-cfm Holley carb.

Factory ATP	Wheelbase	Length	Shipping Weight	Optional 429 V-8	Optional 429 V-8	0-to-60 MPH	¼-Mile
$3,724	109 in.	189.5 in.	3,220 lbs.	(CJ-R) 429 cid/370 hp	(SCJ-R) 429 cid/375 hp	(SCJ-R) 7.1 seconds	(SCJ-R) 14.09 seconds @ 102.85 mph

MCFG Says: $26K (add 20% for SCJ-R)

They Says: *Road Test* (September '70) said, "For those interested in owning a sporty car which reflects up-to-the-minute design, Mustang (Mach 1), an all-around solid vehicle without a significant flaw, can't be a bad choice."

We Says: "You may not be able to break Mach 1 in a Mach 1, but it sure looks like (and feels like) you can."

Phil Kunz

1971 TORINO COBRA 429 CJ-R"

1971 TORINO COBRA 429 CJ-R

Updated trim and a new grille made the '71 Torino Cobra look slightly different. The Cobra was technically a hi-po version of the Torino Brougham. It included all Brougham features, plus a base 285-hp 351 "Cleveland" V-8, a four-speed with a Hurst shifter; Cobra I.D., an H.D. suspension, 7-inch-wide wheels with chrome hub caps, a black-out grille and lower escutcheon panel, a black-finished hood with non-reflective paint, polished aluminum wheel well moldings, F70-14 whitewalls, a 55-amp H.D. battery, dual exhausts, and pleated vinyl seat trim.

In addition to the standard 351, Cobras could be ordered with two 429 V-8s. The 370-hp Cobra-Jet version without Ram Air was $372 and, in addition to the big engine, it included a competition suspension, a "sporty" exhaust note, an 80-amp battery, a 55-amp alternator, dual exhausts, an extra-cooling package, bright engine parts, cast aluminum rocker covers and a non-locking 3.25:1 rear axle. The 370-hp 429 CJ Ram-Air V-8 was $343 extra. It included all the extras that came with the base CJ V-8, plus a "shaker" hood scoop and a Drag Pack.

FORD

Factory ATP	Wheelbase	Length	Shipping Weight	Base V-8	Engine Options	0-to-60 MPH	¼-Mile
* About $4,500	117 in.	206.2 in.	3,586 lbs.	390 cid/370 hp (Ram Air)	Nonee	5.8 seconds	13.99 seconds @ 101 mph

* (429 CJ-R with typical options)

MCFG **Says:** $25K

They Says: *Motor Trend* (February '70) said, "To have had it 16 years ago on Main St. in Lockport, N.Y., with all its shuttered back-lite, fat-tired, shaker-hooded, chopped-top magnificence would have equated with having the Bean Bandit's fuel dragster."

We Says: "It was selected 'Car of the Year' and it could turn out to be one of the 'Muscle Cars of the Century.'"

1980 SVO-MCLAREN TURBO MUSTANG

1980 SVO-MCLAREN TURBO MUSTANG

The McLaren Mustang was created by Ford's new Special Vehicle Operations (SVO) group. The "semi-aftermarket" muscle car hit the market in late '80. It represented the ultimate-for-the-era small-block performance car, though its $25,000 price was not small. Under the hood was a high-tech 2.3-liter turbo four with a special variable-boost turbo providing 5-11 psi and optimum road and track performance. Compared to a stock turbo-four, with a set pressure of 5 psi (131 hp estimated), the McLaren was a screamer—175 hp at 2500 rpm with the turbo boost at 10 psi.

Flared fenders and a functional air dam were among body mods. Designers Todd Gerstenberger and Harry Wykes went after an IMSA image. The air dam directed cold air to the front discs via a hairy-looking wastegate hood. Other goodies included BBS Euro-styled laced wheels, Firestone 225/55R-15 HPR tires, Koni shocks, S-W gauges and Recaro seats. To complement the racecar look, there was a roll bar inside.

The SVO concept was to showcase hi-po parts in cars like the McLaren to determine the popular ones and make them available in the aftermarket. The idea was to drum up interest in bolt-on hardware for thousands of late-model Mustangs. Consequently, production was extremely limited. No more than 250 cars, including the prototype, were created. Some say the real number was substantially lower.

Factory ADP	Wheelbase	Length	Shipping Weight	Base V-8	Engine Options	0-to-60 MPH	¼-Mile
$20,000-$25,000	100.4 in.	179.1 in.	2,582 lbs.	4.3 liter/175 hp	None	9.76 seconds	17.37 seconds @ 79.20 mph

MCFG Says: $30K

He Says: Bob Nagy, writing in *Motor Trend*, said, "The bright orange police magnet was, however, a bit too obvious to thrash about on residential roads."

We Says: "The SVO-McLaren Turbo 'Stang was a very obvious sign that Ford was finally turning the performance-car battleship around to go after the enthusiast market again."

Jerry Heasley

1989 MUSTANG GT 5.0-LITER HO

1989 MUSTANG GT 5.0-LITER HO

Ford forgot the 25th anniversary of the Mustang in '89, in that it did not release a commemorative edition. There were rumors that Roush Racing was going to build a 400-hp 351-powered twin-turbo anniversary model, but this never happened.

Not that the stock GT V-8 was any slouch. The 5.0L Mustang was back offering go-fast enthusiasts as much performance as the Camaro IROC Z with less bulkiness and a lower price. The Mustang GT came as three-door hatchback and a ragtop.

GTs continued to feature a lower front air dam with integrated fog lamps and air scoops, "Mustang GT" lettering formed into the flared rocker panel moldings (and rear fascia), a large rear spoiler with a high-mounted stop light on hatchbacks, wide taillights covered by a louver-like appliqué, and P225/60VR16 Goodyear Eagle GT Gatorback tires.

The GT suspension was really high-tech, with gas struts, variable-rate coil springs, and a front stabilizer bar. At the rear there were variable-rate springs, a Qudra-gas-shock setup, freon-filled horizontal axle dampers, and a fat stabilizer bar.

Factory ADP	Wheelbase	Length	Shipping Weight	Base V-8	Engine Options	0-to-60 MPH	¼-Mile
(HB) $13,272; (RT) $17,512	100.5 in.	179.6 in.	(HB) 3,194 lbs.; (RT) 3,333 lbs.	302 cid/225 hp	None	6.2 seconds	14.5 seconds @ 96 mph

MCFG Says: (HB) $3.5K; (RT) $7.5K

They Says: Said *Motor Trend's Automotive Yearbook* for 1989, "It's a very hot package with a '60s ring and a torque curve that'll tighten your skin, all for the price of a Honda Accord. Ford has vowed to keep the V-8 Mustang as you see it here through the early '90s. And you thought Santa had forgotten."

We Says: The '89 GT may not be the best-looking Mustang that came down the pike, but it sure packs a knockout punch on the street or strip.

1993 MUSTANG COBRA

1993 MUSTANG COBRA

Model year '93 could easily have been one in the "live bait" category for the Ford Mustang. It was in the last year of a long run (since '79) before the all-new '94 models bowed. Chevy's Camaro and Pontiac's Firebird were also redesigned and available in performance trim. Both shared a 350-cid 275-hp V-8 that could beat the Mustang's 302-cid 205-hp H.O. V-8.

Ford knew of Steve Saleen's hot Mustangs and other "tuner" versions that were much more powerful than production cars. However, Ford had to meet CAFE standards and warranty claims and couldn't match such aftermarket creations. Still, the Cobra and Cobra R—introduced in mid-'93—turned out to be a great warm-up act for future hi-po Mustangs.

Ford's Special Vehicle Team (SVT) was a "skunkworks" that took production cars, went over them and made a "better mousetrap." For '93 Cobras, they added large-valve GT-40 cast iron cylinder heads, H.D. valve springs, a two-piece intake plenum and manifold, a hotter cam, higher-ratio rocker arms, higher-flow fuel injectors, and air management and a less-restrictive exhaust. SVT and road racer Paul Rossi also built about 100 heavily modified Cobra Rs for racing-only purposes. The price for the Cobra R was $25,692.

Factory ADP	Wheelbase	Length	Shipping Weight	Base V-8	Engine Options	0-to-60 MPH	¼-Mile
$18,505 ($25,692 for Cobra R)	100.5 in.	179.6 in.	3,255 lbs.	302 cid/235 hp	None	8 seconds	14.4 seconds @ 97.4 mph

MCPG Says: $17.5K (add 40% for Cobra R)

They Says: "It is the hardest accelerating, quickest stopping, best handling pony car from Ford yet," said *Road & Track* of the Cobra.

We Says: "The '93 Mustang Cobra and Cobra-R kicked the whole 5.0-liter movement up a couple of notches."

2000 SVT MUSTANG COBRA R

2000 SVT MUSTANG COBRA R

Ford's Special Vehicles Team built the 2000 Mustang Cobra R to go, turn, and stop very quickly. A steep price tag and production limitations held sales down. Only 300 were scheduled to be built, but that was a lot compared to 109 Cobra R's in '93 and 250 in '95. The 2000 Cobra R had a lot of goodies to make it look fast and handle well. There was a massive front spoiler, a functional stationary rear airfoil, and a front air splitter that could be attached to the nose with Dzuz fasteners. It was only for show or racing purposes, as street use might damage it. The R was offered only in Performance Red. The interior was Dark Charcoal.

Under the louvered hood scoop sat a 9.6:1 compression 5.4-liter V-8 with port fuel injection system. The engine was fitted with a number of hardware items from the Ford parts bin, such as a special cylindrical K & N air filter, a larger single-bore throttle body, hi-po heads from Ford's off-road truck racing program, higher-lift camshafts, flat-top aluminum pistons, Carrillo billet steel connecting rods and tubular steel exhaust manifolds connected to Borla mufflers with a beautiful rumble. The redline was 6,500 rpm and the top speed was 175 mph.

The suspension had Bilstein gas shocks up front, twin-tube gas shocks in the rear, H.D. Eibach springs and fat anti-roll bars at each end. The 9.5-18 5-spoke alloy rims carried 265/40ZR-18 B.F. Goodrich g-Force KD radials. And you no longer had to have SCCA or NHRA credentials or a competition license to buy a Cobra R.

Factory ADP	Wheelbase	Length	Shipping Weight	Base V-8	Engine Options	0-to-60 MPH	¼-Mile
$55,845	97 in.	178 in.	3,590 lbs.	330 cid/385 hp	None	4.7 seconds	13.2 seconds @ 110 mph

MCFG **Says:** $50K

They Says: *Car and Driver* (April 2000) described it as "The fastest Mustang ever."

We Says: "Mustang collectors were right on top of this modern muscle car and all 300 units were sold before the first one made it to a showroom."

2001 FORD BULLITT MUSTANG

2001 FORD BULLITT MUSTANG

Ford's young styling chief J Mays, who created the retro T-bird, was also responsible for the "Bullitt." Named for the '68 Mustang GT that Steve McQueen drove as detective Frank Bullitt in a classic cult film, the hot '01 model was based on a Mustang GT with $3,695 in upgrades. The car's body was modified to reduce the size of the rear quarter windows and it was lowered 3/4-inch all around. The traditional Mustang side scoops were covered, a brushed-aluminum flip-up gas filler was added and the Bullitt Mustang rode on Troq Thrust D-style American Racing Wheels.

Under the hood, the 4.6-liter (281-cid) SOHC V-8 featured the SVT Cobra model's cast-aluminum intake manifold, a twin-bore 57-mm throttle body, special heads and a high-flow exhaust.

The engine was attached to a five-speed manual gearbox. The Bullitt had H.D. shocks, special anti-roll bars and 17-inch diameter Goodyear Eagle tires. The Bullitt included perforated black leather upholstery and interior trim, a black leather steering wheel, white-faced gauges and an aluminum gearshift knob. The car came in Dark Highland Green—a shade just like the famous movie car—as well as optional True Blue or Black. Ford said it planned to build 6,500 copies. The first cars were delivered on May 10, 2001, at Dean Sellers Ford in Dearborn, Michigan.

Factory ADP	Wheelbase	Length	Shipping Weight	Base V-8	Engine Options	0-to-60 MPH	¼-Mile
$27,000	97 in.	178 in.	3,273 lbs.	281 cid/265 hp	None	5.7 seconds	14.1 seconds @ 98 mph

MCFG Says: $25,000

They Says: *Muscle Mustangs & Fast Fords* said: "In stock form, with nearly 1,500 miles on the odometer, the Bullitt turned out 239 rear-wheel horsepower, or about 275 to the flywheel."

We Says: "Much like Mr. McQueen himself, the car named after one of his toughest characterizations was as tough as they come on the street or strip. Cool ride!"

Jerry Heasley

1965 COMET CYCLONE

1965 COMET CYCLONE

A '65 restyling gave the Comet vertically stacked headlights that made it look more like a Ford than a Mercury. The grille used a horizontal-bars theme. Side chrome was limited to the roof quarter panel and three thin horizontal pieces on the front fenders. The hi-po Cyclone came only as a hardtop. It had a special grille with only two groups of horizontal blades and blackout finish around its perimeter. Cyclones had all the standard equipment that came on Calientes, plus bucket seats, a console, a tach, unique wheel covers, curb moldings and a 289-cid "Cyclone" V-8 engine with a two-barrel carb. A distinctive twin-air-scoop fiberglass hood was optional.

Motor Trend (May '65) liked the Comet's new front end, higher horsepower, improved handling, and large trunk. Technical editor John Ethridge's major criticism was the Cyclone's wheel spinning and rear axle hop, which hurt acceleration times. The Cyclone's non-power-assisted brakes were good. Stopping distance from 60 mph was 161 feet.

The base 195-hp "Cyclone" V-8 had a 9.3:1 compression ratio. In addition, there was a 220-hp "Super Cyclone 289" with a 10.0:1 compression ratio and a four-barrel carb. This engine cost $45 extra in Cyclones. A three-speed manual gearbox was standard with all engines. A four-speed was $188 extra. Multi-Drive Merc-O-Matic ran $90 additional. This was a three-speed automatic, comparable to the Ford Cruise-O-Matic.

Factory ATP	Wheelbase	Length	Shipping Weight	Base V-8	Engine Options	0-to-60 MPH	¼-Mile
$3,544	114 in.	195.3 in.	3,060 lbs.	289 cid/225 hp	289 cid/271 hp	8.8 seconds	17.1 seconds @ 82 mph

MCFG Says: $17K

He Says: John Ethridge said, "The Cyclone's 225-hp engine had what you'd consider a healthy feeling at any speed between idle and 3000 rpm. Then it felt like four more cylinders were suddenly added and came on very strongly."

We Says: "This Comet was as whip-lashingly fast as the Coney Island roller coaster that it shared the Cyclone name with."

Jerry Heasley

1966 CYCLONE GT/GTA

1966 CYCLONE GT/GTA

The Cyclone version of the Comet premiered in mid-'65. The '66 became a mid-size car. For hi-po buffs, this made the Cyclone perfect for muscle car treatment. Mercury went full blast and brought out the Cyclone GT. Powered by Ford's 335-hp 390 V-8, the GT had an optional handling package, front disc brakes, a standard three-speed manual gearbox, dual exhausts, a fiberglass hood with twin non-functional scoops and GT identification and stripes.

The 390-cid had a four-barrel carb and 10.5:1 compression. The optional Merc-O-Matic came only with the GT Sport Shift allowing manual-type shifting via a floor-mounted lever.

A Cyclone GT paced the Indy 500. The two actual pace cars were Candy Apple Red ragtops capable of 115-mph cruising speeds. Modifications and engine blueprinting were done at Bud Moore Engineering in Spartanburg, South Carolina. The pace car rode on 7.75 x 14 Firestone Wide-Oval Super Sport tires mounted on optional styled steel wheels. Benson Ford was behind the wheel for the Cyclone GT's parade lap.

Graham Hill won the 500-miler that day, but the Cyclone GT subsequently proved to be a loser in showrooms. Only 13,812 hardtops and 2,158 ragtops were built.

MERCURY

Factory ADP	Wheelbase	Length	Shipping Weight	Base V-8	Engine Options	0-to-60 MPH	¼-Mile
(HT) $2,891; (RT) $3,152	115 in.	195.9 in.	(HT) 3,315 lbs.; (RT) 3,595 lbs.	390 cid/335 hp	None	6.6 seconds	15.20 seconds @ 90 mph

MCFG **Says:** (HT) $15K; (RT) $21K

They Says: Mercury said, "This one will start a glow in any red-blooded American driver." *Car Life* said, "Supercar status for Lincoln's little brother."

We Says: "Dyno Don's drag racing Comets brought many muscle car maniacs into Mercury showrooms in '66. Few of them were disappointed with what they found there."

David Hooten

1967 COMET CYCLONE GT 390/427

1967 COMET CYCLONE GT 390/427

For '66, the formerly compact Comet was upgraded to the same wheelbase the mid-sized Fairlane. When the mildly face-lifted '67 models came along, the Comet name was only applied to the lowest-priced series. For the performance buyer, Mercury continued its Cyclone series. Knowledgeable buyers selected the GT option. Doing so provided a Ford "FE" big-block 390 V-8.

The Cyclone GT included a four-barrel carb, dual exhausts, an engine dress-up kit, a hood with two non-functional air scoops, 5 1/2 x 14-inch wheels, Wide-Oval tires, H.D. shocks and springs, a thick front sway bar, 3.25:1 gearing, side stripes, and GT badging. Cyclones also came standard with front buckets. Options included a four-speed.

The recession of '67 was not kind to car sales and Mercury intermediates took a beating. Only 6,910 were made. Cars with the GT option included 3,419 hardtops and 378 ragtops, so GTs outnumbered the regular Cyclones, although both models were rare.

Racing promotion for the '67 Cyclone was limited to its body being used atop funny cars for drag racing, but these cars earned the one-step-up Ford division lots of attention.

Factory ADP	Wheelbase	Length	Shipping Weight	Base V-8	Engine Options	0-to-60 MPH	¼-Mile
* (HT) $3,061; (RT) $3,353	116 in.	203.5 in.	* (HT) 3,372 lbs.; (RT) 3,632 lbs.	390 cid/320 hp	427 cid/425 hp	(427) 6.2 seconds	(427) 13.81 seconds @ 102 mph

* (Cyclone GT 390)

MCFG Says: (Cyclone GT 390) (HT) $16K; (RT) $19K (add 40% for 427)

He Says: Tom Shaw wrote in *Musclecar Review* (November 1991): "The "R" word—rare—gets the muscle car lover's blood pumpin' like nothing else, with the exception of the phrase 'big-block.' Combine the two and you've got (a) '67 Comet Cyclone 427."

We Says: "If you'd like to drive a beast that can pull up next to a Ferrari at a light, without attracting attention, and blow the Italian job's doors off, this just might be it."

1967 COUGAR GT-390

1967 COUGAR GT-390

Car Life called the Cougar a "Mustang with class." It had a shapely, graceful appearance and jewel-like trimmings. Only a coupe was available. While based on the Mustang platform, the Cougar had suspension upgrades like a hook-and-eye joint in the lower front A-frames to dampen ride harshness, longer rear springs, and better-rated rear spring and axle attachments.

The GT came even more firmly sprung with solid rear bushings, stiffer springs all around, bigger 1.1875-inch shocks, and a fatter .84-inch anti-roll bar. Power front disc brakes, 8.95 x 14 Wide-Oval tires, special I.D., and a 390-cid V-8 with a low-restriction exhausts were included. The 390 produced a 1:10 power-to-weight ratio to provide some driving excitement.

A Holley C70F carb with four 1.562-inch venturis and vacuum-operated secondaries sat on top of the 390. With a 10.5:1 compression ratio, the engine required premium fuel. Its horsepower peak came at just 4800 rpm. A husky 427 lbs.-ft. of torque was produced at 3200 rpm. Transmission choices included three- or four-speed, or a three-speed Merc-0-Matic with manual shifting to second below 71 mph or to first below 20 mph.

Specific manual gearboxes were used with the 390. Ratios for the three-speed with the big-block were 2.42:1 and 1.61:1; for the four-speed, 2.32:1, 1.69:1 and 1.29:1. The 390 came standard with a 3.00 "Power Transfer" axle and similar 3.25 axle was optional.

Factory ADP	Wheelbase	Length	Shipping Weight	Base V-8	Engine Options	0-to-60 MPH	¼-Mile
(GT) $3,175	111 in.	190.3 in.	3,015 lbs.;	289 cid/200 hp	289 cid/225 hp; 390 cid/320 hp	8.1 seconds	16 seconds

MCFG **Says:** (base) $18K; (XR7) $19K (add 10 percent for GT option)

They Says: *Car Life* said, "The Mercury Cougar's fascination is finesse in fabrication."

We Says: "The '67 Mercury Cougar GT with the optional 390-cid V-8 was a muscle car for the enthusiast on his or her way to a Thunderbird."

1968 COUGAR XR-7G "DAN GURNEY"

1968 COUGAR XR-7G "DAN GURNEY"

The limited edition Cougar XR-7G was actually an upscale Cougar XR-7 with a personalized option. The "G" stood for "Gurney." Dan Gurney was an American racing hero of the day who was under contract to Mercury. He was on the driving team that piloted Bill Stroppe-prepared '67 Cougars in the SCCA Trans-Am sedan racing series.

The Cougar would be the first of two Mercury specials named for Gurney. The second was a version of the '69 1/2 Cyclone Spoiler. After '69, Gurney's racing and car-building services were contracted by Plymouth and the string of Gurney editions ended.

The Cougar's rare XR-7G option package was mainly an assortment of "gingerbread" and any available power plant from the base 302-cid V-8 on up could be used to power cars with the package. Features of the option included a fiberglass hood scoop, road lamps, a racing mirror, hood pins and a power sunroof.

At the rear of the car, four exhaust tips exited through the valance panel. New spoke pattern styled wheels held radial FR70-14 tires. Badges showing a special emblem decorated the instrument panel, roof pillar, deck lid and grille. The XR-7G Cougars were not widely promoted back in '68 and very few were made, making the survivors highly prized by collectors today.

Factory ADP	Wheelbase	Length	Shipping Weight	Base V-8	Engine Options	0-to-60 MPH	0-to-100 MPH
(Base XR-7) $3,232	111 in.	191 in.	3,157 lbs.	(Early) 302 cid/210 hp; (Late) 289 cid/195 hp	302 cid/240 hp; 390 cid/325 hp; 428 cid/335 hp; 427 cid/390 hp	(427) 7.1 seconds	(427) 15.12 seconds @ 93.6 mph

MCFG Says: $18K (add 40 percent for 427 cid V-8)

They Says: In July '68, *Car Life* magazine said, "The Cougar is the plushest of the 'pony cars.'"

We Says: "A Dan Gurney edition XR-7 with the 427-cid big-block must be just about the hottest and rarest Cougar any collector could own."

1968 CYCLONE GT

1968 CYCLONE GT

The '68 Comet was restyled like a big Merc on a diet with a horizontal grille, bright rocker moldings, side marker lights and vertical taillights. An energy-absorbing steering wheel, safety belts, a padded dash and sun visors, dual brakes and two-speed wiper/washers were standard. Montegos had similar looks and features.

Cyclones had a mid-tire level tape stripe. The GT option added only $168 to the $2,768 base price, but no longer included the four-barrel 390 V-8. A two-barrel 210-hp 302 V-8 was standard. The GT option now brought you bucket seats and trim changes.

A 230-hp 302 with a for-barrel carb, 265- and 325-hp versions of the 390, and a 390-hp edition of the 427 V-8 were options. The 427 was offered just a short time. A few months into production it was axed and replaced, in sparse numbers, by the 335-hp 428CJ V-8.

Cyclones were offered in two-door hardtop and fastback models and both had a base price of $2,768. The public voted overwhelmingly for the fastback, of which 6,105 GT-optioned Cyclones were made compared to 334 for the notchback.

Factory ADP	Wheelbase	Length	Shipping Weight	Base V-8	Engine Options	0-to-60 MPH	¼-Mile
(CPE) $2,768; (FB) $2,768	116 in.	207 in.	(CPE) 3,208 lbs.; (FB) 3,254 lbs.	302 cid/210 hp	302 cid/230 hp; 390 cid/265 hp; 390 cid/325 hp; 427 cid/390 hp; 428 cid/335 hp	(427/390) 7.1 seconds	(427/390) 15.12 seconds @ 93.6 mph

MCFG Says: [302/390] (CPE) $15K; (FB) $16K; [428] (FB) $19K; [427] (CPE) $23K; (FB) $24K

They Says: *Car Life* (July '68) said, "There's a lot of racing engine in the Cobra Jet." The magazine tested a Cyclone with the 428 CJ engine and got 0-to-60 in 6.2 seconds and a 14.4-second quarter-mile at 99.4 mph.

We Says: "We agree with *Car Life* when it said. 'the Mercury is again on its way to being recognized as a car that digs out.'"

Jerry Heasley

1969 COUGAR ELIMINATOR

1969 COUGAR ELIMINATOR

The '69 Cougar grille had horizontal pieces that protruded slightly at the center. Standard equipment included retractable headlights, rocker panel strips, wheelhouse moldings, and twin body pin stripes. The back-up lights wrapped around the fenders. The taillights were trimmed with concave vertical chrome. Foam-padded vinyl bucket seats and carpeting were standard. Though a ragtop was new this year, the mid-season Eliminator muscle car came only as a hardtop.

Eliminators included front and rear spoilers, a black-out grille, a hood scoop, Argent styled wheels, side striping, a rally clock and a tach. Standard was a four-barrel Windsor 351 V-8 with a four-barrel carb and 290 advertised hp—a fraction of actual output. Other options included a 390, 428-CJ, and 428 R-CJ V-8s. The Boss 302 was offered in "street" and "race" tunes. The latter had two four-barrel carbs and its power wasn't advertised. With the 428-CJ option you got a hood scoop, hood hold-down pins, a competition handling package, and hood striping.

The Eliminator and Boss 302 was a curious combination. "Eliminator" comes from drag racing; the Boss 302's forte was sports sedan racing. The wisdom of sticking it in the 3,500-lb. Cougar was questionable. .

Factory ADP	Wheelbase	Length	Shipping Weight	Base V-8	Engine Options	0-to-60 MPH	¼-Mile (automatic)
$3,297	111.1 in.	194 in.	3,221 lbs.	351 cid/300 hp	302 cid/290 hp; 390 cid/320 hp; 428 cid/335 hp	(428/335) 5.6 seconds	(428/335) 14.10 seconds @ 100 mph

MCFG Says: $19K (add 30% for Boss 302; add 50% for 428-CJ)

They Says: *Musclecar Review* (December '86) said, "The name Eliminator was perfect for a muscle pony car and the spoilers, scoops, stripes, and bright colors created the desired response at the drive-in."

We Says: "This cat was prowling the streets from the moment the first one left the factory."

David Hooten

1969 CYCLONE SPOILER II

1969 CYCLONE SPOILER II

When NASCAR Grand National stock car racing teams tested the new '68 body styles, they found the Cyclone fastback to be a bit faster than its Fairlane fastback counterpart. A more aerodynamic nose design was said to be the reason.

Cale Yarborough drove the Wood Brothers Cyclone to victory in the '68 Daytona 500 and the battle of the NASCAR noses was on. Mercury announced the Spoiler as a midyear model in January '69. The main feature in early information was a spoiler bolted on the trunk deck. It was nice, but not legal in NASCAR at the time. An extended nose was an option.

The long-nosed Spoiler became the Cyclone Spoiler II. A total of 519 were made, all with a four-barrel 351 V-8 (despite announcements there would be a 428-cid CJ-R option). At least 500 had to be produced so it could be raced.

Cyclone Spoilers came in two trim versions. A "Dan Gurney" Spoiler had a dark blue roof, dark blue striping and a signature decal on the white lower portion. A "Cale Yarborough" edition featured red trim similar to his Wood Brothers stock car.

Factory ADP	Wheelbase	Length	Shipping Weight	Base Cyclone V-8 GT V-8	Engine Options	0-to-60 MPH	¼-Mile
$3,759	117 in.	210 in.	3,773 lbs.	351 cid/290 hp optional	None	(Spoiler) 7.4 seconds	(Spoiler) 14.4 seconds @ 99 mph

MCFG Says: $17.5K

He Says: Dr. John Craft, writing in *Musclecar Review* (January '89) said, "Just in case new engines weren't enough to worry the Dodge and Plymouth drivers, Mercury homologated its own version of the long-nose Talladega design with a run of similarly configured Cyclones."

We Says: Cars like the Talladega were designed to bring some 'Viagra' to Mercury's performance image in the muscle car era."

Jerry Heasley

1970 COUGAR

1970 COUGAR

The '70 Cougar had a new vertical grille and a forward-thrusting front end. Basic Cougar features included striping, wheel opening and roof moldings, and windshield and rear window chrome accents. The interior featured high-back buckets and a rosewood dash panel. The two-door hardtop cost $2,917. Prices for the ragtop started at $3,264. Only 2,322 ragtops were made.

XR-7s had distinct wheel covers, rocker moldings, a remote-control racing mirror, rear roof pillar emblems, vinyl high-back buckets with leather accents, seat back map pockets, a tach, a trip odometer, a rocker switch display, a burled walnut dash, rear armrests, map and courtesy lights, a visual check panel, loop-yarn carpeting and an electric clock with elapsed-time indicator. The hardtop was $3,201 and the ragtop was $3,465. Only 1,977 ragtops were made.

The Eliminator returned one final time. Now standard was the new 300-hp four-barrel 351 V-8. Options included the Boss 302, the 428 CJ, and a new version of the 385 series big-block 429. This "Boss 429" package included Ram Air and 375 hp. A spoiler, body graphics and a restyled scooped hood returned.

All numbers below are for the Eliminator.

Factory ADP	Wheelbase	Length	Shipping Weight	Base V-8	Engine Options	0-to-60 MPH	¼-Mile (automatic)
(as tested) $5,048	111.1 in.	196.1 in.	(as tested) 4,040 lbs.	351 cid/300 hp	302 cid/290 hp; 428 cid/335 hp; 428 cid/355 hp	7.6 seconds	15.8 seconds @ 90 mph

MCFG Says: $19K (add 30% for Boss 302; add 50% for 428 CJ)

They Says: *Car Life* magazine said, "Think of it as a family car with guts and you'll be happy with it."

We Says: "The term 'Top Eliminator' was familiar to drag racing buffs, but to Mercury buffs the term meant simply 'hot Cougar.'"

1970 CYCLONE

Jerry Heasley

1970 CYCLONE

Mercury Cyclones got all kinds of things when they were restyled for '70. Though the same unitized chassis was used, the Cyclone wheelbase grew and the overall length was extended. The latter alteration was due to a protruding nose and fender design. Cyclones also got a gun sight-type design in the center of their grilles.

The Cyclone came with the 360-hp version of the 429. Standard equipment included a four-speed with floor-mounted Hurst Shifter, a competition handling package, a 3.25:1 ratio rear axle, a blacked-out performance styled grille with vertical running lights, exposed headlights, and a silver- or black-finished lower back panel.

The Cougar GT, once the hottest Cyclone, was now the mildest. It had, among other things, a 250-hp V-8 351 two-barrel V-8, a choice of seven tone-on-tone colors, and a non-functional performance hood with integral air scoop. The new 351-cid "Cleveland" V-8 was available.

A Ram-Air equipped 370-hp 429 was standard motivation for the Cyclone Spoiler.

Factory ADP	Wheelbase	Length	Shipping Weight	Base V-8	Engine Options	0-to-60 MPH	¼-Mile
(Cyclone) $3,238; (GT) $3,226; (Spoiler) $3,759	117 in.	210 in.	(Cyclone) 3,721 lbs.; (GT) 3,462 lbs.; (Spoiler) 3,773 lbs.	429 cid/360 hp	(Base Cyclone GT V-8) 351 cid/250 hp (351 cid/300 hp optional) (Base Spoiler V-8) 429 cid/370 hp	(Spoiler) 6.4 seconds	(Spoiler) 14.5 seconds @ 99 mph

MCFG Says: (Cyclone) $15.5K; (GT) $16.5K; (Spoiler) $17.5K (add 40% for 429 in GT)

They Says: *Motor Trend* (April '70) said, "The Cyclone's racy looks are borne out in the accompanying specs. The Cyclone has the looks and performance."

We Says: "Cyclone hardtops had trunk lines about halfway between the old notch-back hardtop and a true fastback, but there was nothing halfway about the way they went."

Jerry Heasley

1971 COUGAR GT CJ 429

1971 COUGAR GT CJ 429

Cougars had the most dramatic changes since '67. There was a longer wheelbase, a lower silhouette, interior refinements, and a muscular new GT to fill up the gap left by the Eliminator. The styling inspiration for the thin roof and windshield pillars was said to be European. Cougars had better manners than the Mustangs they were based on, as well as more sound deadening materials and nicer interiors. Only big V-8s were used.

There were two series, each with a hardtop and a ragtop. The XR-7 was the sporty version with bucket seats, full instrumentation, and a vinyl half-roof. The $130 GT package was available for the base hardtop. It included a high-ratio rear axle, competition suspension, dual racing mirrors, hood scoop, performance cooling package, tach, rim-blow steering wheel, F78 x 14 whitewall tires, hub caps with bright trim rings, GT fender identification, and a black instrument panel. The hood scoop was non-functional, except when the 429 CJ engine option was installed.

The 429 CJ engine listed for $311 in all Cougars with the Select-Shifter four-speed (which cost $215 extra). This engine also included cast-aluminum rocker arm covers, bright engine accents (on cars without Ram Air), and H.D. battery.

Factory ADP	Wheelbase	Length	As-tested Curb Weight	Tested V-8	Engine Options	0-to-60 MPH	¼-Mile (automatic)
(Cougar 351 ragtop) $5,429	113 in.	197 in.	3,845 lbs.	351 cid/285 hp	343 cid/280 hp; 390 cid/315 hp	(351/285) 8.3 seconds	(351/285) 16.2 seconds @ 89.7 mph

MCFG Says: (HT) $14K; (RT) $15K (add $1,500 for XR-7; add 40% for 429 GT)

They Says: *Motor Trend* (September '70) said, "Driving the Cougar in whatever version you choose is still a fun proposition."

We Says: "The '71 Cougar is an interesting car and the 429 CJ adds about as much performance as you might find—with few exceptions—in the waning years of the muscle era."

OLDSMOBILE 4-4-2

4-BARREL CARBURETOR!
4-ON-THE-FLOOR!
DUAL EXHAUSTS!

1964 4-4-2

1964 4-4-2

The first 4-4-2 was a '64 3/4 offering, option number B-09 Police Apprehender Pursuit. Oldsmobile's *Product Selling Information for Salesmen* guide explained the 4-4-2 like this: "Police needed it—Olds built it—pursuit proved it." This literature clearly pointed out the *original* meaning of the 4-4-2 designation as follows: "4-BARREL CARBURETION— plus high-lift cams boost the power of the "4-4-2" Ultra High-Compression V-8 to 310 hp—up 20 hp over Cutlass V-8. 4-ON-THE-FLOOR—stick shift synchromesh transmission captures every power advantage both up and down the entire gear range. 2 DUAL EXHAUSTS—complete dual exhaust system features less back pressure for better performance … aluminized for longer life."

Other 4-4-2 features included H.D. shocks and springs, a rear stabilizer bar, a dual-snorkel air cleaner, a higher-lift camshaft, and extra-high-quality rod and main bearings.

Motor Trend tested an Olds F-85 Cutlass 4-4-2 two-door hardtop in September '64. The car had a base price of $2,784 and an as-tested price of $3,658.74. Options on the test vehicle included power steering, two-speed windshield wipers, an electric deck-lid release, back-up lights, a crankcase vent, an outside rearview mirror, a power seat, simulated wire wheel covers, and the Police Apprehender Pursuit package. The car had a 3.55:1 non-Positraction rear axle.

Factory ADP	Wheelbase	Length	Shipping Weight	Base V-8	Engine Options	0-to-60 MPH	¼-Mile
4-2-2 Option $285.14	115 in.	204.3 in.	2,799 lbs.	330 cid/310 hp	None	7.4 seconds	15.5 seconds @ 90 mph

MCFG Says: (CPE) $15.6K; (HT) $17.5K; (RT) $21K

They Says: Said *Car Life*. "The 4-4-2 is indeed 'where the action is.' No better Oldsmobile has rolled off the Lansing assembly line in many a year and, though it isn't quite the sports car that corporate brass likes to think, it doesn't miss by much."

We Says: "Now that Olds is gone, look for 4-4-2 prices to skyrocket."

1965 4-4-2

OLDSMOBILE
1965 4-4-2

The Cutlass line was mildly facelifted for '65 and the 4-4-2 performance and handling package gained popularity. Noting the runaway success of the GTO, Olds engineers saw the need to cram more cubes into their creation. Reducing the bore of the new Olds 425-cid engine from 4.125 inches to an even 4.0 produced an engine ideally sized for the 4-4-2 at 400 cid.

This year the 4-4-2 was offered with optional Hydra-Matic. Since the second "4" in the '64 model designation had stood for "four-speed manual transmission," Olds had to explain 4-4-2 in a different way. The company said the first four (4) stood for the new 400-cid V-8, the second four (4) meant four-barrel carb, and the two (2) meant dual exhaust.

The 400-cid V-8 added 35 hp and torque increased 440 lbs.-ft. at 3200 rpm. The new engine had a 10.25:1 compression ratio and a single Rochester four-barrel carb. Said *Car and Driver*, "Summed up, the Oldsmobile 4-4-2 is another one of those 'special purpose' American cars that should really be sold as the *all*-purpose car." A total of 25,003 cars got the 4-4-2 package this year.

Factory ADP	Wheelbase	Length	Shipping Weight	Base V-8	Engine Options	0-to-60 MPH	¼-Mile
(F85) (CPE) $2,695; (HT) $2,727 *	115 in.	203 in.	2,894 to 3,263 lbs.	400 cid/345 hp	None	7.5 seconds	15 seconds @ 98 mph

* Factory ADP (Cutlass) (CPE) $2,800; (HT) $2,940; (RT) $3,140.

MCFG Says: (CPE) $14.8K; (HT) $17K; (RT) $24K

They Says: *Car Life* magazine (May '65) said, "Olds joins the bigger-inch crowd with another meaning for that first "4" – 400 cu. in."

We Says: "If you want to buy a muscle car that gives you the thrill of a GTO or SS 396 without the headline-high pricing, the 4-dash-4-dash-2 is a great one to get."

1966 4-4-2

Jerry Heasley

1966 4-4-2

Restyled for '66, the Olds Cutlass F-85 took on a more massive, creased-edge look. There was a pronounced "hump" over the rear windows and large C-pillars extending beyond the backlight. The 4-4-2 kit included seat belts, a padded dash, windshield washers, two-speed wipers, a left-hand manual outside rearview mirror, foam padded seat cushions, carpeting on the floor front and rear, chrome roof moldings, a deluxe steering wheel, bucket or Custom seats, 7.35 x 14 tires, and seat upholstery in either vinyl or cloth.

Under the hood of the 4-4-2, the 400-cid V-8 had been tweaked by another 5 hp (to 350) thanks to a slight increase in compression. Late in the model year, the 4-4-2 received another adrenalin injection (to 360 hp) with the one-year-only triple two-barrel carb setup. A new W-30 air-induction setup, including front bumper air intakes and internal engine modifications, was available for the Tri-Power cars. An endless assortment of options was available, including five gearboxes and eight rear axle ratios.

From the standpoints of both performance and rarity, the '66 Olds Cutlass 4-4-2 equipped with the 360-hp factory Tri-Power installation is the most desirable example of these production years to a real muscle car enthusiast.

Factory ADP	Wheelbase	Length	Shipping Weight	Base V-8	Engine Options	0-to-60 MPH	¼-Mile
4-4-2 kit $152 on F-85 and Cutlass two-doors	115 in.	205 in.	3,146-3,338 lbs.	400 cid/ 350 hp	400 cid/360 hp	(360 hp) 6.3 seconds	(360 hp) 14.8 seconds @ 97 mph

MCFG Says: (CPE) $18K; (HT) $20K; (RT) $27K (add 30% for Tri-Power)

They Says: *Car Life* said, "Together with the relative scarcity of the Oldsmobile 4-4-2, the purchaser is assured of a highly individualistic and truly personalized specialty car."

We Says: "The 4-4-2 always got a lot of good press because it was always a lot of good car."

1967 CUTLASS SUPREME 4-4-2

1967 CUTLASS SUPREME 4-4-2

The '67 4-4-2 option was available for Cutlass Supreme two-doors. Base prices were $2,694 for the coupe, $2,831 for the hardtop, and $3,145 for the ragtop. Checking option box L78 added the 4-4-2 option and $184 to your sticker. For that you got a 350-hp 400 V-8, H.D. suspension, wheels and engine mounts, F70 x 14 Red Line tires, bucket seats and 4-4-2 badges front, rear, sides and inside. Another $184 added a four-speed and the whole package could be delivered to the pavement via a limited-slip differential for $42. Axle ratios ranged to 4.33:1.

For those who preferred something simpler to drive, 4-4-2's could be had with THM for $236. Less sport-minded buyers could delete the front bucket seats in favor of a bench seat. However, those interested in a sportier car could get buckets with a console.

Standard again was the 350-hp V-8, but Tri-Power was gone. The flush hood louvers over the 4-4-2 air cleaner were functional, but had no Ram Air effect. Using factory ducting from the front of the car, the W-30 option rammed air to the motor and upped output to 360 hp.

Factory ADP	Wheelbase	Length	Shipping Weight	Base V-8	Engine Options	0-to-60 MPH	¼-Mile
(CPE) $2,878; (HT) $3,015; (RT) $3,210	115 in.	205 in.	(CPE) 3,454 lbs.; (HT) 3,478 lbs.; (RT) 3,574 lbs.	400 cid/350 hp	400 cid/360 hp	(360 hp) 6.7 seconds	(360 hp) 14.98 seconds @ 95 mph

MCFG **Says:** (CPE) $18K; (HT) $21K; (RT) $28K (add 70% for W-30)

They Says: An Oldsmobile ad summed up the '67 Cutlass Supreme 4-4-2 by stating: "Sedate it ain't!"

We Says: "The original 4-4-2 kit of '64 started as a kind of cop car package and Oldsmobile didn't 'cop out' of the muscle car niche as the '60s went on."

1968 4-4-2

1968 4-4-2

The 4-4-2 was a model in '68—not a Cutlass option. It had more curves on its long hood, a short rear deck, razor-edge fenders, a swoopy rear, big 4-4-2 emblems, and dual through-the-bumper exhausts. A coil spring front suspension with anti-roll bar was mated with a coil spring link-coil live axle rear suspension. Brakes were discs up front and drums rear. Tires were F70-14s.

A new 400-cid V-8 had a 3.87 x 4.25-inch bore and stroke versus 4 x 3.975-inch in '67. Of three four-barrel versions of this 10.5:1 compression V-8 engine, the hottest had the W-30 Force Air package. A two-barrel "Turnpike Cruiser" economy engine with 9.0:1 compression and 290 hp was optional. Olds offered a three-speed, wide- and close-ratio four-speeds, THM, and a slew of rear axles.

Buyers who ordered the Force Air induction system got large 15 x 2-inch air scoops below the front bumper, a special camshaft for a higher torque peak, modified intake and exhaust ports, a free-flowing exhaust system, and low-friction componentry.

Production of the '68 Olds 4-4-2 totaled 4,282 sports coupes, 5,142 ragtops, and 24,183 Holiday hardtops for a total of 33,607 units, compared to 24,829 the previous year.

Factory ADP	Wheelbase	Length	Shipping Weight	Base V-8	Engine Options	0-to-60 MPH	0-to-100 MPH
(CPE) $3,087; (HT) $3,150; (RT) $3,341	112 in.	201.6 in.	(CPE) 3,505 lbs.; (HT) 3,512 lbs.; (RT) 3,580 lbs.	400 cid/325 hp	400 cid/290 hp; 400 cid/350 hp; 400 cid/360 hp	(350 hp) 7.0 seconds	(350 hp) 15.13 seconds @ 92.2 mph

MCFG **Says:** (CPE) $18K; (HT) $20K; (RT) $24K (add 30% for W30)

They Says: *Car Life* said, "The 442 Holiday Coupe looked every bit as quick and strong as it really is. A true hi-po car and the best handling of today's supercars"

We Says: "Oldsmobile deserved congratulations."

1968 HURST/OLDS

Jerry Heasley

1968 HURST/OLDS

GM would not OK putting the new 455 into the 4-4-2, but this didn't stop George Hurst from doing it. Then Oldsmobile supplier John Demmer, of Lansing, Michigan, assembled clones of Hurst's car in his own facility. This is how the limited edition Hurst/Olds was born!

The big W45 Force-Air 455 motor was based on the Toronado engine, but built with a special crankshaft, a custom-curved distributor, special carb jets, a 308-degree cam with a .474-inch lift, and hand-assembled Ram-Air cylinder heads. It was hooked to a modified THM with a Hurst Dual-Gate shifter that worked a manual gearbox or an automatic. (Note: Air-conditioned cars had different heads and 10 less hp).

The H.D. rear end incorporated a standard 3.91:1 rear axle. Also included as part of the package were specially calibrated power disc-drum brakes, H.D. suspension, H.D. cooling system with a high-capacity radiator and viscous-drive fan, and G70-14 Goodyear Polyglas tires. The entire car was dressed up in special silver-and-black finish. A total of 515 Hurst/Olds were built for '68. Of these, 451 were based on the 4-4-2 Holiday two-door hardtop, while the remaining 64 were originally 4-4-2 coupes. No Hurst/Olds were produced in ragtop form.

The Hurst/Olds partnership proved to be quite an image-boosting program and the two companies went on to team up on other Hurst/Olds models for many years.

Factory ADP	Wheelbase	Length	Shipping Weight	Base V-8	Engine Options	0-to-60 MPH	¼-Mile
$4,000 (approx.)	112 in.	201.9	3,870 lbs. (approx.)	455 cid/390 hp	(With A/C) 455 cid/380 hp	5.9 seconds	13.77 seconds @ 103.91 mph

MCFG Says: (CPE) $21K; (HT) $23K

He Says: Writing in *Super Stock* magazine, Jim McCraw said "These executive supercars won't last very long."

We Says: "They didn't."

1969 4-4-2

1969 4-4-2

A new pitchman named Dr. Olds prescribed image enhancements for the 4-4-2 in '69. They included a bolder split grille, fat hood stripes and new name badges. Also, the two-barrel "Turnpike Cruiser" option was eliminated to purify Olds' muscle car. Four-barrel engines and transmission options were basically unchanged. Hurst shifters came in stick cars. THM buyers got a column shift, but a console mount was optional. Axle ratios were expanded. The 4.33:1 rear was now standard only with a close-ratio four-speed. A 3.42:1 axle came with wide-ratio four-speeds, as well as THM. The 3.08:1, 3.23:1, and 3.91:1 axles were back and a 4.66:1 was new.

A body-color divider between the grilles carried big 4-4-2 identifiers. W-30s had special hood stripes and front fender decals. The front parking lights were moved from between the headlights into the front bumper. Strato bucket seats, red-stripe Wide-Oval tires, a juicy battery, dual exhausts and a beefy suspension were included. An anti-spin rear axle was mandatory.

Output by body style included 2,475 coupes, 19,587 hardtops, and 4,295 ragtops. Only 1,389 cars had W-30 Force-Air. One percent of all Olds were W-31s.

Factory ADP	Wheelbase	Length	Shipping Weight	Base V-8	Engine Options	0-to-60 MPH	¼-Mile
(CPE) $3,204; (HT) $3,141; (RT) $3,395	112 in.	202 in.	(CPE) 3,512 lbs.; (HT) 3,502 lbs. (RT) 3,580 lbs.	400 cid/350 hp	400/325; 400 cid/360 hp	(350 hp) 7.0 seconds	(350 hp) 15.13 seconds @ 92.2 mph

MCFG Says: (CPE) $18K; (HT) $20K; (RT) $24K (add 30% for W30)

They Says: Oldsmobile advertised that the 4-4-2 was, "Built like a 1 3/4-ton watch."

We Says: "Hotter than all but the Hurst model, the heavy-breathing W-30 option was about the same as in '68, except for the torque rating, which went up."

1969 HURST/OLDS

Jerry Heasley

1969 HURST/OLDS

Hurst/Olds styling was altered only slightly for '69. The headlights were brought closer together. The central grille and bumper area had a less cluttered appearance. New recessed, vertical taillights were seen. Production nearly doubled, with a total of 906 (all hardtops) being built.

Stimulated by a special 380-hp "Rocket 455" V-8, this year's Hurst Olds, while slightly heavier, bettered the original version's 0-to-60 mph acceleration time.

At a price that ranged from $4,300-$4,900, the Hurst/Olds buyer had to part with a few more pennies than it took to buy Oldsmobile's factory hot rod, the 4-4-2. But in return for paying that premium, the Hurst/Olds buyer got the optimum balance of luxury and performance available in an Oldsmobile muscle car.

Power was transmitted from the engine through a H.D. THM or the buyer's choice of a close- or wide-ratio four-speed, all Hurst-shifted, of course. The package was finished off with an eye-popping gold and white color scheme complete with strut-mounted rear deck spoiler.

Factory ATP	Wheelbase	Length	Shipping Weight	Base V-8	Engine Options	0-to-60 MPH	¼-Mile
$4,300	112 in.	201.9 in.	3,716 lbs.	455 cid/380 hp	None	6.0 seconds	13.9 seconds @ 102.27 mph

MCFG Says: $24K

He Says: *Super Stock* magazine (July '69) said, "Ah yes friends, there really is a supercar without lumps in it."

We Says: "In George Hurst's 'magic kingdom' the hairy Hurst/Olds sat on the golden throne."

Jerry Heasley

1970 4-4-2 W-30

1970 4-4-2 W-30

The W-30-equipped 4-4-2 was Oldsmobile's response to the lifting of GM's mandate prohibiting the use of engines exceeding 400 cid in its A-bodied cars. The 4-4-2 had, since '64, enjoyed a deserved reputation for handling. The 370-hp W-30 maintained the tradition of being a handler. There was nothing magical or exotic about the W-30 suspension, which consisted of front coil and rear leaf springs. Like all 4-4-2s, the W-30 was equipped with a rear stabilizer bar.

The W-30 version of the 455 V-8 had specs that looked a lot like those of the base 4-4-2 engine, but it developed 5 additional ponies at a higher spin rate. 10.88-inch front power disc brakes were standard. 9.5 x 2.0-inch rear drums were utilized. The W-30 fiberglass hood had twin air intakes that rammed a flow of cool air through a mesh filter. They were linked to a low-restriction air intake by a sponge-like material that acted as a gasket seal with the hood.

The standard W-30 tranny was a close-ratio Muncie. *Car Life called it* "Olds' version of Chevy's M22 'Rock Crusher.'" For $227 extra, the M40-type THM 400 was available. Compared to a normal THM, the M40 had higher shift points and sharper shifts. All floor shifts made for the W-30 were made by Hurst.

Factory ADP	Wheelbase	Length	Shipping Weight	Base 4-4-2 V-8	W-30 V-8	0-to-60 MPH	¼-Mile
(sport coupe as tested) $5,016	112 in.	203.2 in.	(sport coupe as tested) 4,195 lbs.	455 cid/ 370 hp	455 cid/ 365 hp	(W-30) 5.7 seconds	(W-30) 14.36 seconds @ 100.22 mph

MCFG **Says:** (CPE) $20K; (HT) $24K; (RT) $27K (add 30% for W-30)

They Says: *Car Life* magazine said, "If we had a getaway to make, we'd do it in a W-30 4-4-2."

We Says: "Forget about your Hemi and your GTO and get a W-30 4-4-2 if you really want to go!"

Jerry Heasley

1970 RALLYE 350

1970 RALLYE 350

What the Rallye 350 lacked in brawn it made up for in brightness. Sebring Yellow paint on the body, urethane-clad bumpers and Rally wheels made it stand out. Bold orange and black stripes trimmed the rear fenders and backlight. Introduced in February '70, the car was planned as a Hurst/Olds, but wound up as an option for F-85 coupes and Cutlass 'S' coupes or hardtops. It combined muscle car looks with a more "streetable" power train. It could be added to either.

The base 350 V-8 had a 4.06 x 3.39-inch bore and stroke. A W-31 Force-Air package raised compression from 10.25:1 to 10.5:1. W-31s had an aluminum intake manifold, a H.D. clutch, front disc brakes, a special hood, decals, paint stripes and emblems. When Rallye 350 equipment was added to an F-85 or Cutlass 'S', some extras were mandatory: Rallye Sport suspension, Force-Air fiberglass hood, dual Sport mirrors and a Sport steering wheel.

Buyers could get a three-speed, four-speed or close-ratio four-speed on the floor with a Hurst shifter. Like the GTO "Judge," this trendy-looking Only 3,547 of these "Yellow Perils" were assembled: 2,527 were Cutlass 'S' based and 1,020 were F-85s. Many of the cars came with a rear deck lid spoiler, which cost $74 extra.

Factory ADP	Wheelbase	Length	Shipping Weight	Base V-8	Engine Options	0-to-60 MPH	¼-Mile
(Car Life test car) $3,814 (*)	112 in.	203.2 in.	(Car Life test car) 4,155 lbs.	350 cid/310 hp	W-31 350 cid/325 hp	7.0 seconds	15.27 seconds @ 94.33 mph

(*) Base Rallye 350 prices were: (F-85) $3,163; (Cutlass 'S' coupe) $3,283; (Cutlass 'S' hardtop) $3,346

MCFG **Says:** $23K

They Says: *Car Life* opined, "Beneath that gaudy paint and wing lurks bargains in performance and handling."

We Says: "Sends feathers flying like a screaming yellow honker."

1971 4-4-2

1971 4-4-2

For its last year as a separate series, the 4-4-2's equipment included a special 455-cid V-8, a dual exhausts, carpeting, special springs, stabilizer bars, special engine mounts, Strato bucket seats, H.D. wheels, special emblems, and a deluxe steering wheel. Olds offered a choice of vinyl or cloth upholstery. The standard tires were G70-14s. The W-31 version of the 350-cid Cutlass V-8 had to be discontinued in '71 since it couldn't pass emission control tests that were coming online at the time, but W-30-optioned 4-4-2 models were continued in '71. The W-30s had an 8.5:1 compression ratio, accomplished by using a piston with a dished-out top.

Hot Rod drove a dual-disc equipped W-30 Olds 4-4-2 with a 455-cid engine and four-speed gearbox and found the shifts "startlingly quick and effortless." The writers said, "You really have to get used to using a light foot." An H.D. close-ratio four-speed gearbox could be ordered on the W-30 machines. *Hot Rod* magazine went on record saying, "It isn't recommended for sustained street driving." W-30 machines also got a full complement of suspension pieces for taking on all kinds of highway outings. Disc front brakes were also available. Olds built 1,304 ragtops and 6,285 hardtops.

Factory ADP	Wheelbase	Length	Shipping Weight	Base V-8	Engine Options	0-to-60 MPH	¼-Mile
(HT) $3,551; (RT) $3,742	112 in.	203.6 in.	(HT) 3,835 lbs.; (RT) 3,792 lbs.	455 cid/270 hp	(W-30) 455 cid/300 hp	6.1 seconds	13.89 seconds @ 101.1 mph

MCFG Says: (HT) $23K; (RT) $27K (add 30% for W-30)

They Says: *Car & Driver* said, "strictly speaking, a muscle car, but one ... too gentlemanly to display the gutter habits of its competitors."

We Says: "While Oldsmobile was reluctant to give out the W-30's ratings for '71, the '70 rating was 470 gross horsepower."

Jerry Heasley

1964 SAVOY 426-R/426-S

1964 SAVOY 426-R/426-S

In '64, Plymouth continued to offer the S/S Max Wedge Stage III 426-cid V-8. It was a competition-only option and carried the code 426-R, with "R" indicating "racing." It had an option price in the $500 range. The 426-R came with 415- and 425 hp. The former had an 11.0:1 compression ratio; the latter a 13.5:1 ratio. The 426-R also had nifty "Tri-Y" exhaust headers.

New this year was a 426-S "street" version rated at 365 hp, but actually producing around 410 hp. This engine did not include most of the Max Wedge hardware, but because of the similar displacement numbers, buyers believed it was the same. It ran a single four-barrel carb on a cast-iron intake with 10.3:1 compression and standard exhausts. With 470 lbs.-ft. of torque at 3200 rpm, it was no slouch and it was far more "streetable" than the "race" versions of the 426.

Most of 426-R engines went into Savoy coupes—the lightest full-size cars made by Plymouth. NASCAR racing cars carried four-barrel carbs. Drag racers went for two four-barrels, lightweight aluminum front sheet metal, large hood scoops, etc. The 426-S came in any model from the Savoy to the Sport Fury. A '64 Sport Fury hardtop with the 426-cid 365-hp V-8 carried about 9.5 lbs. per horsepower and could turn in 6.8-second 0-to-60 runs. The same combination was good for a 15.2-second quarter-mile run.

Factory ADP	Wheelbase	Length	Shipping Weight	426-S V-8	426-R V-8s	0-to-60 MPH	¼-Mile
$2,813	116 in.	205 in.	3,200 lbs.	426 cid/365 hp	426 cid/415 hp; 426 cid/425 hp	(425-hp) 5.8 seconds	(425-hp) 13.7 seconds @ 107.3 mph

MCFG **Says:** (Max Wedge) $65K

He Says: Greg Rager in *Musclecar Review* (February '89) said, "The Super Stock was not designed for milk and egg runs to the 7-11."

We Says: "The Chrysler guys got caught up racing Fords and Pontiacs on Woodward Avenue and pressured MoPar to build a racecar for the streets."

1965 BARRACUDA "FORMULA S"

1965 BARRACUDA "FORMULA S"

The "big window" Barracuda returned in '65 with a hotter engine and a rally-bred suspension. While the standard Barracuda had no real changes other than elimination of "Valiant" nameplates on the exterior, *Car and Driver* (October '64) liked the performance version. "Our test Barracuda, with its warmed-up 273 engine, is everything you'd like it to be," it said. "In fact, it may well be the most satisfactory enthusiast's car of all three of the sporty compacts."

The new "Golden Commando" V-8 was a step towards improving the breed. It upped compression to 10.5:1 and added a single four-barrel carb. This boosted horsepower and produced 280 lbs.-ft. of torque at 4000 rpm. In terms of performance, a Barracuda with a 3.23:1 rear axle and all-synchro four-speed was hot.

Base Barracuda pricing started at $2,535, but the hot engine was merchandised as part of the Formula 'S' package, which also included H.D. front torsion bars, H.D. rear springs, firm ride shock absorbers, a sway bar, Rally stripes, extra-wide wheel rims, Goodyear Blue Streak Wide-Oval tires, and "Formula S" medallions ahead of the front wheel openings. A total of 64,596 Barracudas were built.

Factory ADP	Wheelbase	Length	Shipping Weight	Hi-Po V-8	Engine Options	0-to-60 MPH	¼-Mile
$3,169	106 in.	189 in.	2,945 lbs.	273 cid/235 hp	None	8.2 seconds	15.9 seconds @ 85 mph

MCFG Says: $27.5K

They Says: *Car Life* magazine (June '65) said, "Infinitely more sporting and a lot more satisfactory."

We Says: "Back in the muscle car era, we always wanted one of these and we really kick ourselves for not buying the gold, moon-roofed, factory-show-car version that was in the flea market at Hershey for $5,500 about 20 years ago."

PLYMOUTH

1965 SATELLITE MAX WEDGE STAGE III/RACE HEMI

1965 SATELLITE MAX WEDGE STAGE III/RACE HEMI

Promoted as "the roaring '65s," midsized Plymouths had lower bodies, carryover roofs, single headlights, and a new hi-po Satellite. A four-section aluminum grille and crisp, tapering lines dominated the round-cornered, square styling. Dummy louvers decorated the rear fenders.

Bucket seats, a console, and vinyl trim were standard in hardtops and ragtops. The 426 Max Wedge Stage III was a race-bred V-8 with a unique combustion chamber configuration. It had 12.5:1 compression, NASCAR "Tri-Y" exhausts, a 320-degree cam, reworked combustion chambers, notched valves, and twin four-barrels with giant air cleaners. Chrysler did not warrantee this engine, which was "not recommended for general driving." The 365-hp 426 Street Wedge, with 10.3:1 compression and a single four-barrel on a cast-iron intake had better street driveability.

The 426 "Race Hemi" introduced in '64 for "off-road" use had a forged and shotpeened crank, impact extruded pistons, cross-bolt mains, forged rods, solid lifters, and other racing stuff. Chrysler built 360 and about 60 percent went in Plymouths.

Factory ADP	Wheelbase	Length	Shipping Weight	Base Satellite V-8	Engine Options	0-to-60 MPH	¼-Mile
(HT) $2,612; (RT) $2,827 *	116 in.	203.4 in.	(HT) 3,220 lbs.; (RT) 3,325 lbs. *	273 cid/180 hp	318 cid/230 hp; 383 cid/325 hp; 426 cid/425 hp (Opt. Hemi V-8) 426 cid/425 hp	(Hemi) 5.3 seconds	(Hemi) 13.81 seconds @ 104 mph

* *(Base Satellite)*

MCFG **Says:** (HT) $20K; (RT) $30K (add 75% for Max Wedge; 100% for Hemi)

They Says: *Musclecar Review* (July '90) said, "It had the gusto to run at the head of the pack, and styling wise we scored it high."

We Says: "A Max Wedge or Hemi Satellite would launch into outer space like the best of Cape Canaveral's Titan rockets."

David Temple

1966 SATELLITE "STREET HEMI"

1966 SATELLITE "STREET HEMI"

Some 844 Hemi Satellites were built in '66: 817 hardtops (including 503 with four-speeds and 314 with TorqueFlite) and 27 ragtops. All had the "Street Hemi." Though similar to a race Hemi, this 426 used a dual four-barrel aluminum intake, milder valve specs, different 10.25:1 pistons, and a big air cleaner. A pair of tubes on the right-hand exhaust manifold handled heat riser functions. The engine was rated 425 hp at 5,000 rpm and 490 lbs.-ft. of torque at 4,000 rpm.

Like other Belvederes, Satellites were restyled. The slab-sided body had crisper fenders and mild sculpturing. Cantilevered hardtop rooflines continued, with the pillars slightly widened. The windshield was larger and flatter. Up front, the old rectangular parking lamps changed to circles located in the grille. Satellites had bucket seats, consoles, full wheel covers, and vinyl trim.

Early in the season, the biggest engine for Satellites was the 325-hp 383 V-8. Dodges got the Hemi first, a few months into the season, then Plymouth. Included in the $1,105 engine package were an H.D. suspension, larger drum brakes, wide wheels, and 7.75 x 14 Goodyear high-speed tires. Three-on-the-tree couldn't handle the Hemi's torque, so a four-speed or TorqueFlite had to be added. The automatic included a transmission fluid cooler.

Factory ADP	Wheelbase	Length	Shipping Weight	Base V-8	Engine Options	0-to-60 MPH	¼-Mile
(HT) $3,800; (RT) $4,015	116 in.	203.4 in.	(HT) 3,220 lbs.; (RT) 3,325 lbs.	273 cid/180 hp	318 cid/230 hp; 383/325; 426/425 hp	Street Hemi 7.1 seconds	Street Hemi 14.5 seconds @ 95 mph

MCFG Says: $70K

They Says: *Car Life* (July '66) said, "That the Hemi-Satellite accelerates in a straight line in astonishing fashion cannot be disputed."

We Says: "Eight wins by Richard Petty announced the Hemi's induction into NASCAR circles. USAC saw the Hemi-powered cars take its annual championship."

PLYMOUTH

1967 BARRACUDA FORMULA S

1967 BARRACUDA FORMULA S

The Barracuda arrived two months after other '67 Plymouths. There were now three body styles: a smooth-looking fastback, a unique hardtop, and a ragtop. Barracudas retained Valiant influences, but were a separate car-line and looked mostly different on the outside. Curved side glass, many unique body panels, distinctive roofs, and 4.4 inches more length made the Barracuda stand by itself. A split grille with parking lights inside added to its sporty flair.

One way to assure getting all the goodies was to order the Formula S package, which included a Commando 273 engine, 14-inch Wide-Oval tires, H.D. suspension, an anti-sway bar and 'S' badges. You could now get a production B-block V-8 in a Barracuda, supposedly only as part of a second, midyear Formula S option including the 383.

The new styling got rave reviews in the press and Plymouth delivered 30,110 fastbacks, 28,196 notchbacks, and 4,228 ragtops. It was the most popular Barracuda model ever.

PLYMOUTH

Factory ADP	Wheelbase	Length	Shipping Weight	Base V-8	Engine Options	0-to-60 MPH	0-to-100 MPH
(Base V-8) (FB) $2,720; (HT) $2,530; (RT) $2,860	108 in.	192.8 in.	(FB) 2,940 lbs.; (HT) 2,865 lbs.; (RT) 2,975 lbs.	273 cid/180 hp	273 cid/235 hp; 383 cid/280 hp	(383 V-8) 6.8 seconds	(383 V-8) 15.4 seconds @ 92 mph

MCFG Says: (FB) $23K; (HT) $22K; (RT) $25K (add 10% for 'S' and 40% for 383)

They Says: *Car Life* (December '66) said, "The game is pony car poker and Plymouth raises one—who'll call?"

We Says: "Magazines of the time compared the '67 Barracuda's looks to those of the sporty Buick Riviera, but the muscle car crowd was more into the big new power under the hood."

1967 GTX HEMI

Jerry Heasley

1967 GTX HEMI

Having a big-inch performance model in your midsize line up was mandatory if you wanted to market a muscle car in the mid-'60s. One of the last "supercars" to arrive was the '67 GTX.

With lightweight Super Stockers, big Wedge V-8s and Hemis, Plymouth had already built cars that were far faster than the GTO, but only in limited numbers. The automaker was slow to develop a package that put all the parts together.

Vital to creation of the first GTX was the '66 introduction of the Street Hemi and the release of the '67 "Super Commando" 440-cid Wedge engine. Combining these with the Belvedere's top-of-the-line bucket seats, fake scoops, and stripes made the GTX.

The exact number of GTXs sold during the model year is not known, since their total was included with that of Satellites. What is known is that the Hemi-optioned GTXs are rare. Only 720 of the approximately 12,500 GTXs built were equipped with the Hemi. Of those, 312 had four-speeds and 408 were had TorqueFlite. Estimates put the number of Hemi ragtops built at only 17.

Factory ADP	Wheelbase	Length	Shipping Weight	Base V-8	Engine Options	0-to-60 MPH	¼-Mile
(HT) $3,178; (RT) $3,418	116 in.	200.5 in.	(HT) 3,535 lbs.; (RT) 3,615 lbs.	440 cid/375 hp	426 cid/425 hp (Hemi)	6.6 seconds	15.2 seconds @ 97 mph

MCFG Says: (HT) $28K; (RT) $32K ($65K Hemi Satellite)

They Says: Dodge advertised, "The idle alone sounds like the William Tell Overature. It goes rumpety-rumpety-rumpety, rumpety-rumpety-rumpety, rumpety!"

We Says: "Even a better bargain with the Hemi, if you consider what such cars go for in the collector market today."

1968 GTX HEMI

Jerry Heasley

1968 GTX HEMI

The GTX was a high-content muscle car with an assortment of big-block V-8s. It shared a new Belvedere body—including a special hi-po hood—with the Road Runner.

For '68, the Super Commando 440-cid V-8 again came as standard equipment in the GTX. It had a 4.32 x 3.75-inch bore and stroke, hydraulic valve lifters, a 10.1:1 compression ratio and a single Carter AFB four-barrel carb. *Car Life* road tested a 375-hp 440-powered GTX with automatic transmission and reported a top speed was about 121 mph. This version of the GTX did 0-to-60 mph in 6.8 seconds. It could cover the quarter-mile in 14.6 seconds with a 96-mph terminal speed. *Car Life* described the 440 GTX like this, "Exciting, enjoyable, extremely capable ... to those who like supercars, they just may be the epitome."

Plymouth built 17,914 GTX hardtops and 2,026 GTX ragtops in '68. The numbers were surely higher than those for '67 models. However, they paled in comparison to the 44,599 Road Runners that came off the assembly line.

For $605 extra, you could get the 426-cid Street Hemi stuffed into your GTX. Hemi-equipped GTXs continued to be rare, with only 410 hardtops and about 36 ragtops believed to have been made.

Factory ADP	Wheelbase	Length	Shipping Weight	Base V-8	Engine Options	0-to-60 MPH	¼-Mile
(Hemi) (HT) $3,960; (RT) $4,195	116 in.	203 in.	(HT) 3,470 lbs.; (RT) 3,595 lbs.	440 cid/375 hp	426 cid/425 hp	(Hemi ragtop) 6.3 seconds	(Hemi ragtop) 14.0 seconds @ 96.5 mph

MCFG Says: (HT) $32K; (RT) $40K (We suggest adding 50% for Hemi)

They Says: *Car Life* said, "The Hemi GTX will appeal to the acceleration enthusiast who wants the ultimate—the fastest standard car on the market."

We Says: "The GTX was more like the GTO than any other member of Plymouth's muscle car fleet."

1968 ROAD RUNNER

Jerry Heasley

1968 ROAD RUNNER

Plymouth was first to exploit the market for a low-buck performance car with the '68 Road Runner. The idea of putting a powerful engine in the cheapest, lightest model was not a new, but the Road Runner, Plymouth did all the work for the customer. With a low price youthful buyers could afford and a gimmicky Warner Bros. cartoon character as its namesake, the car caught on.

Using Road Runner identification and a horn that emulated the cartoon bird's "beep-beep" got attention in the marketplace. A "stripper" Belvedere coupe was the basis for the Road Runner. It came with a bench seat, rubber floor mats, a hot V-8, a standard four-speed manual tranny, a H.D. suspension, 11-inch drum brakes and Red Stripe tires.

The kicker with the Road Runner was its low price. If you wanted some interior niceties such as carpeting and bright trim, you had to invest $79 for the Road Runner Decor Group. If you wanted to kick the toy image, you had to ante up $714 extra for the 426-cid/425-hp Street Hemi.

A two-door hardtop was added midyear and its 15,359 production run was added to the coupe's 29,240 tally to make the Road Runner a winner. Of those, 1,019 were Hemi powered.

Factory ADP	Wheelbase	Length	Shipping Weight	Base V-8	Engine Options	0-to-60 MPH	¼-Mile
(CPE) $2,896; (HT) $3,034	116 in.	203 in.	(CPE) 3,390 lbs.; (HT) 3,400 lbs.	383 cid/335 hp	440 cid/350 hp; 440 cid/375 hp; 426 cid/425 hp	(383/335) 7.3 seconds	(383/335) 15.37 seconds @ 91.4 mph

MCFG Says: (CPE) $31K; (HT) $33K (add 50% for 440 and 100% for Hemi)

They Says: *Car Life* said that the Road Runner, "emulates what a young, performance-minded buyer might do on his own if properly experienced and motivated."

We Says: "The Road Runner was what you'd have if J.C. Whitney sent you all the neat stuff they had for your car and installed it for you."

GTX Hardtop
(also available as Convertible)

1969 GTX

1969 GTX

The '69 GTX was again based on the Roadrunner. The GTX received modest restylings at the front and rear. New features included new side markers and slightly revised grille and taillight treatments.

There were a number of technical improvements. The GTX was now offered with a wider choice of rear axles. A Hurst shifter could be ordered. Also new was the optional "Air Grabber" system. This was comprised of dual functional hood air intakes that could be opened and closed through the use of a dashboard shutoff. The Street Hemi V-8 was a $701 option. This hairy V-8 was ordered for just 198 hardtops and only 11 ragtops.

GTX sales continued to slip to taper off and only around 15,000 of the cars were built. Part of the reason for this was the expansion of body styles in the Road Runner line, which gained a hardtop and ragtop in '69.

A third engine for the GTX was introduced at midyear. Plymouth mounted three two-barrel carbs on the 440 to make the "440+6" option. This cost $119 and gave the buyer 375 hp. Also known as a "Six Pack," this version was good for a 13.70-second quarter-mile at 102.8 mph.

Factory ADP	Wheelbase	Length	Shipping Weight	Base V-8	Engine Options	0-to-60 MPH	¼-Mile
(HT) $3,416; (RT) $3,635	116 in.	203 in.	(HT) 3,465 lbs.; (RT) 3,590 lbs.	440 cid/375 hp	440 cid/390 hp; 426 cid/425 hp	(440/3785) 6.8 seconds	(440/375) 14.6 seconds @ 95.6 mph

MCFG **Says:** (HT) $31K; (RT) $40K (add 40% for 440+6; add 100% for Hemi)

He Says: "One primary purpose of a supercar is to get from here to there, from this light to the next, in the shortest elapsed time," said *Motor Trend's* Bill Sanders. "To this end, the Plymouth GTX is the flat out best qualifier of all."

We Says: "'Plymouth tells it like it is,' was the '69 sales slogan and it only took three letters to tell the world that GTX was king-konging it again."

1969 ROAD RUNNER

Jerry Heasley

1969 ROAD RUNNER

New grille and rear styling characterized the '69 Road Runner coupe, hardtop and ragtop. Standard H.D. features included suspension, brakes and shocks. Road Runner nameplates decorated the dash, deck and doors. Top-opening hood scoops, chrome engine parts, an un-silenced air cleaner, red or white streak tires, a four-speed transmission with a Hurst gear shifter, a fake walnut shift knob, back-up lights, and a Deluxe steering wheel were included.

The standard Road Runner V-8 was the 383, which had a 4.250 x 3.338-inch bore and stroke. With a Carter AVS four-barrel carb and 10.0:1 compression ratio, the Road Runner 383 produced 335 hp at 4600 rpm. Options included the 440-cid V-8 and the 426-cid Street Hemi.

Car and Driver had a Hemi Road Runner coupe in a January '69 comparison test of six "econo-racers." As tested, the car cost $4,362, including the Hemi ($813), an automatic transmission ($40 over the base four-speed), a performance axle package ($64), the décor package ($82), power steering ($100), power disc brakes ($92), and other options. The Street Hemi had a slightly larger 3.75-inch stroke, but the hemi heads, a 10.25:1 compression ratio, and dual four-barrel Carter carbs boosted its output considerably.

Factory ADP	Wheelbase	Length	Shipping Weight	Base V-8	Engine Options	0-to-60 MPH	¼-Mile
(CPE) $2,945; (HT) $3,083; (RT) $3,313	116 in.	203 in.	(Hemi) (CPE) 3,435 lbs.; (HT) 3,450 lbs.; (RT) 3,790 lbs.	383 cid/ 335 hp	440 cid/375 hp, 426 cid/425 hp	(Hemi) 5.1 seconds	(Hemi) 13.54 seconds @ 105.14 mph

MCFG Says: (CPE) $30K, (HT) $33K, (RT) $40K (add 70% for 440; add 100% for Hemi)

They Says: *Car Life* said the Road Runner "Gives immediate identification as a member of an exclusive club—a 'beep-beep' and a wave."

We Says: "The Road Runner may have been inspired by a funny paper character, but it was not a car to laugh at."

1970 AAR 'CUDA

Jerry Heasley

1970 AAR 'CUDA

SCCA Trans-Am racing was a must for hot pony car makers. Plymouth/Dodge participation came together because of new Barracuda and Challenger designs and rules changes saying the 5.0-liter racing V-8s didn't have to be exactly the same as production version. This meant MoPar's potent 340-cid small-block could be de-stroked to 303.8 inches and meet the limit. Plymouth could legalize its Trans-Am V-8 by building 1,900 or more special AAR 'Cudas.

The new option package for the Barracuda hardtop was named after Dan Gurney's All-American Racers. Powering the car was a 340 with hi-po heads. Thicker webbing in the block allowed the racing team to use four-bolt mains. A single four-barrel carb was used in Trans-Am racing, but triple two-barrel Holleys were used on production models. A fiberglass, cold-air-induction hood let them breathe.

Other parts of the package for Plymouth's E-body model were a rear spoiler, front and rear sway bars, side-exit exhaust and rally wheels with E40 x 15 front tires and G60 rear tires. Transmission choices included the A-833 four-speed with Hurst shifter or the Chrysler 727 TorqueFlite. AAR decals and striping identified the package. Plymouth built 2,724 AAR 'Cudas.

Factory ATP	Wheelbase	Length	As tested Weight	Base V-8	Engine Options	0-to-60 MPH	¼-Mile
$4,340	108 in.	186.7 in.	3,585 lbs.	340 cid/390 hp	None	5.8 seconds	14.3 seconds @ 99.5 mph

MCFG Says: $38K

They Says: "Everything makes sense if you forget all about Dan Gurney and think of it in terms of the Burbank Blue Bombers," said *Car and Driver* (July '70). "The new AAR 'Cuda is every inch a hot rod."

We Says: "One very fast small-block Plymouth."

1970 'CUDA

Jerry Heasley

1970 'CUDA

The '70 'Cuda came standard with the 335-hp 383. The Hemi was an $871 option for both hardtops and ragtops. No wonder the 'Cuda was part of Chrysler's "Rapid Transit System."

Street Hemis got new hydraulic lifters for '70, but a new cam profile gave the Mopar engineers no reason to alter the 425 horsepower rating. Two Carter AFB four-barrels breathed through an Air Grabber hood. In order to get the ponies to the pavement, Hemi-powered 'Cudas relied on H.D. driveline parts. There was a choice of the New Process A-833 four-speed or the 727 TorqueFlite. A Dana 9 3/4-inch rear was held a leaf-spring suspension with six leafs on the right and five (plus two half-leafs) on the left. Seven-inch-wide wheels held F60 x 15 tires.

In short, power was the Hemi 'Cuda's long suit. Not long was the list of buyers. Insurance companies did not look kindly on Hemi 'Cudas and did not care if they could do 0-to-60 mph in under 6 seconds and run down the quarter-mile turning 14s. By the time the '70 run came to an end, only 652 hardtops had left the factory with Hemi power and 284 of them had four-speeds. Far rarer was the ragtop, with only 14 being made (five with stick shift).

Factory ADP	Wheelbase	Length	Shipping Weight	Base V-8	Engine Options	0-to-60 MPH	¼-Mile
(base 'Cuda) (HT) $3,164; (RT) $3,433	108 in.	187 in.	(base 'Cuda) (HT) 3,395 lbs.; (RT) 3,480 lbs.	383 cid/ 335 hp	383 cid/290 hp; 426 cid/425 hp	5.8 seconds	14 seconds @ 102 mph

MCFG Says: (HT) $30K; (RT) $40K (add 100% for Hemi)

They Says: *MoPar Muscle* magazine said, "Together with the Challenger, the new E-bodies offered a new home for ol' King Kong hisself, the 426 Hemi."

We Says: "Plymouth's resounding message in the case of the Hemi 'Cuda was 'Damn the insurance companies—full speed ahead.'"

1970 'CUDA 340

Phil Kunz

1970 'CUDA 340

The 'Cuda entered its third generation in '70. It was longer. The space between the front wheels could comfortably swallow everything from a slant six to a Hemi. Width went to 74.9 inches and height was 5.9 inches. At 59.7 inches the front track was a bit narrower than the 60.7-inch rear track. The fastback was axed, but attractive hardtop and ragtop models were left.

Attracting less media attention than the big-block 'Cudas was the 'Cuda 340, which continued as an option (a 383-cid V-8 was standard). The 340, with its 4.04 x 3.31-inch bore and stroke, was a nice alternative, especially for youthful muscle car buyers who couldn't quite hack the price of a 440 or a Hemi. It had 10.5:1 compression and a single four-barrel carb and that was enough to generate 275 hp at 5000 rpm and 340 lbs.-ft. of torque at 3200 rpm.

Motor Trend ran a comparison test between 'Cudas with all three engines. The 340 needed about a half a second more to go 0-to-60 compared to the 440's 5.9 seconds and the Hemi's 5.8 seconds. The 340's quarter-mile performance also stacked up well against 14.4 seconds and 100 mph for the 440 and 14 seconds and 102 mph for the Hemi.

For all-around use, the 'Cuda 340 was a nicely balanced package.

Factory ADP	Wheelbase	Length	Shipping Weight	Base V-8	Engine Options	0-to-60 MPH	¼-Mile
(base 'Cuda 383) (HT) $3,164; (RT) $3,433	108 in.	187 in.	(HT) 3,395 lbs.; (RT) 3,480 lbs.	383 cid/335 hp; (Optional small-block V-8) 340 cid/275 hp	440 cid/375 hp; 340 cid/ 275 hp; Hemi 426 cid/425 hp	'Cuda 340 7.5 seconds	'Cuda 340 15 seconds @ 95 mph

MCFG Says: ('Cuda 340) (HT) $33K; (RT) $44K

He Says: A.B. Shuman wrote, "From the foregoing you may have detected a 'slight' preference for the 340 'Cuda. This was intentional. It was the best of the lot!"

We Says: "If you're the 'I'll-drive-my-muscle car-everyday-and-die-with-a-smile-on-my-face' type, check out the 'Cuda 340."

1970 GTX

1970 GTX

A redesigned grille, a new hood, and restyled front fenders characterized '70 midsize Plymouths. The GTX featured much of the same standard equipment as the Road Runner, including H.D. suspension and brakes, dual exhausts, a hi-po hood with an "Air Grabber" scoop, front and rear bumper guards, a 150-mph speedo, F70-14 red or white stripe tires, three-speed wipers, H.D. shocks, roof and door moldings, a Super Commando 440 V-8, a deluxe vinyl interior, new high-back front bucket seats, a rear bench seat, body side reflective tape stripes, side markers, and bright exhaust trumpets.

Only a coupe was offered and it drew only 7,748 orders. Only 72 cars got the Street Hemi, which cost $711. GTX buyers could also get the 440-cid six-pack with three two-barrel carbs for just $119 above the price of the base 440. "A GTX six-barrel is no slouch in the performance department either," said *Motor Trend* in its fall '69 review of the hot '70s models.

TorqueFlite was standard in the '70 GTX. A four-speed was available at no extra cost. The Trak Pak option was $143 and Super Trak Pak was $236. Also available was a Super Performance Axle Package with a 9 3/4-inch Dana rear axle, a 4.10:1 axle ratio, and power front disc brakes.

Factory ADP	Wheelbase	Length	Shipping Weight	Base V-8	Engine Options	0-to-60 MPH	¼-Mile
$3,535	116 in.	204 in.	3,515 lbs.	440 cid/ 375 hp	440 cid/390 hp; 440 cid/350 hp; 426 cid/425 hp	(440 Six-Pack) 6.8 seconds	(440 Six-Pack) 13.85 seconds @ 104 mph

MCFG Says: $30K (add 100% for Hemi)

He Says: Writing in the November '86 issue of *Musclecar Review*, Paul Zazarine said, "The Plymouth GTX was always considered an upscale version of the Road Runner—it could still boil the hides, but in a classy sort of way."

We Says: "The difference between First Class and Parcel Post is a matter of money and speed—kind of like the GTX."

1970 ROAD RUNNER

1970 ROAD RUNNER

The Road Runner again utilized the Belvedere body. Standard equipment included a three-speed transmission with floor shift, front armrests, rear armrests, cigar lighter, glove box light, "beep-beep" horn, hi-po hood, front bumper guards, 150-mph speedo, Road Runner emblems, 383-cid Road Runner V-8, F70-14 white line tires on wide safety rim wheels, three-speed windshield wipers, roof-drip rail and upper door frame moldings, and H.D. shock absorbers.

To a degree, Plymouth was gradually changing the original Road Runner concept of being a "stripper" muscle car with a low price tag. Replacing the four-speed with a three-speed was one sign of this, as was the use of hydraulic valve lifters in the Hemi, which cost $841 extra. You could also get the 440-cid six-pack engine for $250 extra, as long as you could live without air conditioning and added either the four-speed or TorqueFlite.

Another Road Runner option for owners with drag racing in mind was the A33 Super Trak Pak. It included an H.D. 9 3/4-inch Dana Sure-Grip 3.55:1 rear axle, a dual breaker point distributor, a wood-grained shift knob and recessed warning light and the H.D. four-speed manual gearbox with Hurst shifter.

Factory ADP	Wheelbase	Length	Shipping Weight	Base V-8	Engine Options	0-to-60 MPH	¼-Mile
(CPE) $2,945; (HT*) $3,083; (RT) $3,313	116 in.	203.8 in.	(CPE) 3,435 lbs.; (HT*) 3,450 lbs.; (RT) 3,790 lbs.	383 cid/ 335 hp	440 cid/375 hp; 440 cid/390 hp; 426 cid/425 hp	6.6 seconds	14.4 seconds @ 99.0 mph

(*) Hardtop as tested by Motor Trend cost $4,417 and weighed 3,935 lbs.

MCFG Says: (CPE) $27K; (HT) $30K; (RT) $40K (add 40% for 440; add 100% for Hemi)

He Says: Motor Trend's A.B. Shuman said, "It's no longer just a stripped down Belvedere with a big engine and heavy suspension."

We Says: "Plymouth's 'beep-beep' bomb still did a great job of kicking its feathers up in the stop light grand prix."

1970 SUPERBIRD

1970 SUPERBIRD

The final volley in the battle of muscle car aerodynamics was the '70 Superbird. With a 7.0-liter engine limit, competing automakers turned to wind-cheating body designs, like the "winged warriors" from Chrysler—'69 Dodge Daytona and '70 Superbird. Designed for NASCAR superspeedways, these Mopars both featured a long peaked nose and a rear-deck airfoil mounted on struts. NASCAR's '69 rules called for 500 copies of a model to be built to make it "race legal." For '70, the rule was one car per dealer. Experts believe 1,971 Superbirds were built.

The most popular engine was the 440-cid Super Commando V-8 with a four-barrel carb. A total of 1,120 Superbirds came this way. Another 716 cars were equipped with the 440 Six-Pack. That leaves 135 Hemi 'Birds (77 with automatic and 58 with four-speed).

Racecars used the Race Hemi and the combo was enough to lure Richard Petty back to racing Plymouths. Petty Engineering hired Pete Hamilton to run a second Superbird at selected events in '70 and he promptly won the Daytona 500.

Midsized Plymouths were redone for '71. There was no Superbird follow up.

Factory ADP	Wheelbase	Length	Shipping Weight	Base V-8	Engine Options	0-to-60 MPH	¼-Mile
(base) $4,298	117 in.	204 in.	3,841 lbs.	383 cid/225 hp	383 cid/290 hp; 440 cid/350 hp; 440 cid/375 hp; 440 cid/390 hp; 425 cid/426 hp	5.9 seconds	14.26 seconds @ 103.7 mph

MCFG Says: $66K (add 60% for 440 6-Pack; 75% for Hemi)

They Says: *Road Test* magazine said, "The Superbird in concept is a vehicle for the raw competition of NASCAR tracks. But in street versions, it is also a fun car when you get used to being stared at."

We Says: "We remember a neighbor buying a Superbird at a clear-out price and letting it sit out all winter. If only we knew then what we know now."

1971 GTX

Jerry Heasley

1971 GTX

With sales of Plymouth's upscale hi-po model running below expectations for several years, many were surprised when it showed up for one more appearance in the '71 Plymouth lineup. This year it again came only in two-door hardtop form.

GTX equipment picked up where the Road Runner's left off. Additional items included a 375-hp Super Commando 440 V-8, TorqueFlite, high-back buckets, low-restriction dual exhausts with chrome tips, dual horns, vinyl trim, a 70-amp battery, sill moldings, wheel opening moldings, drip rail moldings, an extra-H.D. suspension (front and rear), and G70 x 14 RWL tires.

A bench seat with cloth-and-vinyl trim and a center armrest was a no-charge option and white sidewall tires could be substituted in place of the white-lettered style at no extra cost. GTX buyers could also opt for a three-speed floor shift. The Hemi V-8 was available for $747.

On Hemi GTXs, an Air Grabber hood was standard and a four-speed was a no-charge opton. This was the last year for the Street Hemi. Only 356 were used in all Chrysler cars. Only 30 GTX Hemis were made and only 11 had a four-speed. Only 2,942 were GTXs were built in '71.

Factory ADP	Wheel-base	Length	Shipping Weight	Base V-8	Engine Options	0-to-60 MPH	¼-Mile
$3,733	117 in.	203.2 in.	3,675 lbs.	440 cid/375 hp	440 cid (Six-Pack)/385 hp; 426 cid/425 hp	(440 Six-Pack) 5.7 seconds	13.70 seconds @ 102 mph

MCFG Says: $19.5K (add 40% for 440 Six-Pack; add 100% for Hemi)

He Says: Greg Rader, writing in *Musclecar Review* (February '88) said, "Obviously a slight drop in horsepower and compression had not hurt the big wedge engine."

We Says: "This 'fancy-pants' Road Runner often went unappreciated in its own era, but is starting to attract much attention now."

Jerry Heasley

'71 HEMI 'CUDA

1971 HEMI 'CUDA

Sox & Martin and PeeWee Wallace were burning up the drag strips in Barracudas back in '71 and also helping to generate interest in Plymouth's "fish car." Most sales went to non-Hemi-powered cars. The $884 Hemi option was ordered for just 108 hardtops (60 with four-speeds) and a mere seven ragtops. Two of the ragtops had four-speeds.

Seven other engines were offered, including a 125-hp 198 slant six, a 145-hp 225 slant six, and a 230-hp 318 V-8. The 275-hp 340 V-8 with a four-barrel carb was a little hotter. Then came the 383 big-block V-8, which was offered in two-barrel (275-hp) and four-barrel (300-hp) versions. That left two V-8s for the muscle car crowd—the 385-hp 440 Six Pack and the 425-hp 426 Hemi.

The '71 Hemi engine featured a 10.2:1 compression ratio and a single four-barrel carb. It came attached to either a four-speed or automatic. The standard rear axle had a 3.23:1 ratio. Sure-Grip-only options included 3.55:1, 3.54:1, and 4.10:1. Plymouth's nifty S15 H.D. suspension package was standard with the Hemi 'Cuda.

After model year '71, Barracudas continued to be offered by Plymouth, but Hemi versions and ragtops didn't make the cut after the season came to its end.

Factory ADP	Wheelbase	Length	Shipping Weight	Optional Hemi V-8	Engine Options	0-to-60 MPH	¼-Mile
(HT) $4,040; (RT) $4,296	108 in.	186.6 in.	(HT) 3,475 lbs.; (RT) 3,550 lbs.	426 cid/425 hp	None	5.8 seconds	13.53 seconds @ 106.8 mph

MCFG Says: (HT) $30K; (RT) $40K (add 100% for Hemi)

He Says: In *Musclecar Review* Paul Zazarine said, "If you're looking for the ultimate MoPar, look no further than the Hemi 'Cuda."

We Says: "Pretty beyond comparison and potent beyond imagination."

Jerry Heasley

1971 ROAD RUNNER

1971 ROAD RUNNER

Performance cars of all sizes continued to be available in large numbers of models and options during '71, but low sales numbers put them on the endangered species list. In the Plymouth stable, only the Road Runner hardtop returned. Its new grille looked like a big loop around the front end. New sheet metal was shared with the Sebring and Sebring Plus coupes. The sedan and ragtop were not translated onto the new Mopar midsize body shell.

With the more expensive GTX still around, the Road Runner again filled its low-priced muscle car niche with its trick "beep-beep" horn, hot graphics, and more. Standard in the Road Runner was a 383 V-8 with a single four-barrel carb, a floor-mounted three-speed, H.D., deep-pile carpeting, a Rallye gauge cluster, a performance hood, low-restriction dual exhausts, H.D. brakes, F70-14 whitewalls, and all-vinyl bench seats with foam rubber front cushions.

For $242 you could add the 440 Six-Pack. The Hemi was an $884 option and still came with an advertised 425 hp. Other interesting options included the Air Grabber pop-up hood scoop for $67 and a bolt-on rear deck spoiler. Plymouth built 14,218 Road Runners including 55 Hemis.

Factory ADP	Wheelbase	Length	Shipping Weight	Base V-8	Engine Options	0-to-60 MPH	¼-Mile
$4,266	115 in.	203.2 in.	3,750 lbs.	383 cid/300 hp	440 cid/370 hp; 440 cid/38 hp; 426 cid/425 hp	(383/300) 6.9 seconds	(383/300) 14.92 seconds @ 94.5 mph

MCFG Says: $23K

They Says: *Road Test* (January '71) said, "Youth of all ages took a fancy to the idea and they've been beep-beeping at each other ever since. This in turn bred an owner's cult."

We Says: *Road Test* magazine named the Plymouth Road Runner its "1971 U.S. Car of the Year", saying, "When the performance-minded think Plymouth they think Road Runner."

Jerry Heasley

1972 ROAD RUNNER

1972 ROAD RUNNER

The '72 Road Runner had minor cosmetic changes, like a slightly different grille. Although Plymouth offered 16 colors, the psychedelic hues of prior years were gone. The standard bench seat came in blue, green or black vinyl. Production dropped nearly 50 percent to 7,628 cars.

Road Runners included all Satellite features, plus the following additions or substitutions: three-speed tranny with floor-mounted shifter, H.D. suspension, H.D. brakes, front and rear sway bars, and other goodies.

The 440 four-barrel V-8 cost $153, but couldn't be ordered with the three-speed. You had to add either a four-speed ($202), or TorqueFlite ($232). Sales literature did not list the output of this engine, but sources put it at 280 nhp at 4800 rpm and 375 net lbs.-ft. of torque at 3200 rpm.

A $67 "Air-Grabber" scoop required different stripes (a $22 option). A 3.23:1 axle was standard. Options included a 2.76:1 (with 340- or 400-cid four-barrel V-8s only). Hood lock pins were $16. A tach cost $52. A $94 performance axle package included a Sure Grip differential, a H.D. 3.55:1 rear axle, a seven-blade torque fan, a 26-inch hi-po radiator and a fan shroud. This package wasn't available with the 440-cid V-8 and four-speed. A $160 Trak Pak option included the same items, but with a 3.54:1 Dana axle.

Factory ADP	Wheelbase	Length	Shipping Weight	Base V-8	Engine Options	0-to-60 MPH	¼-Mile
$3,080	115 in.	203.2 in.	3,495 lbs.	440 cid/255 hp (340 cid/240 hp alternate)	400 cid/265 hp; 440 cid/ 280/290/330 hp	(340/240) 7.8 seconds	15.50 seconds @ 90 mph

MCFG Says: $22K

They Says: *Musclecar Review* (August-September '95) said, "Road Runner continued as Plymouth's premier performer. The 383 gave way to a 255-horsepower 400."

We Says: "This momentum muscle car struggled valiantly to keep the dwindling interest in high-performance motoring alive."

Jerry Heasley

1962 SUPER-DUTY CATALINA 421

1962 SUPER-DUTY CATALINA 421

Pontiac was first to make factory lightweight drag cars. After releasing NASCAR engine options in '57, PMD learned racing sold cars. By '60, the "Poncho" performance image put Pontiac third in U.S. sales for the first time. Chevy's new-for-'62 409 was a threat and Pontiac's answer was the '61 S-D Catalina, which had a 368-hp 389 with Tri-Power. Maybe 25 were built.

More power and less weight was needed to keep Pontiacs competitive, so PMD put its lightest, most-powerful car on a diet with a horsepower supplement. Extensive use of aluminum body parts and a special 405-hp 421 V-8 created the 3,600-lb. '62 Super-Duty Catalina. The 421 featured four-bolt mains, forged pistons and twin four-barrel carbs on a special manifold linked to either a B-W T-85 three-speed or a T-10 four-speed. The 421's actual output was over 500 hp.

Lightweight parts—in addition to front fenders, hood and grille sections—included an aluminum back bumper and dealer-optional Plexiglas windows. Many of the S-D Cats used a functional hood scoop.

Pontiac drag racing PR man Jim Wangers found the '62 S-D Catalina to his liking and turned in performances like a 12.38-second quarter-mile at 116.23 mph at Detroit Dragway. In all, 225 of the 421-cid motors were built in '62. They went into 162 cars and 63 served as replacement engines.

PONTIAC

Factory ADP	Wheelbase	Length	Shipping Weight	Base Super Duty V-8	Engine Options	0-to-60 MPH	¼-Mile
Approx. $4,500	120 in.	211.6 in.	Approx. 3,425 lbs.	421 cid/405 hp	426 cid/415 hp; 426 cid/425 hp	(Estimated) 5-second bracket	12.38 seconds @ 116.23 mph

MCFG Says: $70K
He Says: Jerry Heasley, writing in *Car Review* (December '85) said, "The '62 Catalina lightweight sings precious memories from the pre-GTO performance era."
We Says: "Shakes the tarmac like a barrel of maniacal monkeys playing catch with a box of ammonium nitrate."

1963 SUPER-DUTY 421 CATALINA

1963 SUPER-DUTY 421 CATALINA

Pontiac took the '63 S-D 421 further. The heads got higher intake ports, oval exhaust ports, larger valves and 12.5:1 heads. A new McKellar No. 10 solid lifter cam was used with dual valve springs. A transistor ignition was new. A few cars had 13.0:1 compression. Rating for the hottest setup went to 410 hp, but the actual was 540-550 hp. Factory lightweights also lost about 100 lbs. due to Plexiglas windows and aluminum trunks. Also available were aluminum splash pans, radiator core supports, and bumper parts. Some Catalina frames were "Swiss cheesed" by drilling large holes in them. The cars weighed about 3,325 lbs. in ultimate lightweight form.

Arnie "Farmer" Beswick raced one of 15 "Swiss Cheese" cars built before GM's ban on factory racing in January '63. The rare "Swiss Cheese" cars didn't qualify as Super Stockers and ran in F/SX Factory Experimental.

In addition to 77 S-D Catalinas and Grand Prixs, 11 S-D Tempests were constructed. Mickey Thompson dreamed up this combination for A/FX competition. Another pair of A/FX class 421-powered Tempests—a coupe and a wagon—were campaigned by Beswick.

Today, an S-D 421 Catalina factory lightweight should fetch at least $65,000 in the collector's market. A car with a famous racing history that's documented could bring $100,000. A Swiss Cheese car will go even higher.

Factory ADP	Wheelbase	Length	Shipping Weight	SD-421 V-8	Engine Options	0-to-60 MPH	¼-Mile
About $5,000	119 in.	211.9 in.	3,800 lbs.	421 cid/405 hp	None	5.4 seconds	13.9 seconds @ 107 mph

***MCFG* Says:** $65K-$100K

He Says: Writing in *MUSCLECARS* (fall '85), Scott Stevens said "Pontiac's 421 Super-Duty Catalinas were the terror of the drag strip in their day and were simply outrageous when unleashed on the street."

We Says: "Growing up on Staten Island in the '60s, we recall a street-driven "Swiss Cheese" car that was really awesome in the stoplight drags."

1964 GTO

Jerry Heasley

1964 GTO

The first true muscle car, the '64 GTO, was not really a "model." Due to GM's '63 ban on hi-po marketing, Pontiac wasn't supposed to put an engine with more than 300 cubic inches into a mid-sized car. So Pontiac's "young Turk" executives and ad man Jim Wangers snuck the GTO into existence as an extra-cost package for the Tempest LeMans.

In late October '63, the $295 Grand Turismo Omologato option came out for the LeMans coupe, hardtop, and ragtop. It included a 325-hp 389 V-8 with a special cam, special hydraulic lifters and 421-style heads. It had a single Carter four-barrel, specially-valved shocks, a seven-blade fan with a cut-off clutch, dual exhausts, special 6-inch rims, red stripe tires, GTO I.D., twin hood scoops, an engine-turned dash, bucket seats, special springs, and longer rear stabilizers.

Desirable options included a center console, a Hurst shifter, custom exhaust splitters, no-cost whitewalls, special wheel covers, and a 348-hp Tri-Power option with three two-barrel carbs. By the year's end, the GTO was considered a huge sales success. Pontiac records showed production of 7,384 GTO coupes, 18,422 two-door hardtops, and 6,644 ragtops. Wow!

Factory ADP	Wheelbase	Length	Shipping Weight	Base GTO Tri-Power V-8	Engine Options	0-to-60 MPH	¼-Mile
(CPE) $2,852; (HT) $2,963; (RT) $3,081	115 in.	203 in.	(CPE) 3,106 lbs.; (HT) 3,126 lbs.; (RT) 3,360 lbs.	389 cid/348 hp	None	7.7 seconds	15.80 seconds @ 93 mph

MCFG Says: (CPE) $21K; (HT) $23K; (RT) $27K

They Says: "GTO—a car for go" stated the cover of *Car Life* magazine (June '64). Inside it said, "A special sort of Pontiac for a special type of customer—the enthusiast."

We Says: "We think an ad for the GTO summed it up pretty well: 'GTO is kicking up the kind of storm that others just talk up!'"

1965 CATALINA 2+2

1965 CATALINA 2+2

Along with the GTO, the 2+2 further contributed to Pontiac's mid-'60s performance image that has become a modern day legend. Exciting to look at, exciting to drive, and most of all exciting to own, the Catalina 2+2 was in a class by itself among American automobiles.

In its second season, the 2+2 was available in two-door hardtop and ragtop forms. It was possible to add a "Ride and Handling Package" with extra-stiff front and rear springs, H.D. shocks, a front sway bar, aluminum wheels, quicker-ratio power steering, a tach, a gauge package, and a close-ratio four-speed.

The base V-8 was Pontiac's 421 with a 10.5:1 compression ratio and four-barrel carb. Pontiac also offered a 421 HO version with a Tri-Power setup featuring three two-barrel carb. A Catalina 2+2 prepared by Royal Pontiac was another possibility. Featuring a modified 421 HO V-8, such a car was tested by *Car and Driver* against a Ferrari 2+2. With a top speed of 132 mph and a 4-second 0-to-60 time, the Pontiac 2+2 gave the Italian exotic a run for its money.

With a modest list price, the Catalina 2+2 was a tremendous performance bargain.

Factory ADP	Wheelbase	Length	Shipping Weight	Base four-barrel V-8	Optional 421 HO Tri-Power	0-to-60 MPH	¼-Mile
(HT) $3,228; (RT) $3,500	124 in.	215 in.	(HT) 3,748 lbs.; (RT) 3,795 lbs.	421 cid/338 hp	V-8 421 cid/376 hp	(421) 7.2 seconds; (421 HO) 7.2 seconds	(421) 15.8 sec. @ 88 mph; (HO) 15.5 sec. @ 95 mph

MCFG **Says:** (HT) $15,500; (RT) $18,000 (add 10% for 2 + 2 and 30% for 421 HO)

He Says: *Car Life*, April '65, quoted one happy 421 HO owner as saying "I will say this is the finest road machine I have ever driven—foreign cars included. It has comfort, performance and, in my opinion, handling that should satisfy anyone but a road course driver."

We Says: "Definitely the 'sleeping giant' of the muscle car brigade—a great combination of size and comfort with power and performance."

Jerry Heasley

1965 GTO

1965 GTO

In '65, the GTO option was again offered on Tempest LeMans coupes, two-door hardtops, and ragtops. The '65 model had twin stacked headlights and the front fenders had small hoods. While sales of the '64 model had been held back by UAW strikes and an abbreviated model year, this year Pontiac was ready to open the flood gates.

Ad promotions included five huge 26 x 11 1/2-inch full-color photos of the so-called "GeeTO Tiger" in action for 25 cents and a GeeTO Tiger record for 50 cents. The latter captured the sounds made as a test driver put a '65 "Goat" through its paces at the GM Proving Ground.

Pontiac held the price of the GTO option at $296 for '65. It included most of the same items it did in '64, except that a single dummy hood scoop was used in place of two. The 421-style cylinder heads were re-cored to improve the flow of gases.

The GTO ragtop was available for as little as $3,093 and 11,311 were made. The coupe had a base price of $2,787 and 8,319 assemblies. The sales leader was the two-door hardtop that could be had for as little as $2,855. It was the choice of 55,722 buyers.

Factory ADP	Wheelbase	Length	Shipping Weight	Base GTO V-8	Optional GTO Tri-Power V-8	0-to-60 MPH	0-to-100 MPH
(CPE) $2,787; (HT) $2,855; (RT) $3,093	115 in.	206.2 in.	(CPE) 3,478 lbs.; (HT) 3,478 lbs.; (RT) 3,700 lbs.	389 cid/335 hp	389 cid/360 hp	7.2 seconds	(335 hp) 16.1 seconds @ 89 mph

MCFG Says: (CPE) $23K; (HT) $25K; (RT) $29K

He Says: "Pontiac Tempest-GTO order-blank-building produces a winner," said muscle car expert Roger Huntington.

We Says: "We went to buy one once. It was too rusty to take home, but it ran perfect and it sure was fun to take on a road test"

Jerry Heasley

1966 GTO

1966 GTO

The '66 GTO had a smoother, rounder appearance with wide wheel openings and a recessed split grille. There was now a separate GTO series. GTO features included a distinctive mesh grille, bucket seats, a single hood scoop, walnut-grain dash inserts, specific ornamentation, dual exhausts, H.D. suspension, and 7.75 x 14 red-line or white-stripe tires.

Car Life magazine (May '66) asked for and almost got a "standard" GTO to test drive. Pontiac supplied a sport coupe with the 335-hp 389, four-speed gearbox, a console, tinted glass, Rally gauges, a tach, Rally wheels, a radio, a remote rearview mirror and air conditioning. It priced out at $3,589 with a 3.08:1 rear axle and dual reverse-flow exhaust system.

The 389-cid V-8 had a 4.064 x 3.75-inch bore and stroke. It featured a single Carter four-barrel carb, a 10.75:1 compression ratio and hydraulic lifters. Output was rated at 335 hp at 5000 rpm and 431 lbs.-ft. of torque at 3200 rpm. *Car Life's* 3,950-lb. GTO carried 11.6 lbs. per horsepower and delivered outstanding performance. Another publication tested a heavier '66 GTO ragtop with the 360-hp Tri-Power V-8 and didn't do any better, running 0-to-60 mph in the same 6.8 seconds and using 15.5 seconds for the quarter-mile.

Factory ADP	Wheelbase	Length	Shipping Weight	Base V-8	Engine Options	0-to-60 MPH	¼-Mile
(CPE) $2,783; (HT) $2,847; (RT) $3,082	115 in.	207 in.	(CPE) 3,465 lbs.; (HT) 3,465 lbs.; (RT) 3,555 lbs.	389 cid/ 335 hp	389 cid/ 360 hp	(335 hp) 6.8 seconds	(335 hp) 15.4 seconds @ 92.0 mph

MCFG **Says:** (CPE) $20K; (HT) $22K; (RT) $27K (add 20% for Tri-Power)

They Says: *Car Life* (May '66) said, "The GTO always surprises *Car Life* drivers with its ability to perform well."

We Says: "Smooth new styling, added power, and some outstanding new colors made the '66 'Goat' the 'King of the Hill' one more time."

PONTIAC

1967 FIREBIRD 400

1967 FIREBIRD 400

John DeLorean gave the Firebird a strong send-off, noting, "The personal sports car field is probably the most rapidly growing in the industry. With the Firebird we hope to attract new buyers who want to step up to something extra in styling as well as performance in this segment."

The most potent of five new Pontiacs Firebirds, the 400, boasted a 400 V-8 with a four-barrel carb and 10.75:1 compression, and included either a four-speed or THM. The 400 had twin traction bars to allow the use of a single-leaf-spring rear suspension.

Since the Firebird 400 and GTO V-8s had identical specs, enthusiasts wondered why the Firebird had less horsepower. A small steel tab on the linkage between the Rochester carb's primary and secondary barrels limited the second venturi's opening to 90 percent of capacity. Added in the name of corporate policy prohibiting any GM product to have less than 10 lbs. per horsepower, this restriction could be circumvented by removing or bending the tab.

When the Ram Air option was ordered, it added direct-air induction, a longer-duration cam with more overlap, a more efficient cast-iron exhaust manifold and different valve springs with flat metal dampers. Only 65 Firebird 400s were so equipped.

Factory ADP	Wheelbase	Length	Shipping Weight	Base V-8	Engine Options	0-to-60 MPH	¼-Mile
(400) (HT) $3,110; (RT) $3,347 *	108 in.	189 in.	(HT) 2,955 lbs.; (RT) 3,247 lbs.	400 cid/325 hp	(Ram Air) 400 cid/325 hp	6.2 seconds	14.70 seconds @ 98.0 mph

Factory ADP: (400 Ram Air) (HT) $3,372; (RT) $3,347

MCFG Says: (HT) $19K; (RT) $23K (add 15% for 400; add 30% for Ram Air)

They Says: Car Life said, "The Firebird 400 has acceleration in spades" and dubbed this version of the Firebird "the enthusiast's choice."

We Says: "The hot-looking new Firebird came in five zesty flavors and the 400 was the spiciest of them all."

Jerry Heasley

1967 GTO RAM AIR 400

1967 GTO RAM AIR 400

Minor revisions and wide body underscores identified '67 "Goats." The GTO included all LeMans equipment, plus a specific V-8, bucket seats, striping, a walnut dashboard, dual exhausts, H.D. shocks, springs and stabilizer bars and red line or white sidewall tires. Pontiac built 7,029 coupes, 65,176 hardtops and 9,517 ragtops. This year, 29,128 had stick shift.

A new 400 cid V-8 replaced the 389-cid. The base version, used in 64,177 cars, had 10.75:1 compression and a Rochester 4-barrel carb. A 2-barrel "economy" version with an 8.6:1 compression ratio went into 2,967 GTOs. This motor was available at no extra cost in cars with automatic. Another option was the 400 HO, which went in 13,827 cars. The HO engine had a 10.75:1 compression ratio. It developed 360 hp.

Pontiac's RA I V-8 was installed in 751 GTOs (138 with automatic). This V-8 was $263 with either transmission. It had the same basic specs as the HO engine, but different power and torque curves. *Car Life* reported (October '67), "The GTO may be the oldest of the current supercars, but it remains a worthy target for would-be competitors. Performance, brakes and styling continue to set the pace for other manufacturers."

PONTIAC

Factory ADP	Wheelbase	Length	Shipping Weight	Base V-8	Engine Options	0-to-60 MPH	¼-Mile
(Base 400 V-8) (CPE) $2,871; (HT) $2,935; (RT) $3,165	115 in.	207 in.	(CPE) 3,425 lbs.; (HT) 3,430 lbs.; (RT) 3,515 lbs.	400 cid/ 335 hp	400 cid/225 hp; 400 cid/360 hp (Ram Air I)	6.1 seconds	14.5 seconds @ 102 mph

MCFG **Says:** (CPE) $18K; (HT) $21K; (RT) $24K (add 10% for Ram Air I)

They Says: *Car Life* drove the 400-cid 360-hp GTO and raved, "Ram Air GTO! Hail to the king. The super supercar!"

We Says: "This is not your father's Pontiac," was the message of the GTO, and it came through loud and clear throughout America.

1968 GTO

Jerry Heasley

1968 GTO

A long hood/short deck format highlighted a more streamlined GTO on a shorter wheelbase. GTOs featured dual exhaust, a three-speed with a Hurst shifter, H.D. underpinnings, red line tires, bucket or notchback-bench seats, a cigar lighter, carpeting, disappearing windshield wipers, and a 350-hp 400 V-8. New was the highly touted Endura front bumper, GTO emblems, distinctive taillights, and hood scoops.

Pontiac dropped the post-coupe style. Production came to 77,704 hardtops and 9,980 ragtops. Although the Endura bumper was a hit, those who didn't like it could get the '68 Tempest chrome bumper as a delete option. Engine choices for '68 were the same as in '67.

The '67 GTO production figures included: 2,841 hardtops and 432 ragtops with the 400-cid 255-hp two-barrel V-8 and automatic; 39,215 hardtops and 5,091 ragtops with the 400-cid 335-hp four-barrel V-8 and automatic; 25,371 hardtops and 3,116 ragtops with the 400-cid 335-hp four-barrel V-8 and manual transmission; 3,140 hardtops and 461 ragtops with the 360-hp 400 HO V-8 and automatic; 6,197 hardtops and 766 ragtops with the 360-hp 400 HO V-8 and stick shift; 183 hardtops and 22 ragtops with the Ram Air 400 V-8 and automatic; and 757 hardtops and 92 ragtops with the Ram Air 400 V-8 and a stick shift.

Motor Trend named the '68 GTO "Car of the Year."

Factory ADP	Wheelbase	Length	Shipping Weight	Base V-8	Engine Options	0-to-60 MPH	¼-Mile
(base 400 V-8) (HT) $3,101; (RT) $3,996	112 in.	189 in.	(HT) 3,506 lbs.; (RT) 3,590 lbs.	400 cid/ 330 hp	400 cid/265 hp; 400 cid/350 hp; 400 cid RA/360 hp; 400 cid RA/366 hp	(360 hp) 6.5 seconds	(360 hp) 14.45 seconds @ 98.2 mph

MCFG Says: (HT) $20K; (RT) $24K (add 25% for RA I; add 40% for RA II)

They Says: *Car Life* raved, "If press reaction to the '68 lineup is any indication, Pontiac's third place in sales is in no jeopardy for another year."

We Says: "The king of Woodward Avenue was back on the throne for another 12 months."

Jerry Heasley

1969 GTO "JUDGE"

1969 GTO "JUDGE"

"Born Great" was the slogan used for the '69 "Judge." *Car and Driver* called it an "econo racer"—a well-loaded muscle car priced to give you a lot for your money. It was a machine that you could take drag racing pretty much "as is"—and win.

Pontiac released its "The Judge" option on December 19, 1968. It came only in bright orange with tri-color striping, but was later offered in the full range of GTO colors. Standard features of the package included a black-out grille, Rally II wheels (less trim rings), functional hood scoops, "The Judge" front fender decals, and "Ram Air" decals on the hood scoops. At the rear was a 60-inch-wide "floating" airfoil with a "The Judge" decal on the upper right-hand surface.

The standard engine was the 366-hp 400 with Ram Air III linked to a three-speed with a Hurst T-handle shifter and a 3.55:1 rear axle. A total of 8,491 GTOs *and* Judges were sold with this motor and only 362 of them were ragtops. The 400-cid 370-hp Ram Air IV engine was installed in 759 cars in the same two lines and 59 of these were ragtops.

"The Judge" option was added to 6,725 GTO hardtops and only 108 GTO ragtops. The editors of *Car Life* whipped a Judge through the quarter-mile at 14.45 seconds and 97.8 mph. *Supercars Annual* covered the same distance in a Judge with THM transmission and racked up a 13.99 seconds at 107 mph run!

Factory ADP	Wheelbase	Length	Shipping Weight	Base V-8	Engine Options	0-to-60 MPH	¼-Mile
(HT) $3,161; (RT) $4,212	112 in.	201.5 in.	(HT) 3,080 lbs.; (RT) 3,553 lbs.	400 cid/366 hp (RAIII)	400 cid/370 hp (RAIV)	6.2 seconds	14.45 seconds @ 97.80 mph

MCFG Says: (HT) $30.8K; (RT) $50.4K (add 20% for RAIV)

They Says: *Car Life* said, "Pontiac invented the supercar for this generation … and The Judge is one of the best."

We Says: "Any car inspired by 'Here Come 'de Judge' skits on Rowan & Martin's 'Laugh In' was sure to be a bit crazy, but the GTO Judge was crazy fast."

1970-71 GT-37

1970-71 GT-37

An economy wave swept the auto industry in '70, with cheap sixes seeing renewed popularity. PMD—with its '60s performance image—was a little out of step with the new trend that inspired Vegas, Mavericks, and Dusters. When Plymouth knocked PMD out of third in sales, PMD did a midyear de-contenting of its Tempest hardtop to slash its price. The "El Cheapo" T-37 was aimed at entry-level buyers. While the "37" in the designation was based on GM's two-door hardtop code, PMD soon bent the "rules" and released a T-37 coupe, as well as the hardtop. With a $2,683 base price tag, the T-37 generated 20,883 sales in half a year.

Not long after the T-37 appeared, someone decided to issue a sporty version. To create this budget muscle car, the plain-looking coupe was dressed up with GTO extras and called the GT-37. The new model was a stripped-down muscle car with a V-8, and the fastest production car that PMD built in '70 turned out to be the GT-37 coupe with the Ram Air III engine.

The hottest GT-37 engine was the '70 1/2 stick-shift 400 cid V-8. This was the Ram Air III V-8 without a Ram Air hood and dual-snorkel air cleaner. It did have bigger Ram Air III valves. Pontiac built 1,419 of the '70 1/2 GT-37 coupes.

Factory ATP	Wheelbase	Length	Shipping Weight	Base V-8	Engine Options	0-to-60 MPH	¼-Mile
$4,332	112 in.	202.8 in.	3,675 lbs.	350 cid/250 hp	400 cid/265 hp; 400 cid/300 hp	(400/300) 7.2 seconds	(400/300) 14.40 seconds @ 97.5 mph

MCFG Says: $16K

He Says: In *Hot Rod* magazine, Steve Kelly wrote, "We call it high-performance on a low-test diet."

We Says: The great guru of GT-37 groupies, John Sawruk, described the GT-37 as a "lightweight car that was great for performance, but not in the up-level image of Pontiac."

1970 GTO

1970 GTO

Prominent styling changes on the '70 GTO included smaller, split oval grilles, dual rectangular headlight housings (with round lenses), and creased body sides. The hood had twin air scoops and a GTO nameplate was seen on the left-hand grille. The rear end also sported flared fenders and the exhaust pipes exited through a valance panel below the rear bumper. The "Goat" featured a total Endura nosepiece without a metal bumper and had cleaner styling than other Tempests.

GTO engines had innovations including special spherical-wedge cylinder heads and a computer-perfected cam design. 366-hp Ram Air III V-8s were used in 1,302 hardtops and 114 ragtops with stick shift, and 3,054 hardtops and 174 ragtops with THM. 370-hp Ram Air IV engines were used in 140 hardtops and 13 ragtops with stick and 627 hardtops and 24 ragtops with THM. Also available in non-Judges was a 455-cid 360-hp V-8. This engine was installed in 2,227 stick cars (241 ragtops) and 1,919 cars with THM (including 158 ragtops).

Car Life found the RA 400 GTO faster than the 455-powered GTO.

Factory ADP	Wheelbase	Length	Shipping Weight	400 V-8	455 V-8	0-to-60 MPH	¼-Mile
(Car Life Test Cars) (400 RA) $5,057; (455) $5,251	112 in.	202.9 in.	(400 RA) 4,230 lbs.; (455) 4,455 lbs.	400 cid/350 hp 400 RA V-8 (RA III) 400 cid/366 hp; (RA IV) 400 cid/370 hp	455 cid/ 360 hp	(400 cid/336 hp) 6.0 seconds; (455 cid /360 hp) 6.6 seconds	(400/366 hp) 14.6 seconds @ 99.5 mph; (455/360 hp) 14.76 seconds @ 95.94 mph

MCFG Says: (HT) $23K; (RT) $27K

They Says: Car Life said, "It got to the end of the drag strip first and it was going faster when it arrived, so the Ram Air 400 does have more power than the 455."

We Says: "The 455 goes fast and it's docile and domesticated enough to be a daily driver, but the Ram Air 400 is the engine to take racing."

1970 GTO "JUDGE"

Jerry Heasley

1970 GTO "JUDGE"

"The Judge" option was available for '71 GTOs. This 332-WT1 accessory group included a Ram Air V-8, Rally II wheels (less trim rings), G70-14 tires, a T-handle-shifted stick shift, a rear deck lid airfoil, and specific side stripes, "The Judge" decals, stripes and a black-textured grille.

Contrary to some reports, GTO Judges were not cheaper than base models—unless the base models had all of the same accessories installed individually. The base price of a hardtop with "Judge" equipment was about $3,604 and there may have been some mandatory options that added a little more. Judge ragtop prices started at about $3,829.

Those who wanted to get their Judge with a more powerful Ram Air IV engine had to shell out $558 extra. In addition, Ram Air IV cars could only be built with either a three-speed THM or a four-speed. Pontiac engine production records show that 42 GTO hardtops and 288 ragtops were built with Ram Air (a.k.a. Ram Air III) V-8s The Ram Air IV V-8 was used in 767 hardtops and 37 ragtops. (These figures are for plain GTOs and Judges lumped together.) Pontiac's base '70 GTO "The Judge" hardtop with the 350-hp 400 was good for 0-to-60 mph in 6.6 seconds. It did the quarter-mile in 14.6 seconds.

Factory ATP	Wheelbase	Length	Shipping Weight	Base Judge V-8	Optional Judge V-8	0-to-60 MPH	¼-Mile
(hardtop) $4,748	112 in.	202.9 in.	(hardtop) 3,691 lbs.	(RA III) 400 cid/366 hp	(RA IV) 400 cid/370 hp	(RA IV) 5.1 seconds	(RA IV) 13.9 seconds @ 107 mph

MCFG Says: (HT) $32.2K; (RT) $37.8K (add 25% for RA IV)
Note: Base price for the Judge ragtop was $3,829.
They Says: *Road Test* (March '70) said, "It's a fun car built by people who had a good idea and weren't afraid to carry it out."
We Says: "Pontiac advertised that the Judge was 'born great.' John DeLorean and Jim Wangers were there to see that the delivery went without complications."

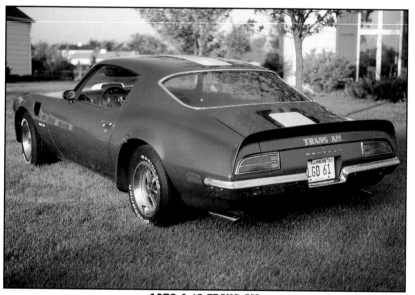

1970 1/2 TRANS AM

1970 1/2 TRANS AM

The introduction of '70 Firebirds was delayed until the winter of '70. When they appeared they had a sleek new, half-inch-longer body shell on the same wheelbase. There were now four separate Firebird series called Firebird, Espirit, Formula 400, and T/A. A Maserati-like, semi-fastback body made the second-generation T/A a sophisticated muscle car.

The T/A suspension was upgraded. The base V-8 was the Ram Air 400 connected to a wide-ratio four-speed with a Hurst shifter. Only coupes were available. In addition to white paint with blue stripes, Pontiac now offered Lucerne Blue T/As with white stripes. Standard equipment included a front air dam, front and rear spoilers, a shaker hood, side air extractors, a rear spoiler, aerodynamic mirrors, 1 1/4-inch front and 7/8-inch rear stabilizer bars, H.D. shocks and springs, an engine-turned aluminum instrument panel with a Rally gauge cluster, concealed wipers, bucket seats, carpets, all-vinyl upholstery, power brakes and steering, and 15-inch Rally II wheels.

A higher 10.5:1 compression ratio gave the base "Ram Air III" V-8 more hp. This engine went into 1,339 cars with automatic and 1,769 with stick. In addition to the standard four-speed, THM (also with a floor shifter) was a no-cost extra. Fifty-nine automatics and 29 sticks were built with the Ram Air IV option.

Factory ATP	Wheelbase	Length	Shipping Weight	Base V-8	Optional V-8	0-to-60 MPH	1/4-Mile
$4,305	108 in.	191.6 in.	3,550 lbs.	400 cid/345 hp (RA III)	400 cid/370 hp (RA IV)	(RA IV) 5.7 seconds	(RA IV) 14.1 seconds @ 103.2 mph

MCFG **Says:** $20K (add 10% for four-speed; add 25% for RA IV)

They Says: *Road Test* (March '70) said, "The standard Trans Am engine transforms the Firebird into a true muscle car."

We Says: "The '70 T/A is one of our favorite muscle cars and we'd buy one if the prices didn't keep climbing out of our range every time we get close."

1971 GTO "JUDGE"

Jerry Heasley

1971 GTO "JUDGE"

The '71 "Goat" was based on the LeMans Sport, which included all LeMans equipment, plus dual horns, pedal trim plates, a lamp package, carpeted lower door panels, a custom cushion steering wheel, and wheel opening moldings. Moving up to the GTO got buyers an engine-turned aluminum instrument panel, an exclusive Endura front end treatment, a special scooped hood, a 300-hp 400 V-8 with a 4-barrel carb, a H.D. 3-speed with floor shift, dual exhausts, a power-flex fan, a 1 1/8-inch front stabilizer bar, a beefed-up rear stabilizer, high-rate shock absorbers and springs, G70-14 blackwall tires and GTO badges.

The $395 Judge option for the hardtop and ragtop added the 455 HO four-barrel V-8, Rally II wheels less trim rings, a hood air inlet, a T-handle shifter (with stick shift), a rear deck lid airfoil, specific body side stripes, "Judge" decals, Ram Air decals, and a black texture in the grille.

Adding the option price to the base price of the hardtop gives you a total of $3,840 for "The Judge" of that body style. The very rare ragtop version (only 17 1971 GTO Judge ragtops were actually built) went out the door for as little as $4,070 when no extras were added in.

PONTIAC

Factory ADP	Wheelbase	Length	Shipping Weight	Base V-8	Engine Options	0-to-60 MPH	¼-Mile
(Judge) (HT) $3,840; (RT) $4,070	112 in.	203.3 in.	(HT) 3,446 lbs.; (RT) 3,676 lbs.	400 cid/ 300 hp	455 cid/ 335 hp	N/A	(400 cid/300 hp) 14.4 seconds @ 98 mph

MCFG Says: (HT) $21K; (RT) $29K (add 40% for Judge option)

He Says: Paul Zazarine (*Musclecar Review* November '90) said, "This 455 HO Judge can still deal out some judicial action on the street."

We Says: "Street justice is rarely as much fun to experience as it is in a '71 GTO Judge 455."

Jerry Heasley

1971 TRANS AM

1971 TRANS AM

1971 F-cars were a near direct carryover of the late-arriving '70 1/2 models. The big change between the two years was new high-back bucket seats in '71s. The Firebird, Espirit, and Formula had new front fender air extractors and a few detail changes, but the '70 and '71 T/As looked virtually identical, except for the seats. Only 2,116 T/As were made.

Standard equipment in T/As included all mandatory safety features, vinyl bucket seats, Rally gauges, a clock, a tach, a Formula steering wheel, an Endura front bumper, body-color mirrors, honeycomb wheels, functional front fender air extractors, a rear deck lid spoiler, a black textured grille with bright moldings, front and rear wheel opening flares, concealed wipers, I.D. badges, performance dual exhausts, a special air cleaner, a rear-facing cold-air hood intake with throttle control, a Power Flex fan, dual horns, front power disc brakes and rear drum brakes, F60-15 RWL tires, a close-rato four-speed with floor shift, and a big 455 HO four-barrel V-8.

With a change to lower compression ratios in '71 (due to leaded gas), PMD found it prudent to substitute the 455 V-8 for the 400. The HO version had a 4.15 x 4.21-inch bore and stroke and used a single four-barrel carb. T/A buyers who preferred an automatic could substitute a three-speed THM for the Hurst-shifted close-ratio four-speed at no charge.

Factory ADP	Wheelbase	Length	Shipping Weight	Base V-8	Engine Options	0-to-60 MPH	¼-Mile
$4,590	108 in.	191.6 in.	3,578 lbs.	455 cid/335 hp	None	5.92 seconds	13.90 seconds @ 103 mph

MCFG Says: $25K

He Says: Paul Zazarine, writing in *Car Review* (March '86) said, "It probably wouldn't be a good idea to drive it to next week's meeting of the Sierra Club. They still don't like Trans Ams."

We Says: "Looks like a Maserati with a star-spangled paint job and a big-block made-in-the-U.S.A. engine under the hood."

1973 TRANS AM SD 455

Jerry Heasley

1973 TRANS AM SD 455

'73 Firebirds had new colors, redesigned interiors, new hubcaps and more options. The bumpers were redesigned to meet new federal standards. This made the cars slightly longer, which resulted in the new grille being slightly less recessed. The grille had an egg-crate pattern.

Like other T/As that came before it, the '73 had special air dams, spoilers, flares and scoops. The scoops were now sealed and non-functional. A new feature was a large hood decal showing the American Indian Firebird that the car was named for. Enthusiasts dubbed this icon the "screaming chicken." On '73 models, the bird was always black, but the background color varied. It was orange on red cars, black on white cars and light green on Brewster Green cars.

The base engine used in the T/A was a 455-cid V-8 with a single four-barrel carb and 8.0:1 compression ratio that produced 250 hp. Pontiac built 4,550 cars with this engine and 1,420 of them had a stick shift. For real muscle, buyers could add a SD 455 V-8 derived from Pontiac's racing experiences. The SD 455 featured a special block with reinforced webbing, large forged-steel connecting rods, special aluminum pistons, an H.D. oiling system, a high-lift camshaft, four-bolt main bearing caps, a special intake manifold, a dual exhaust system and upgraded valve train components. It had an 8.4:1 compression ratio and cranked out 310 hp.

Factory ADP	Wheelbase	Length	Shipping Weight	Base V-8	Engine Options	0-to-60 MPH	¼-Mile
$4,879	108 in.	192.1 in.	3,504 lbs.	455 cid/310 hp	None	7.3 seconds	13.54 seconds @ 104.29 mph

MCFG Says: $35K

He Says: Writing in *Musclecar Review*, Paul Zazarine said, "When every other car maker had forgotten about muscle cars, Pontiac introduced the '73 455 Super-Duty Trans Am."

We Says: "The T/A had all the visual bells and whistles you needed to feel like a sedan racer—the SD 455 simply added a little sizzle below the scooped hood."

Jerry Heasley

1974 TRANS AM SD 455

1974 TRANS AM SD 455

Extensive front-end styling revisions and an improvement in sales made headlines in the Firebird niche of the American muscle car marketplace in '74. Firebird, Espirit, Formula, and T/A models were carried over. The SD 455 remained in limited availability for the Formula and T/As.

The new John Schinella-designed nose introduced an integrated "soft" bumper treatment, which was repeated at the rear. The front carried a new "shovel nose" grille cap with an "electric shaver" grille made up of slanting, vertical blades. Black rubber bumper-face bars were featured. An air-scoop front valance contributed to a more massive look.

T/As had a Formula steering wheel, Rally gauges, clock, tach, swirl-finish dash trim, rear deck spoiler, power steering, power front disc/rear drum brakes, limited-slip differential, wheel opening air deflectors, front fender air extractors, dual exhausts with chrome extensions, Rally II wheels with trim rings, H.D. suspension, dual Sport mirrors, F60-15 RWL tires, a four-speed, and a 225-hp 400 V-8. The SD 455 V-8 ($578 extra) was installed in 212 T/As with four-speeds and 731 with automatic. Although relatively rare, the engine was popular with the editors of enthusiast magazines, who said it made the T/A the hottest car of the year and slightly faster than the 'Vette!

PONTIAC

Factory ADP	Wheelbase	Length	Shipping Weight	Super-Duty V-8	Engine Options	0-to-60 MPH	¼-Mile
$4,446	108 in.	196 in.	3,655 lbs.	455 cid/290 hp	None	5.9 seconds	13.54 seconds @ 104 mph

MCFG Says: $15.5k (add 40% for SD 455)

He Says: Jerry Heasley, writing in *Car Review* (November '85) said, "Muscle car collector Dan Werner says the T/As through '74 with the big HO and SD engines kept the muscle car era going for a few more years."

We Says: "It was all over but the church service, but no one told Pontiac it didn't have a prayer of keeping the hot-as-a-pistol SD 455 around much longer."

1989 1/2 TRANS AM INDY 500 PACE CAR

1989 1/2 TRANS AM INDY 500 PACE CAR

To commemorate the 20th anniversary of the first T/A, a special series of 1,500 20th Anniversary T/As was produced. These cars were above the level of the GTA model and were really the "ultimate" T/As of this year.

Power was provided by a V-6 with a Garrett T3 turbocharger and air-to-air intercooler. It was coupled to a four-speed automatic and limited-slip axle. All 20th Anniversary T/As were white with camel interiors. The GTA emblem on the nose was changed to a special "20th Anniversary" insignia. A similar cloisonné emblem could be found on the sail panels. "Turbo Trans Am" emblems on the front fenders replaced the standard GTA script in the same location. Also included with this model was a larger, baffled, competition-type 18-gallon fuel tank, four-wheel power disc brakes, 16-inch gold-finished lightweight diamond-spoke aluminum wheels, stainless-steel exhaust splitters, analog gauges with turbo boost gauge, unique contoured rear seats. Each of these cars came with a complete set of Official Indianapolis 500 Pace Car decals for the doors and windshield. These could be owner or dealer installed.

Pontiac originally announced that it would build 1,500 20th Anniversary Pace Cars as part of the total run of Firebirds. Actually, 1,550 turbo V-6 models were made, including two ragtops created by PAS, Inc. (the firm that built the cars) by adding Camaro parts. T-tops were used on 1,515 of the cars and 1,350 had leather interiors.

Factory ADP	Wheelbase	Length	Shipping Weight	Base V-8	Engine Options	0-to-60 MPH	¼-Mile
$32,000	101 in.	188 in.	3,346 lbs.	231 cid/250 hp	None	5.3 seconds	13.91 seconds @ 90 mph

MCFG Says: $19K

They Says: "It might be a good idea to get in the Turbo Trans Am line now," *Road & Track* recommended in its January '89 issue.

We Says: "We wrangled a brief spin in one of the actual Indy Pace Cars, strobes and all, and it went like a V-6 jet."

Jerry Heasley

1994 25TH ANNIVERSARY T/A

1994 25TH ANNIVERSARY T/A

The 25th Anniversary T/A arrived on January 7, 1989. At first it was only announced for the T/A GT coupe. A month later, at the Chicago Auto Show, a 25th Anniversary T/A GT ragtop was put on display. The theme was obviously taken from the original '69 1/2 T/A, since the car's Bright White exterior was decorated with a Bright Blue center stripe. There were also anniversary logos, door badges, special 16-inch white alloy wheels, white Prado leather seating surfaces with blue embroidered logos, and a special commemorative portfolio.

The price for all of this was only $995. Of course you had to come up with the base price $22,309 for the GT coupe or $27,279 for the GT ragtop.

Despite its 3,668-lb. curb weight and automatic transmission, the 25th Anniversary ragtop was a good performer.

While certainly not as rare as the first T/A ragtop (only eight of those were made), the '94 ragtop is certainly a keeper. Its production was low. Seeing that it is part of a set of special editions, its collector value is fairly high.

Factory ADP	Wheelbase	Length	Shipping Weight	Base V-8	Engine Options	0-to-60 MPH	¼-Mile
(CPE) $23,304; (RT) $28,274	101.1 in.	195.6 in.	(CPE) 3,478 lbs.; (RT) 3,588 lbs.	350 cid/275 hp	None	6.1 seconds	14.40 seconds @ 99 mph

MCFG **Says:** (CPE) $14.5K; (RT) $15.5K (add 10% for 25th Anniversary)

They Says: "The result is a white-on-white stunner of a car, with the highest profile in traffic this side of a presidential motorcade," said *Car and Driver*.

We Says: "We'll go along with the Pontiac ad that said this beauty had 'the power to change minds.'"

1996 FORMULA WS6 RAM AIR

1996 FORMULA WS6 RAM AIR

The '96 Formula shared the new WS6 Ram Air performance-and-handling package with T/As. The business end of the WS6 was under the hood, where the LT1 V-8 featured sequential-port fuel injection and an Opti-Spark ignition system. While providing '60s-like acceleration, it ran smoothly on 91-octane.

The '96 Formula WS6 came with fat 17-inch Goodyear Eagle GS-C tires. The front springs were increased from the normal stiffness. Rear-spring stiffness was variable from equal to more than a normal Firebird. WS6 suspension upgrades included rear sway bars, higher-rate front-and-rear springs, unique shocks, stiffer tranny mounts, and stiffer Panhard-bar bushings.

The '96 Formula's V-8 was OBD II compliant, meaning that it met stage II on-board-diagnostic system regulations. OBD II monitored the EGR valve, oxygen sensor and crankshaft- and camshaft-position sensors to detect misfiring. Also new for the year was a theft-deterrent system with a personal security key fob available, a new Taupe interior, optional steering-wheel-mounted radio controls for all but the W51 sound system, a new Red-Orange Metallic body color, zinc brake-corrosion protection on all models, and other upgrades.

PONTIAC

Factory ADP	Wheelbase	Length	Shipping Weight	Base V-8	WS6 V-8	0-to-60 MPH	¼-Mile
(base Formula V-8) (CPE) $19,464; (RT) $23,135	101.1 in.	195.6 in.	(CPE) 3,345 lbs.; (RT) 3,610 lbs.	350 cid/285 hp	350 cid/ 305 hp	4.9 seconds	13.5 seconds @ 103.5 mph

MCFG Says: (CPE) $12K; (RT) $14.5K (add 20% for WS6)

They Says: Pontiac said that the WS6 "bridged the gap between the raw power of the Muscle Car Era and today's sophisticated performance and safety technology."

We Says: "Collectors are latching on to these hairy-looking, twin-nostril jobs as they start showing up in the used-car market and now is the time to buy ahead of the curve."

ABBREVIATIONS & MUSCLE CAR TERMS

AA/S	drag racing class
ABS	antilock braking system
Ad	advertisement
ADP	As Delivered Price
AFB	type of carburetor
A-frame	A-shaped front suspension part
AHRA	American Hot Road Association
Air Grabber	functional Mopar hood scoop
AMC	American Motors Corp.
Amp	ampere
AMX	AMC model
ASC	Automobile Specialty Co.
ATP	As Tested Price
Autolite	Ford parts branch
BBS	type of plastic used for wheels
B-W	Borg-Warner
Bee-Liever	Mopar hi-po option
B/FX	drag racing class
Big-block	large displacement engine
Borla	performance exhaust system maker
Buffs	enthusiasts
CAFÉ	Corporate Average Fuel Economy
Caliente	Mercury Comet with Mexican name
Cam	camshaft
Can-Am	type of racing
Carb	carburetor
Cfm	cubic feet per minute
Chevy	Chevrolet
CHP	California Highway Patrol
CID	cubic-inch displacement
CJ	Cobra-Jet
C/L	Car Life magazine
COPO	Central Office Production Order
Cpe	coupe
Cruise-O-Matic	Ford automatic tranny
CS	California Special
'Cuda	hi-po Barracuda
Dana	axle maker
Discs	disc brakes
DOHC	double overhead camshafts
Drag	drag race
Dyno	engine dynometer
Dyno Don	famous drag racer
Dzuz	type of automotive fastener
Econo	inexpensive
Euro	European-like
Fastback	streamlined car
FB	fastback
FoMoCo	Ford Motor Company
Four (by itself)	four-cylinder
Lbs.-ft.	pounds-feet
Funnycar	type of drag racer

Gearbox	transmission
GeeTO	GTO (Pontiac)
GM	General Motors
GN	Grand National
GT	grand touring (Ford and others)
GTA	grand touring – automatic (Ford)
GTO	Gran Turismo Omologato
GTS	GT Sport (Dodge Dart model)
GS	Gran Sport
GSX	Buick model
H.D.	heavy-duty
Header	smooth-flowing exhaust manifold
Hemi	type of engine or car with it
Hertz	rent-a-car company
Hi-po	high-performance
Hi-Tech	high-technology; leading edge
HO	high-output
Holley	carburetor maker
Holman & Moody	NASCAR team (Fords)
Hop-up	modify for speed
HP	horsepower
HRM	Hot Rod Magazine
HT	hardtop
Hurst	hi-po equipment maker; shifters especially
Hydra-Matic	GM automatic transmission
I.D.	identification
Intake	intake manifold
Intro'ed	introduced
IMSA	International Motor Sports Association
IROC	International Race of Champions
Jav	Javelin
J.C. Whitney	aftermarket parts cataloger
K	thousands
King Kong	slang for big or powerful
K & N	performance air filter maker
Koni	shock absorber maker
KR	King of the Road (Shelby Mustang)
Kruncher	Mopar hi-po option
L88	hi-po Chevy V-8
LBJ	President Lyndon B. Johnson
LeMans	French race or Pontiac model
LS1	hi-po Chevy V-8
LS5	hi-po Chevy V-8
LS6	hi-po Chevy V-8
LT1	hi-po Chevy V-8
Mach 1	hot Mustang
Mags	mag wheels
Max Wedge	hot Dodge or Plymouth
MCFG	Muscle Car Field Guide
Merc-O-Matic	Mercury automatic tranny
Mill	engine
Mini	small

Mopar	Motor Parts (Chrysler)
"mucho"	slang for lots
MPG	miles per gallon
MPH	mile per hour
MSRP	manufacturer suggested retail price
MT	Motor Trend
N/A	not available
Nailhead	type of Buick V-8
NASCAR	National Association for Stock Car Automobile Racing
NHP	net horsepower
NHRA	National Hot Rod Assoc.
Notchback	model with a regular trunk
Olds	the dearly departed Oldsmobile
Opti-Spark	a hot-spark ignition system
"Park Bench"	slang for plain bench-type seat
PMD	Pontiac Motor Division
Poncho	Pontiac
Ponies	horsepower
Posi	Positraction locking differential
Positraction	GM locking differential
Power-Flex	plastic cooling fan that flexes
Psi	pressure per square inch
Quadrajet	type of carburetor
Quadra-Shocks	four-shock suspension set up

RA III	Ram Air III (Pontiac)
RA IV	Ram Air IV (Pontiac)
Ragtop	convertible
Red line	"redwall" tires instead of whitewalls
Regs	regulations
Retro	old-fashioned design
Rev	engine rpms
Rim-blow	squeeze the steering wheel, the horn blows
Rpm	revolutions per minute
RPO	Regular Production Order
Rock Crusher	bullet-proof type of tranny from GM
Royal Pontiac	a hi-po dealer in Michigan; not the king's GTO
RS	Rally Sport
RT	ragtop (convertible)
R/T	Dodge model name (Road/Track)
RWL	raised white letter
Scat Pack	Mopar muscle
SCCA	Sports Car Club of America
SCJ	Super Cobra-Jet (FoMoCo)
SC/Rambler	AMC model
S-D	Super-Duty Pontiac
SE	Special Edition (Dodge model)
SelectShift	Ford's have-it-both-ways tranny
Six-Pack	triple 2-barrel carbs (Mopar)
Spec	Specifications
Speedo	Speedometer

Sohc	single overhead camshaft
Sox & Martin	drag racing team (Mopar)
SS	Super Sport
SS/B	Super Stock drag racing class
S/S	Super Stock
Stang	Mustang
Stick	manual tranny (stick shift)
Supercar	same as muscle car
Super Trak Pak	performance option (Mopar)
Sure-Grip	type of locking differential
SVO	Special Vehicle Operations (Ford)
SVT	Special Vehicle Team (Ford)
SW	Stewart-Warner
Swiss cheese	car with holes drilled in frame for racing
Synchro	gearbox with synchronizers
T-Bolt	Fairlane-based drag car
T-10	type of B-W 4-speed transmission
T/A	Trans Am (Dodge or slang for Pontiac)
Tach	tachometer
THM	Turbo-Hydra-Matic
TorqueFlite	Mopar tranny
TPI	tuned port Injection
Tuner	modern modified car—often imported

Turbo	turbocharged
Turbo-Hydra-Matic	GM automatic transmission
Traction-Lok	locking differential transmission
Tranny	transmission
Trans Am	Pontiac Firebird model
Trans-Am	type of racing
Tri-Power	triple two-barrel carbs (usually GM)
Tri-Y	exotic exhaust system
UAW	United Auto Workers
USA	good old United States of
USAC	U. S. Automobile Club
V-8	type of engine
V-10	type of engine
VP	vice president
Vette	Corvette
W-30, W-31	Olds hi-po packages
WCFB	type of carburetor
WS6	Pontiac hi-po engine
XR-7	Mercury Cougar performance model
Yenko	Chevy dealer Don Yenko
Z11	hi-po Chevy
Z06	hi-po Vette
Z28	hi-po Camaro ("Z/28" in 1967-1969)
2+2	four-seat sports car

MUSCLE CAR CLUBS AND ORGANIZATIONS

GENERAL

National Muscle Car Association
3404 Democrat Road
Memphis, TN 38118

AMC

Classic AMX Club International
7963 Depew St.
Arvada, CO 8003-2527

National American Motors Drivers & Racers
Assoc.
PO Box 987
Twin Lakes, WI 53181-0987

BUICK

Buick GS Club of America
625 Pine Point Circle
Valdosta, GA 31602

CHEVROLET

American Chevelle Enthusiasts
4636 Lebanon Piike
Suite 195
Nashville, TN 37076-1316

International Camaro Club
2001 Pittston Ave.
Scranton, PA 18505

National Council of Corvette Clubs
3701 S. 92nd Street
Milwaukee, WI 53228-1611

National Corvette Owners Association
900 S. Washington Street G-13
Falls Church, VA 22046

National Chevelle Owners Association
7343-J Friendly Ave.
Greensboro, NC 27410

National Nostalgic Nova
PO Box 2344
York, PA 17405

FORD

Fairlane Club of America
340 Clicktown Road
Church Hill, TN 37642-6622

Ford Galaxie Club of America
PO Box 178
Hollister, MO 65672

Mustang Club of America
3588 Highway 138 St. 365
Stockbridge, GA 30281

Mustang Owners Club International
2720 Tennessee NE
Albuquerque, NM 87110

Shelby American Automobile Club
PO Box 788
Sharon, CT 06069

Shelby Owners of America
PO Drawer 1429
Great Bend, KS 67530

MERCURY
Cougar Club of America
1637 Skyline Drive
Norfolk, VA 23518-4327

International Mercury Owners Association
6445 West Grand Avenue
Chicago, IL 60707-3410

MOPAR
Daytona-Superbird Auto Club
13717 W. Green Meadow Drive
New Berlin, WI 53151

Dodge Charger National Registry
PO Box 184
Greenbay, VA 23942

OLDSMOBILE
Hurst/Olds Club of America
455 131st Avenue
Wayland, MI 49348

PLYMOUTH
Plymouth Owners Club, Inc.
PO Box 416
Cavalier, ND 58220

PONTIAC
GTO Association of America
5829 Stroebel Road
Saginaw, MI 48609-5249

National Firebird & Trans Am Club
PO Box 11238
Chicago, IL 60611

Pontiac Oakland Club International (POCI)
PO Box 9569
Bradenton, FL 34205

The Judge GTO International
114 Prince George Drive
Hampton, VA 23669-3604

Royal Pontiac Club of America
PO Box 252402
West Bloomfield, MI 48325

1971 DODGE CHALLENGER R/T

Jerry Heasley

The latest and greatest Muscle Cars

Standard Catalog of® American Muscle Cars 1973-Present

by John Gunnell
Gain key production data — including VIN decoding information, pricing and performance data for the hottest models of muscle cars of the last 30 years. Plus, 300+ stellar color photos.
Softcover • 8-1/4 x 10-7/8 • 304 pages
300+ color photos
Item# Z0754 • $27.99

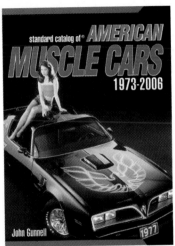

Order directly from the publisher at **www.krausebooks.com**

Krause Publications, Offer **AUB9**
P.O. Box 5009
Iola, WI 54945-5009
www.krausebooks.com

Call 800-258-0929 M-F 8 a.m. - 5 p.m. to order direct from the publisher, or shop booksellers nationwide and select coin shops.

Please reference offer **AUB9** with all direct-to-publisher orders

Tune up your car connections at www.oldcarsweekly.com

Return to the Golden Era of Muscle Cars

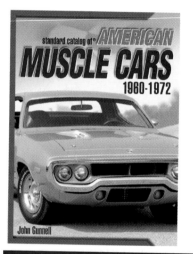

Standard Catalog of® American Muscle Cars 1960-1972

by John Gunnell
This one-stop shop for muscle car details features every model of muscle car produced in the hey-day of high performance; with more than 300 color photos, and production data.
Softcover • 8-¼ x 10-7/8 • 304 pages
300+ color photos
Item# Z0376 • $27.99

Order directly from the publisher at **www.krausebooks.com**

Krause Publications, Offer **AUB9**
P.O. Box 5009
Iola, WI 54945-5009
www.krausebooks.com

Call 800-258-0929 M-F 8 a.m. - 5 p.m. to order direct from the publisher, or shop booksellers nationwide and select coin shops.

Please reference offer **AUB9** with all direct-to-publisher orders

Tune up your car connections at www.oldcarsweekly.com

The Little Car That Could

Chevy II - Nova

The Ultimate Guide to Chevy's Gas Sipping Sizzler
by Doug Marion
From mild to wild experience every heart-racing moment of Chevy Nova Innovation in this exploration of the history, performance and production of every model of Nova.
Softcover • 8-¼ x 10-7/8 • 224 pages
15 b&w photos • 260 color photos
Item# Z2099 • **$24.99**

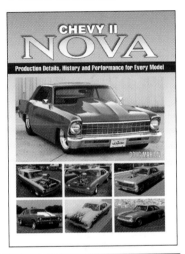

Order directly from the publisher at **www.krausebooks.com**

Krause Publications, Offer **AUB9**
P.O. Box 5009
Iola, WI 54945-5009
www.krausebooks.com

Call **800-258-0929** M-F 8 a.m. - 5 p.m. to order direct from the publisher, or shop booksellers nationwide and select coin shops.

Please reference offer **AUB9** with all direct-to-publisher orders

Tune up your car connections at www.oldcarsweekly.com

Remember when muscle cars ruled the road?

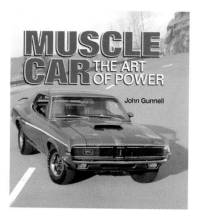

Muscle Car
The Art of Power

by John Gunnell
A treasury of beautiful, classic Muscle Cars from Detroit's golden age are featured along with essays and commentary on each mighty model. Includes the 1965 Pontiac GTO, the 1969 Charger and the 1971 Plymouth GTX. Softcover • 10-3/4 x 10-3/4 • 192 pages 350 color photos
Item# Z1808 • $27.99

Order directly from the publisher at **www.krausebooks.com**

Krause Publications, Offer **AUB9**
P.O. Box 5009
Iola, WI 54945-5009
www.krausebooks.com

Call 800-258-0929 M-F 8 a.m. - 5 p.m. to order direct from the publisher, or shop booksellers nationwide and select coin shops.

Please reference offer **AUB9** with all direct-to-publisher orders

Tune up your car connections at www.oldcarsweekly.com

Mad Modern Muscle

Resto-Mod Muscle Cars

*A Showcase of the World's Best Builds
Plus Ideas for Designing Your Own*
by Bill Holder & Phil Kunz
This brilliant color showcase of the best
resto-mods on the street includes charts
and tables of parts and supply outlets,
and contact to rest-mod groups.
Softcover • 8-¼ x 10-7/8 • 176 pages
200 color photos
Item# Z1807 • $24.99

Order directly from the publisher at **www.krausebooks.com**

Krause Publications, Offer **AUB9**
P.O. Box 5009
Iola, WI 54945-5009
www.krausebooks.com

Call 800-258-0929 M-F 8 a.m. - 5 p.m. to order direct from the publisher, or shop
booksellers nationwide and select coin shops.

Please reference offer **AUB9** with all direct-to-publisher orders

Tune up your car connections at www.oldcarsweekly.com

Celebrate Shelby's Marvelous Mustangs

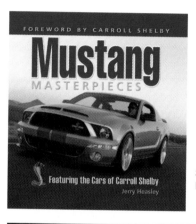

FOREWORD BY CARROLL SHELBY

Mustang
MASTERPIECES

Featuring the Cars of Carroll Shelby

Jerry Heasley

Mustang Masterpieces

Featuring the Cars of Carroll Shelby
by Jerry Heasley
A pictorial feast of the best muscle cars ever built, with accompanying historical essays and commentary set this book above the rest of the pack. Features mighty muscle models including, the 1965 Pontiac GTO, 1970 Ford Mustang Boss and the 1969 Charger.
Hardcover • 10-3/4 x 10-3/4 • 256 pages
300 color photos
Item# Z2640 • $35

Order directly from the publisher at **www.krausebooks.com**

Krause Publications, Offer **AUB9**
P.O. Box 5009
Iola, WI 54945-5009
www.krausebooks.com

Call 800-258-0929 M-F 8 a.m. - 5 p.m. to order direct from the publisher, or shop booksellers nationwide and select coin shops.

Please reference offer **AUB9** with all direct-to-publisher orders

Tune up your car connections at www.oldcarsweekly.com

Muscle Car Mastery

Standard Guide to American Muscle Cars

A Supercar Source Book 1960-2005
4th Edition
by John Gunnell
Delivers high-performance details including historical notes, original factory specifications, available options, original price, and current collector value for 300 muscle cars of the 1970s, 80s, 90s and early 2000s.·
Softcover • 8-¼ x 10-7/8 • 400 pages
400+ color photos
Item# AM04 • $27.99

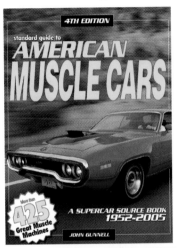

Order directly from the publisher at **www.krausebooks.com**

Krause Publications, Offer **AUB9**
P.O. Box 5009
Iola, WI 54945-5009
www.krausebooks.com

Call 800-258-0929 M-F 8 a.m. - 5 p.m. to order direct from the publisher, or shop booksellers nationwide and select coin shops.

Please reference offer **AUB9** with all direct-to-publisher orders

Tune up your car connections at www.oldcarsweekly.com

Affordable and Portable
Take these field guides along for the ride!

Corvette Field Guide 1953-Present
by Jerry Heasley

200 eye-popping color photos of 70 stunning 'Vettes including the most collectible and memorable models are complemented with captions detailing available options and other facts of interest about the evolution of the Corvette.

Softcover • 5-3/16 x 4-3/16 • 408 pages • 200+ color photos
Item# VETFG • $12.99

Mustang Field Guide 1964-1/2-Present
by Brad Bowling

200+ brilliant color photos, featuring the early 1964-½, the powerful 2005s and everything in between, accompany detailed captions outlining performance data, historical details and available options for Mustang — the original Pony car.

Softcover • 5-3/16 x 4-3/16 • 408 pages • 200+ color photos
Item# TNGFG • $12.99

Harley-Davidson Field Guide All-American Bikes 1903-2004
by Doug Mitchel

Featuring color photos accompanied by a detailed caption with information on options and equipment of 200 Harley-Davidson motorcycles, enthusiasts will see the evolution of the bikes from 1903 to today's most popular models.

Softcover • 5-3/16 x 4-3/16 • 408 pages • 200+ color photos
Item# HDFG • $12.99

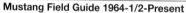

Order directly from the publisher at **www.krausebooks.com**

Krause Publications, Offer **AUB9**
P.O. Box 5009
Iola, WI 54945-5009
www.krausebooks.com

Call 800-258-0929 M-F 8 a.m. - 5 p.m. to order direct from the publisher, or shop booksellers nationwide and select coin shops.

Please reference offer **AUB9** with all direct-to-publisher orders

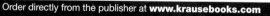

Tune up your car connections at www.oldcarsweekly.com